ORIG. PLANECRAFT
(CHAMPION + CLIFFORD, RECORD)
PUBL. 1934, REV'D 1950 + 1959
MUCH OF ORIG. IN THIS BOOK,
WHICH IS A REWRITING OF ORIG.

Planecraft:
A Woodworker's Handbook

JOHN SAINSBURY

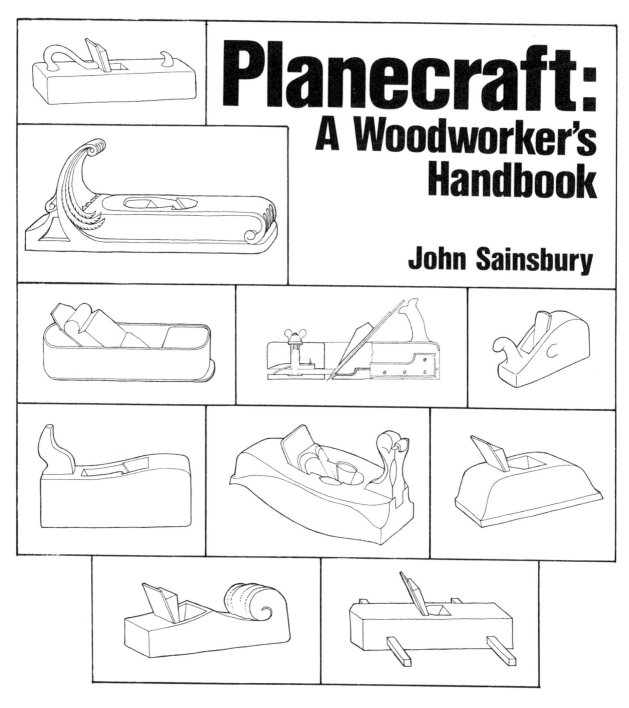

Planecraft:
A Woodworker's Handbook

John Sainsbury

 Sterling Publishing Co., Inc. New York

Library of Congress Cataloging in Publication Data

Sainsbury, John A.
  Planecraft: a woodworker's handbook.

  Rev. ed. of: Planecraft / [C.W. Hampton]. Completely
rev. & enl. 1959, 1974 printing.
  Includes index.
  1. Planes (Hand tools) I. Hampton, C.W. (Charles
William). Planecraft. II. Title.
TJ1201.P55S35 1984   684′.082   83-24217
ISBN 0-8069-5520-1
ISBN 0-8069-7848-1 (pbk.)

Edited by Michael Cea

Third Printing, 1986

Table of Contents

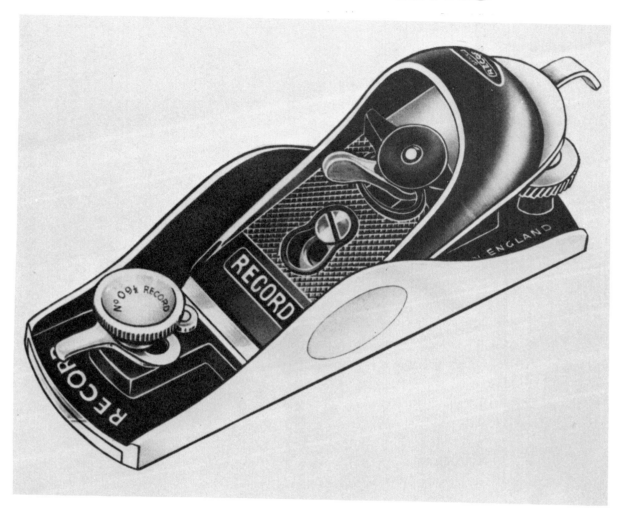

Preface 7
1 The History of the Plane 8
2 Bench Planes 24
3 Maintenance of Plane Cutters 32
4 Using the Planes 41
5 The Block Plane 69
6 Rebate Planes 73
7 Plow Planes 85
8 Combination Planes Nos. 050 and 050C 92
9 The Multi-Plane 103
10 Router Planes 112
11 The Circular Plane 120
12 Spokeshaves 124

13 Scrapers 130
14 Wooden Bench Planes 133
15 Difficulties in Planing, and Their Solutions 142
16 Contemporary Plane Makers 149
17 Power Planes 158
  Glossary 167
  Metric Equivalency Chart 184
  Index 185
  Acknowledgments 191

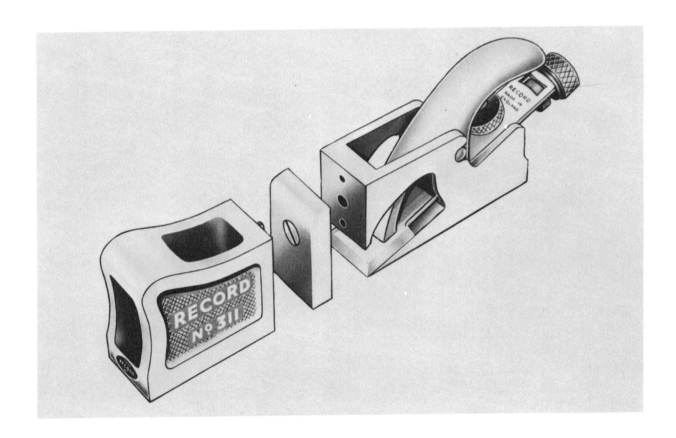

Preface

The pride of craftsmanship which has distinguished all woodworkers since the birth of the craft is undoubtedly traceable in great measure to the intimacy that must exist between the craftsman, the tools and the material. That intimacy is responsible for the critical attitude that every woodworker assumes in the choice of his tools, and also for the opinion generally held that good work can only be done with good tools that respond to the skill of the user. Such tools are a constant delight to use, and because of their beauty and finish are a joy to possess.

Planecraft was first published in 1934 and revised in 1950 and 1959, when it reached its seventh printing. Much of the material in this book was written by Charles Hampton and E. Clifford and published by C. & J. Hampton, the makers of Record Planes in Sheffield, England. Charles Hampton was a highly skilled engineer and chairman of C. & J. Hampton. "Cliff" was probably one of the most knowledgeable plane men of his time. I am indebted to Mark A. Alexander and R. H. McKears, Directors of Record Ridgway Tools Ltd., for permission to rewrite *Planecraft*.

Many of the planes described are no longer manufactured, but many thousands were produced and are still in use. These tools were sold with accompanying "How to Use" booklets, of which most booklets have probably been lost by now. It is hoped that this book will serve to fill that gap, be of service to all workers in wood, and serve as a workshop companion.

1
The History of the Plane

In tracing the story of the carpenter's plane through the ages, one has to rely mainly on the work of the archeologists to shed some light on the past. Although their researches have revealed something about early craftsmanship, very little has come to light about the tools used in early days. This may be explained to some extent by the fact that until recent times the craftsman working in wood received very little recognition for his contribution as an artist. Many examples of the craftsman's work still exist as monuments to his skill in craftsmanship and design, for in ear-

Fig. 1. Erecting a wood-framed house, about AD 1420 (MS 18850, fol. 15b, British Museum).

lier times the worker was often his own designer.

The lack of documentary evidence on craftsmanship and woodworking tools in early days may also be due to the social gap which separated those who were learned enough to compile written works and those who worked with their hands. One class had little in common with the other. Therefore, we have to rely on evidence other than that of the written word. Furthermore, in the days of the guilds, the craft was taught in the workshop by example and the spoken word.

Manuals of craftsmanship only appeared a comparatively short time ago.

In ancient Egypt the craft of the woodworker was on a high level. Work that has been buried in tombs shows such accepted constructions as mortise-and-tenon joints. In one tomb a model of a contemporary carpenter's shop has been found. This is now in the Metropolitan Museum of Art in New York, to whom we are indebted for the reproduction of a photograph of the model (Fig. 2). It is interesting because, while it shows several

Fig. 2. Model of ancient Egyptian's shop.

carpenters busily employed at their trade, and some of the partly finished work, not one of the carpenters is using a plane. Instead, they are shown trimming their boards with an adze and smoothing them after the manner of the stonemason, by scouring them with a stone.

The mummy cases in the British Museum also show evidence of this method of finish. It would be safe to assume that in those days the plane was quite unknown, although iron was well known and widely used.

Although it is a natural assumption that the first plane was a chisel fixed in a block of wood (the mortising in Fig. 2 is in principle the same as in modern practice, and the chisel is similar to modern chisels), who first tried it and by whom it was copied and improved is still one of the hidden mysteries of the past that will probably never be solved.* What is certain, however, is that by the time of Roman civilization the plane was in a very advanced stage.

Between the time of the ancient Egyptians and the Romans, considerable development had taken place, and the carpenter's plane had become a highly specialized tool. No specimen of a Roman wooden plane has so far been traced, though doubtless such were used, but Flinders Petrie discovered in Pompeii planes which have a wood core sheathed in iron plate (Fig. 3). The excavations at Silchester yielded an iron plane (Fig. 4) of much sturdier construction, and of a very different pattern, though still probably hav-

ing a wood core also. Excavations in Europe have yielded Roman planes of bronze, one of which, at Cologne, is all metal with no wood core. This era of development presents a remarkable similarity with the subsequent development of the plane from 1800 onwards, as will be seen later.

Fig. 4. Iron plane from Silchester, England.

The Pompeii planes are remarkable in several ways. There was evidently a desire on the part of the worker for a more permanently accurate sole, hence the metal sheathing. This sheathing passes around the plane, top, nose and sole, and holes are cut in the sole and top for the mouth and escapement. The hand hole is pierced in a workmanlike way, in such a position as to get a maximum result for the effort expended, and actually follows modern practice in some respect, though we do not close the top of the handle as is done here. In common with the Silchester plane, the cutter or iron is secured by a wedge, holding against a strong rivet that passes through the middle of the plane. This method is still employed by the Chinese, who use a piece of iron roughly resembling a cut nail.

It is not certain of what material the Roman wedge was made, but it was probably wood. The position of the handle leaves little to be desired, and it has been suggested that the central rivet and wedge are superior to the channel and wedge which to be found on the present planes, but it may be that the rivet and wedge method is more prone to chatter (making irregular, uneven cuts).

The iron plane from Silchester offers a remarkable resemblance in its main lines of design to the most up-to-date planes of today. This may best be demonstrated by comparing a modern metal jack plane with the Roman plane (Fig. 3), which is 13¼

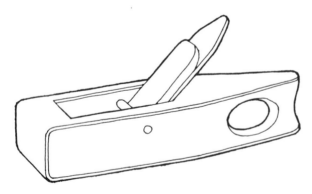

Fig. 3. Roman plane (Pompeii).

---

*Modern research is leaning towards the restriction of the cut of the adze—possibly by the attachment of a block or blocks of wood to the blade—resulting in a shaving rather than a chip (W. L. Goodman, *History of Woodworking Tools*).

inches long and 2¼ inches wide. The cutter is 4¼ inches long and has a pitch of 65°.

Both planes illustrated have single irons, and it has always been assumed that the invention of the cap iron came early in the 19th century, the need for it coinciding with the increased use of mahogany so popular at that period. It is, therefore, interesting to find that among the iron tools which were found in the excavations at the Roman border fortress of Newstead, was what appeared to be a Roman double plane iron (Fig. 5) that is similar to the cap iron in principle.

This double iron appears to be unique, the only specimen until the cap iron appeared early in the 19th century. It may indeed not be a plane iron at all since there were no planes found with it, but its form and design are such that they are very suggestive of an early attempt at a cap iron. The two irons are welded together at the top.

The same "smith's hoard" of tools yielded several chisels, tanged and socketed, quite equal in design and workmanship to modern tools, and also, curiously enough, a moulding plane iron that will cut a moulding about 1 inch wide. This, like the cap-ironed cutter, appears to be the only one of its kind that has been found. Flinders Petrie wondered about this, as mouldings were in great favor by the Roman carpenters. A possible explanation is that most of these mouldings were made with a scratch stock, the blades of which, being small, would be easily lost. The two cutters discussed here, the chisels and fine examples of the wheelwright's art may be seen in the National Museum of Antiquities, in Edinburgh, Scotland.

It is interesting to speculate at this point as to what degree the native craftsman of Britain contributed to the improvement of the plane, but there is little evidence to guide us. Julius Caesar has given vivid descriptions of the chariots used by the ancient Britons. After he had defeated them, they retreated with some 4,000 chariots. He also makes a point of the greatness of the fleet which he had to conquer and its superior seaworthiness to his own. Even allowing for a pardonable exaggeration on the general's part, we are forced to the conclusion that both the smith's and the carpenter's art (and the smith and the carpenter may have been one and the same person) were more advanced than we have usually assumed, and that after the Roman conquest there must have been a fusion of the craft knowledge of both peoples. The Newstead cap iron may indeed have been the work of a British or Pict craftsman.

After the end of the Roman period it is extremely difficult to trace anything at all connected with the plane for several centuries. Yet, the invaders of England came over in wooden ships, lived in houses made of wood and had wooden pails—one of which, an excellent example of workmanship, still survives. Therefore, the craft of the woodworker must have existed and continued even in those perilous times and on through the Norman Conquest.

The Norman castles and churches could not have been built without the stonemason using the prior constructions of the carpenter, though again, the stonemason may have been his own carpenter. Yet, not a vestige of evidence can be found of the tools used. It may be that with the incursion of the Northmen, the plane was lost and its work done with the axe and the adze, for when in later times the carpenter is depicted in illuminated manuscripts he is more often than not using an axe or an adze (see Fig. 1). Also, the few remaining 13th century chests show by the texture of their surfaces that they were worked by the adze.

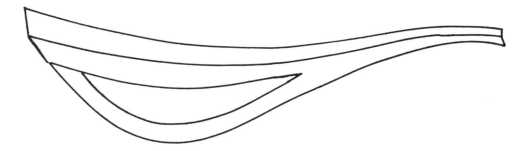

Fig. 5. Roman double plane iron.

By the 14th century the carpenter had a kit of tools very much the same in content as he carries now, and it included a "pleyn." A 14th century poem, anonymous, rendered into modern English by Mr. A. H. Collins, records a humorous and very human conversation in which (in the characteristic style of those days) all the tools speak for themselves and take a part, and from which we extract:

"What, Sir Rule?" then said the plane—
"My master shall not want for gain.
I'll work for him, both day and night
To get him good with all my might.
I'll cleanse the wood on every side
To help my master in his pride."

This type of "pleyn" would most probably be somewhat like the plane which appears in Fig. 1, which is from a manuscript in the British Museum. Apart from the wide variety of tools here depicted, the picture is of value in that it shows the type of long plane then in use. Some of the other manuscripts of the period show only a shorter plane, and that has led some to wonder whether or not the longer plane as used in Roman times had been lost. However, the picture shows that the medieval carpenter was fully aware of the use of the longer plane, as well as the shorter one, for at his feet lies a small smoothing plane which is very similar to one (Fig. 6) that appears in a French manuscript, also in the British Museum. The plane that is in use has two

handles, horizontally fixed, though the carpenter is only using the back one. Does this indicate that on occasion a helper was pressed into service to pull at the front-end—as, we shall see later, was done with some planes of a later date? Or is it merely that at times the plane was pushed and at other times pulled? Or is it that the iron may be set either way? The horizontally placed handle probably persisted for some time, as a variant of it will be seen in a later plane (Fig. 12).

From this time onwards, evidence, though still sketchy, allows us to follow the trend of the design of the tool a little better. Dürer's famous picture, *Melancholia*, gives us a vivid impression of the smoothing plane (Fig. 7) of his time for the minute correctness of the detail of his pictures admirably conveys to us what the plane was like—the shapeliness of the body, the rounded end, the shaping of the forward horn. The detail of the picture is such that we can even see from it the method of fitting the horn into the body. The pictures of the "swan" planes (Figs. 1 and 6) are not so abundantly full of detail, but there also we see how carefully the tool was designed for comfortable handling. (They are called swan planes because their handles resemble the neck of a swan.)

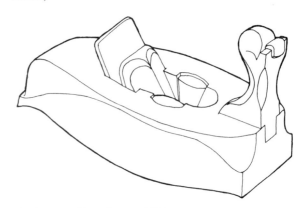

Fig. 7. Smoothing plane c. 1514.

The planes of the 15th, 16th and 17th centuries are almost invariably fitted with a forward horn. This disappeared in England, if indeed it was ever very common, but it has persisted in Europe until now. Almost all the planes of Northern Europe are so fitted. The chestmakers were, of course, pioneers in the craft of the cabinetmaker and they "builded better than they knew."

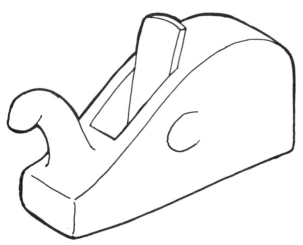

Fig. 6. Early 15th-century small smoothing plane (French). (MS 4431, fol. 196, British Museum.)

The forward horn presented an opportunity for a good deal of variation and individuality. It is a product of an age when time, in terms of hurry and bustle, did not count for much. It was an age when men expressed themselves very freely in their craft. "Designers" in the modern sense had not yet appeared. It was natural that a man who was making his own tools should make them primarily to serve his purpose efficiently, but having made a sound "utilitarian" tool, he frequently satisfied an innate aesthetic urge by incorporating carved decoration in the design. The tools were also open to inspection and undoubtedly sound criticism by fellow members of the guild. It is not unlikely, indeed, that in many cases they were made so as to invite criticism. Such criticism would sometimes lead to suggestions that would help improve the tool. So long as the horn served its primary purpose efficiently, that is, it was comfortable for the hand and was not likely to produce blisters and kindred troubles, it could be, and was, shaped in a variety of ways.

A scroll was a natural suggestion, and the scroll appears very frequently (Fig. 8). The scrolls were not always elegant but all showed a healthy individuality of treatment. One must understand that the apprentice not only struggled to master his craft, but he also spent the majority of his spare time in making his tools, the very instruments of his craft. When we come across a plane of the type shown in Fig. 9, it would, however, not seem that we have the work of an apprentice—this plane is surely the product of a master craftsman.

The scrolls are finished work. The toe and heel are so designed that it is impossible to trap the fingers, yet this design is cleverly hidden in the decoration—in fact, the decoration is the design! It is easy to understand the saying handed down from generation to generation to the present day that a craftsman is known by his tools.

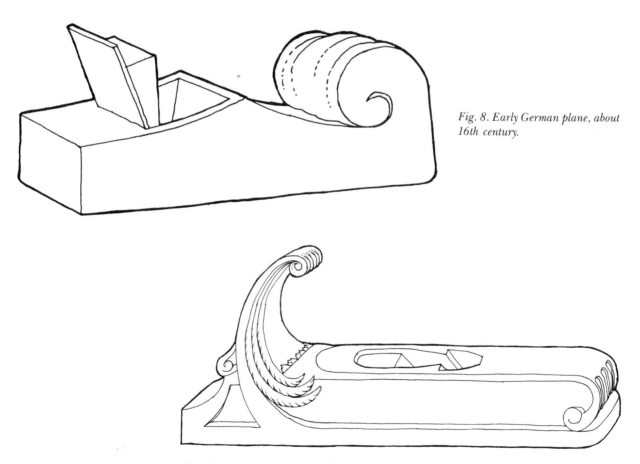

Fig. 8. Early German plane, about 16th century.

Fig. 9. Seventeenth-century cabinetmaker's plane.

It was the custom at one time to incorporate in the carved decoration the owner's initials and the date of manufacture, and several planes thus decorated have survived. Of such, they do not carry evidence of excessive wear; they must have been veritable treasures. Often, they are wide rebate or moulding planes which would not, of course, be subject to as much wear as a jack or smooth plane.

Fig. 10 shows a late example of one of these dated planes, the reproduction of which is inserted by courtesy of the South Kensington Museum, where two similar planes are preserved. One, dated 1688, with the initials P. F., was at one time in the Museum of Antiquities in Edinburgh, Scotland. It was 21 inches long but because it was falling to pieces through decay it was destroyed. As, unfortunately, no photograph of it was taken, a pictorial representation is impossible.

At this point it should be noted that it is a pity that there have been in the past so few museums like the Museum of Antiquities and South Kensington Museum. While museums are teeming with flints and armor, the tools of war, few have any of the craftsman's tools of peace. It is even on record that a well-known museum refused a large collection of Greek tools on the grounds that they had no aesthetic attraction. South Kensington and Edinburgh have appreciated the craftsman's point of view, but against centuries of academic tradition their task has not been easy. With a modern trend towards industrial and folk museums, the position has recently improved. Craftsmen can make a valuable contribution to this effort by presenting to museums specimens of tools which have become obsolete, though their historical value may be considerable.

The smooth plane of the Novaya Zemlya expedition, left by ship's carpenters in 1596 (Rijksmuseum, Amsterdam), has a simpler variant of the forward horn, but its principal interest for us is its iron, not shown in the sketch (Fig. 11). This, both in shape and bevel edge, closely resembles a modern iron, but there is no slot or other provision for a cap iron; it was a single iron plane. The time of the double iron had not yet arrived.

In *The Carpenter's Tool Chest*, Hibben shows two English planes of the 17th century—a smooth and a jack plane—which call for passing comment.

Fig. 10. Moulding plane.

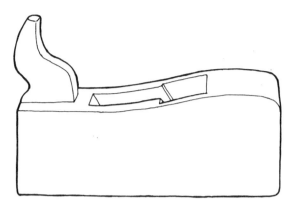

Fig. 11. *Novaya Zemyla smoothing plane of 1596 (Rijksmuseum, Amsterdam).*

jack, while the other was ground as a try plane, dead straight. An illustration is not available, but odd planes of the type can be spotted occasionally in private collections.

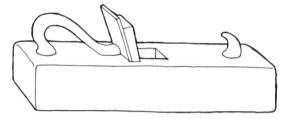

Fig. 12. *Seventeenth-century English jack plane.*

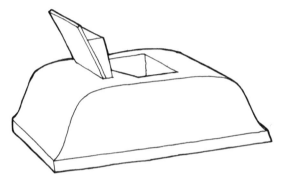

Fig. 13. *Seventeenth-century English smoothing plane.*

The jack is provided with a forward horn reminiscent of the hooked horn of the "swan"-type plane of the 15th century. The handle or toat is of very unusual form (Fig. 12)—a decorative form more like the flat handles of the 15th century plane already noted (Fig. 1).

The smooth plane has neither forward horn nor backward handle, but front and back the shape is ogee, thus leaving enough protection against trapped fingers (Fig. 13). Was the horn discarded because the workman found it in the way when he wished to dislodge the iron by rapping the forward part of the plane on the bench top? On discarding it, did he still continue to grasp his plane around the front of the nose, as when he had the horn, until the later method of holding the plane fingers across the top, thumbdown, was adopted? A projecting toe was certainly very much in favor about this time, and it continued until well into the early part of the 19th century.

Except as regards the toat and the horn, the form of the 17th-century planes differed very little from the form of the wood planes of the 18th and 19th centuries, some of which are still to be found. The hollow toat appeared in the later 18th century. The horn disappeared in England, though in Europe it survives.

An interesting variation has been noted in one or two survivals where a plane has been fitted with two blades, sometimes these being on adjacent faces. The purpose of this is not quite clear, though a possible explanation is that one of the irons was ground slightly round and used as a

Many craftsmen using modern planes during a comparatively long spell of planing frequently adopt a pull on the knob for a time as a relief from a push on the handle. This raises the question as to whether or not planes were always pushed, and it may explain in part the reason for the horn. *Nouveau Manuel Complet du Charpentier* (Biston Boutereau in Hanus, Paris, 1848) shows a *galère*, or *demi-varlope*, an organ builder's plane (Fig. 14) through which two handles pass, front and back. The accompanying instructions indicate how the plane is pulled by one man and pushed by another at the same time. Hibben shows a similar plane as a 17th century plane. The Chinese plane is fitted with a similar crossbar, and this plane is definitely pulled and not pushed. Some Japanese planes also follow the same lines and method of working.

There are woodworkers who can remember wide architrave moulding planes being used that

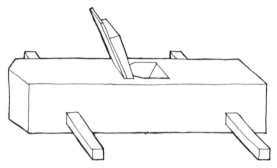

Fig. 14. Galère *or* demí-varlope *(1848)*.

were bored with a hole in the front part. The craftsman pushed the plane in the usual way while the apprentice standing at the other end of the work assisted by hauling on a cord attached to the plane through the hole. It has been very difficult to trace one of these "holed" moulding planes. They were difficult to use, and with the general adoption of the spindle machine they became virtually obsolete. Fig. 15 shows one of these planes. It had two irons (one of which is missing) and was discovered in Gloucester Technical College. The cooper has yet another variation. His plane is neither pulled nor pushed; he works today exactly as he did in the 16th century (Fig. 16).

The 18th century was a time when the art of the cabinetmaker was approaching a very high level, a time when craftsmanship was at its best, and when new and strange woods were being imported plentifully from distant lands. These woods had figure and grain that called for greater and still greater skill in their mastery, and the woodworker responded with more efficient tools. The demand for a finer finish and greater accuracy of work meant much experimenting with planes to achieve this object.

It is a remarkable fact that, except for the lower pitch of the iron, development of the 18th century planes offers a close parallel with that of Roman times. It started with an iron sheathing, like that of the Pompeii planes (discovered at a later date). Figs. 17 and 18 show such a plane discovered in the U.S., dating from about 1800. It is virtually a wooden plane, with a sheathing of iron, a low-set cutting iron and a very narrow mouth, ideal for the shooting of mitres and end grain and for smoothly finishing difficult grained wood. It is said that this plane was made in England, and it was destined to be the forerunner of many similar types. The fixing of the blade is by wedge—the wedge being of such a form that the iron can be

Fig. 15. *"Holed" moulding plane*.

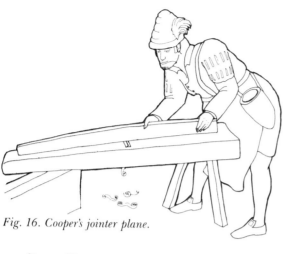

Fig. 16. Cooper's jointer plane.

Fig. 17. Plane with iron sheathing.

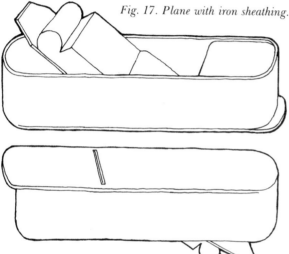

Fig. 18. Plane inverted, to show metal sole with narrow mouth.

Fig. 19. Norwich plane with two-parted sole (top); home-made plane with a centrally pivoted brass wedge held by a screw (middle); and a panel plane by Buck (bottom).

withdrawn without rapping the plane on the bench—and it has a protruding toe!

Belonging to approximately the same time is a similar plane discovered in Norwich, England, Fig. 19 (top). In this case, the sole is made in two parts, one of them notched so as to form an extremely narrow mouth. Countersunk screws attach the sole to the wood core of the body. A striking knob is let into the front part and the plane bears evidence of adjustment at the rear in many hammer marks. On the side of the plane are two well-worn ebony strips, indicating that it has seen much service on the shooting board. The low pitch of the irons of these two planes would necessitate the use of single irons with which they

are fitted. The Norwich plane has no sheathing on the sides or ends.

It is extremely difficult to assign a definite date to these iron planes. Some of this difficulty stems from the fact that during the 16th, 17th and 18th centuries one part of the world was always more advanced. For example, the iron plane shown in Fig. 20 was in an advanced stage as early as 1719 in France. The plane, approximately 8½ inches long and accommodating a 1½-inch cutter (which has disappeared), is made of plate about ⅛ inch thick. The sides are brazed to the sole, which projects front and back. Presumably, the lining was of wood, and the riveted crossbar held the wedge and cutter. The pitch is about 30°.

A bent-over projection at the front-end is carved or filed into the form of a shell, giving a comfortable front grip, while the rounding of the back would afford a comfortable hold for the right hand. The edges are highly ornate and suggest that the upper surfaces of the wood filling may have been equally decorative in keeping. Sides and end are completely covered with decoration that was probably etched, though it may have been carved when one considers the high degree of skill that the French locksmiths exhibited nearly two centuries prior to this.

The name of the owner (Jaques Boquay), his address (Rue d'Argenteuil, Paris) and the date (1719) appear in the decoration of the rounded-after end and, as befits such a famous violin maker, the front-end is decorated with a trophy of musical instruments. Midway around the sides runs a musical air, with a love song. The plane was in the possession of Messrs. Wm. E. Hill & Sons, violin makers, by whose courtesy permission was given to photograph it.

A beech try plane of approximately the same period (Fig. 21) was also in the possession of Messrs. Hill. It bears the initials I. B. and the date 1713 and is carved on the front part of the top, the escapement being neatly and cleanly finished with three gouge cuts. This plane is remarkable in hav-

ing neither handle nor front grip. Instead, running the whole length of the plane on both sides is a gouged groove, about half an inch from the bottom, into which fingers and thumb may fit as the hand is stretched over the plane. Another unusual feature is the tapering from middle to front and back, this giving an easier grip, especially when the hand is rather small.

Other planes of the early years of the 19th century have survived in which a sheathing or plating of iron is employed. In some cases, this sheathing is dovetailed together, as in the examples shown

Fig. 20. French iron plane (1719).

Fig. 21. Beech try plane (1713).

in Figs. 22 and 23. Fig. 22 is shown by courtesy of the South Kensington Museum, and Fig. 23 is from East Anglia, possibly acquired from a shipwreck. The plates of this latter plane are not dovetailed in the strict sense of the word, but are rather notched into each other and brazed.

After the fashion of the Roman development, however unwittingly, this plane shows the central rivet and not side channels for the blade and wedge. The rivet is rectangular in section and set at the appropriate angle in the body, parallel with the line of the cutter. The wood core still persisted; considering the technique of the time it was easier to make the plane with a wood core, and tradition dies hard. Even when later the wedge was made of brass and centrally pivoted, and the hold maintained by a screw, lever fashion (Fig. 19, middle), the body core was still of wood.

Fig. 22. Mitre plane (1820).

Fig. 23. Nineteenth-century iron-sheathed plane.

Fig. 19 (middle) is a plane of mid-19th century (probably "homemade," but typical of many of that time and later) which was retrieved from an attic in Dundee where it had lain for many years. By this time the craft of the toolmaker had developed, and many planes from 1800 onwards trace their origin to Sheffield and London.

The plane shown in Fig. 22 was made by Nelson, of Edgware Road, London, about 1820, whose business was taken over in 1824 by J. Buck, the maker of the beautiful panel plane shown in Fig. 19 (bottom). The sole and sides of the plane shown in Fig. 19 (bottom) are made very solidly of one piece of iron, and the filling is of rosewood. The wedge is shaped for easy removal, and a striking knob is provided in the usual forward position.

As if to follow the Roman precedent still more closely, craftsmen of yesterday often used bronze for their plane bodies, but usually only in the smaller planes such as bullnose and shoulder planes. Behind all these searchings and experiments was a desire for more permanent accuracy of the sole and mouth. The advantages of metal for this purpose having been demonstrated in practice, it was not long before cast iron was exploited to further this end. Knowles, in 1827, took out a patent for a cast iron plane that required no wood filling.

The fitting of the iron was by wedge, with the usual side channels. Therein lay its weakness, for adjustment by hammer on a cast iron tool is asking for trouble. Hence, inventive minds set about to minimize this defect. In a year or two there appeared a plane on similar lines, that still used a wedge. However, a new pattern adjustment was arranged by forming in the front part of the sole a square hole, through which projected a block of wood. This block could be raised or lowered at will by a screw adjustment on the top of the plane. Thus, the blade was fixed initially by the wedge and the effective amount of cut and the thickness of the shaving were dependent upon the position of the block. This meant that the major part of the sole was not in use, so it was really no solution.

This type of plane had no longer life than the plane with a similar aim (Fig. 24) that appears in *Spon's Mechanic's Own Book* (second edition, 1886). In this case, the plane, a wood jack of conventional pattern, is sawn through horizontally. The two parts are joined by a long hinge plate, pivoted on the upper half. The upper part also retains, by wedge, the cutting iron. By means of a screw stop and spring the amount of available "iron" is controlled. On the return stroke, the pressure naturally being relieved over the nose, the blade does not draw along the work, but rides over it.

About the middle of the 19th century inventors concentrated more on the elimination of the wedge and finding a more satisfactory way of adjusting the iron. In 1844, Sandford patented a screw adjustment of the iron, the top of the iron being turned over at right angles to form a nut for the adjustment.

However, it was Leonard Bailey who brought about improvements to our planes which are still used to the present day. Bailey took the wooden plane and added a metal superstructure having a cam lever cap to secure the cutter. This was in 1858. Nine years later he added a longitudinal adjuster—a "Y" lever operated by a screw set vertically behind the cutting unit. This was later changed to the horizontal position exactly as it is seen in the plane of today. Leonard Bailey was in business in Boston, Massachusetts, but sold out to the Stanley Rule and Level Company in 1869. He was a prolific inventor and Stanley saw the wisdom in employing him as manager of their plane department.

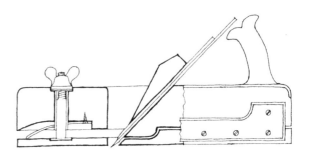

Fig. 24. Wood jack plane.

At the same time, an inventor named G. A. Warren was experimenting with lateral adjustment and mouth adjustment. His improvement on Bailey's work produced lateral adjustment by means of a knurled nut with offset plate and frog to adjust the mouth. His plane looked very much like the Record plane of today, particularly in regard to handling and balance. (The lateral adjusting level was improved by another patentee named J. A. Traut.) Stanley, however, still pays tribute to Leonard Bailey, since every bench plane carries his name on the front-end.

Certainly, we could not have had a thin cutter had it not been for Bailey's cap iron with its curved end, which not only eliminated the possibility of chatter but also served to break, roll and eject the shavings. His lever cap eliminated the necessity for thumbscrews, screws and screwdrivers, and fine adjustment of the cutter became synonymous with his name. Cutter adjustment was effected by a thumb lever devised by J. A. Traut, assisted by Henry Richards.

Even at this time, a cheaper, simpler metal plane is being marketed by Stanley.

Record planes were further improved by the introduction of a separable cap iron which eliminated entirely any possibility of chatter. It simplified grinding and honing and ensured that the cap iron would return to the exact setting. It increased efficiency and also saved the time of the user.

We had to wait until the beginning of the 19th century before examples of the infil plane were produced. Probably the first of these was the mitre plane, although this has not been authenticated. Certainly, planes of the highest quality were designed and made by Stuart Spiers of Ayr, Scotland, around 1840 and Thomas Norris possibly 20 years later. Spiers was undoubtedly copied by others, including Norris. Few would question his high quality of design and workmanship.

Spiers made his stock in the form of a steel box with a core of rosewood. The sides of the stock were dovetailed to the sole. The cutting iron was held in the stock either with a wedge or with a screwed metal lever cap pivoting about two pins located in two holes, one on each side of the escapement of the plane. Planes of this type were also made of iron and gunmetal.

The Spiers planes were intended mainly for the craftsman, and were built with a high degree of perfection. Smoothing planes were 7½ inches long and had three options of cutter width. Panel planes varied from 13½–17½ inches in length, with cutters 2½ inches wide. The jointers, 20½ to 27½ inches long, again had 2½-inch cutters. Rabbet or rebate planes, shoulder planes and bullnose planes made in exactly the same way as the bench planes were an addition to this range of incredible tools.

During a period of 80 years up to 1940, Norris produced a similar group of tools, and just before World War I patented a unit to achieve lateral and front and back adjustment of the cutter. This placed him ahead of Spiers in design. This development was probably prompted by the success of the Justus Traut pattern used extensively by Stanley at that time.

These companies were prepared to make planes for various other firms. Indeed, Norris was prepared to sell unfinished castings to be completed by the worker. That is probably the reason why we see so many pale imitations of the Spiers/Norris planes around. Norris had a wider range of planes than Spiers. They included thumb planes, violin planes, and chariot and bullnose planes.

In 1976, the Henley Optical Company, Oxford, commenced production of similar high-quality metal planes. These are of superb workmanship and very expensive.

About the same time, the Jamestown Tool Company began production of a range of planes similar to Spiers but constructed differently. Bronze castings were soldered to steel soles and filled with mahogany and other hardwoods. The cutting irons were secured with wooden wedges. All these planes were numbered and signed with the casting dated. The list comprised mitre planes, thumb planes, chariot planes and shoulder planes.

Thus, steadily improving through the ages, the modern plane, accurately made and capable of accurate and easy work, is not the invention of any one man but embodies the work and thoughts of many. And though the machine plane is with us, the hand plane will never leave us. Its present form is more efficient than it ever has been; its materials, thanks to endless research, were never better.

Thus far our survey of the plane has been concerned mainly with the form of the plane, important in that it naturally affects the "feel" and the handling of the tool. We have considered very little the material of which the various planes were made, nor have we discussed the character of that most vital part, the cutter or "iron" as it is frequently called by the craftsman.

Fig. 25. Record plane.

As regards the material of the body of the wooden planes, there is no record of what wood those appearing in the early manuscripts were made of. Of the rest, the favorite wood, in England at any rate, was red beech. In Europe, white beech and birch have both been used, as is the case now. With the arrival of the iron-cased planes, mahogany was a favorite wood, later giving way to rosewood.

The original "irons" of the historical planes have mostly disappeared, for in the nature of things the iron is ground away with sharpening and another iron replaces the original. Most of the planes illustrated have seen many years of service, but the cutters found in them are often much more modern than are the bodies. A thicker iron than is at present used was characteristic of the older planes. Some experiment had been made with thinner irons about a century ago—even in wood planes—as the irons of the cased mitre planes were usually of a thinner gauge. A tapered iron was at one time very popular, but it gradually gave way to the parallel iron. Steel facings on iron backs were standard, but it is not easy to discover when this welded or composite cutter was first introduced.

To those who think of engineering as a modern science, and the use of tool steel as a 19th century innovation, it is a puzzle how good carpentry and cabinetmaking were done with the material available for cutters to the earlier workers. We have already hinted at the high degree of skill that

must have existed in Britain long before the Christian era, but when we read in Homer that the hissing of the stake which Ulysses drove into the eye of Polyphemus was like that of the steel quenched in water—an account that was written not later than the 9th century B.C.—we realize that the hardening and tempering of steel, a delicate art at any time, was a familiar process a very long time ago. That steel should have been in common use is not so remarkable—it is likely that most of the iron in use in early times was really steel—because it probably contained sufficient carbon which, together with a good deal of hammering by the blacksmith, would enable it to be hardened.

Jas. Napier (*Manufacturing Arts of Ancient Times*, p. 213*ff.*) suggests that bronze was tipped with steel or iron. Iron tools were used by the ancient Egyptians and the Hebrews. An iron tool was found embedded in one of the tombs dating back to about 3500 B.C. There is a suggestion, however, that the Egyptians considered iron an impure metal—they preferred bronze. That the Egyptians and Hebrews had a method of hardening copper and bronze, which is now a forgotten art, is not borne out by the facts. If it were, the bronze that is found would be hard, and that is not so, unless it has passed through a normalization due to time. Hard edges could be obtained by hammering, and the Romans certainly had small field anvils on which such hammering was done, as when sharpening a scythe. In any case, although bronze was used for a plane body by the Romans, there is no indication that they used bronze for the blades. Those which have survived are of iron or steel.

The steel from which the blades were then made was "natural" steel, the carbon content of which was accidental, and subject to many variations. The cutting and edge-keeping qualities of these blades would vary accordingly. This would be the case until the 15th and 16th centuries, the methods of the iron-founders having varied little except in the magnitude of their output.

Metallurgy is a comparatively new science, and in spite of the work of Huntsman in the mid-18th century, of Bessemer a century later and of many others, the variation in the qualities of plane irons has persisted almost up to the present day. Within living memory, indeed, the purchase of a satisfactory plane iron was largely a matter of luck. It might be too hard or too soft; it might hold its edge or it might not.

The contribution of Huntsman to the development of the plane was an indirect one, but important in that it very materially improved the qualities of the steels available for the cutting irons. It was about 1740 that he introduced the "crucible process" of melting steel in small crucibles. The effect of this was that the slag or rich iron silicate which was present, mechanically mixed with the steel, could be freed readily. The removal of this cinder greatly improves the steel. The process was costly then and it remains costly today, but the quality of the steel is so suitable for plane blades and so incomparably better than the cheaper produced Bessemer open-hearth steel of later introduction.

Record plane cutters were originally made from the best crucible cast steel, and further improved through the application of modern scientific knowledge, advanced metallurgical research and wide practical experience. The details of this laboratory research and workshop experiment need not be traced here. It will be sufficient to note that the main lines of the research were devoted to careful analysis and accurate heat treatment, the ultimate result being the well-known and proved tungsten steel cutter, fitted to all Record planes.

The reader will naturally ask: "Why is this tungsten steel better than ordinary steel?" There are two reasons which stand out most clearly. The first is that tungsten has the property of uniting with the carbon in the steel and forming tungsten carbide. Tungsten carbide is the main constituent of all high-speed cutting materials, and is used in modern machine tools for metal working, turning lathes, boring machines, milling machines, gear-cutting machines, etc.

This material will cut at very high speeds, even when working on hard steel. In fact, its introduction caused great changes in the design of machines. It is therefore logical that a plane iron containing the correct amount of tungsten is harder and more resistant to wear, and will take a keener cutting edge, and hold it for a longer period than would an ordinary steel plane. This has been proved beyond doubt in Record cutters.

Secondly, the correct and proper introduction of tungsten is greatly beneficial in steel for plane irons as it prevents grain growth in the steel. This means that in the fully hardened cutter the steel is of very small grain size, which is immediately obvious when a blade is fractured. Because the grain size is small, the steel is more resistant to shock, and therefore the keen edge will suffer less damage when cutting than any other steel.

Modern science has brought engineering aids to the plane maker which were not available years ago, enabling the maximum grade of skill to be employed on every operation. Thus, through skilled engineering, not only is the bevel of the cutter correctly ground, but a uniform thickness and parallelism are attained in every blade (a factor which has so much to do with the efficiency of the whole assembly). Also, looseness and chatter when the plane is in service is eliminated.

The whole of the heat treatment (annealing, hardening, tempering) is controlled scientifically by delicate pyrometric instruments that are so sensitive they record the slightest variation of temperature, eliminating all "hit or miss" methods and discounting human error.

2
Bench Planes

On account of their more frequent use, three planes have by common usage acquired the description "bench planes." Taken in order of their size, they are the smooth, the jack and the trying (jointer) plane. Of the latter variety, the shorter ones are sometimes called "fore" planes.

Apart from relatively small work, the jack plane No. 05 and No. 05½, 14 inches and 15 inches long respectively, are generally the first to be used, and are called into action more frequently than any other. Their use is in the preliminary cleaning and squaring of wood, and they can be used also

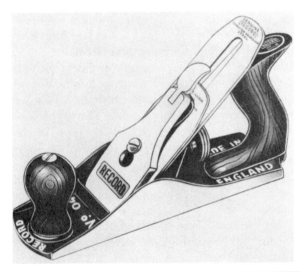

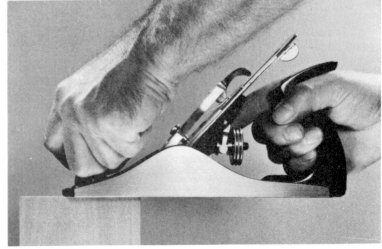

Fig. 26. Smoothing plane.

Fig. 27. Planing end grain on a narrow board.

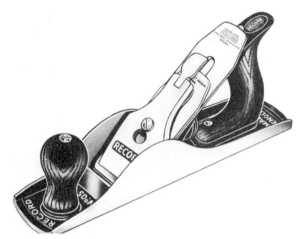

Fig. 28. Jack plane.

its 9-pound weight, this plane is exceedingly pleasant to handle. Its weight keeps it well down to its job, and the positioning of the knob and handle makes control quite easy, and accurate work a regular feature.

The smooth plane obtained its name from the fact that it was generally brought into use for smoothing away any irregularities left after using the jack plane. By virtue of its shorter length, it can be used easily over a small surface, and while it was useful for smoothing joints and cleaning blemishes it is today perhaps the most appreciated plane in use where "odd jobs" are concerned.

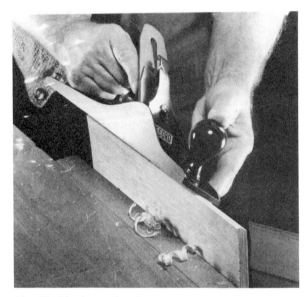

Fig. 29. Planing a chamfer.

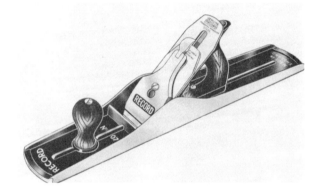

Fig. 30. Trying plane.

Fig. 31. Trying plane in use.

for accurate shooting of moderately long edges, provided the cutter is suitably ground and honed for that purpose. (See Chapters 4 and 5.)

For work on very long edges or surfaces, however, the jointer plane should be used. No. 06 has a cutter 2⅜ inches wide, and a length of 18 inches. No. 07 has a similar cutter, with an increased length of 22 inches, and will be found equal to most of the work occurring in joiners' and cabinetmakers' shops. When extra long lengths have frequently to be jointed, the No. 07, having a 2⅝-inch cutter, and a length of 24 inches, is strongly recommended. In spite of its length and

Fig. 32. Planing an edge for rub jointing.

Unless the work involved is of fairly large dimensions, it is always the smoothing plane which is used, especially by the amateur, when household jobs are involved. Short lengths of wood are very conveniently worked with the 04 (2-inch smoothing plane). If extra width is required, the 04½ (2⅜ inches) is used.

Fig. 33 suggests that the metal plane may well be complicated in construction and use. This really is not so. A few minutes examination will quickly reveal that this plane has a simplicity combined with an efficiency that was impossible with the earlier wooden planes. This is particularly important in an age when many people who haven't the craft skills attained after long practice are using planes in their homes. Before continuing to read this chapter, the reader should study the exploded view and acquaint himself with the names of the component parts.

Frequent honing of the cutter is necessary. It should always be honed before use or possibly after use, the cutting unit being retracted before the plane is put away. To remove the cutting unit from the plane, lift the trigger of the lever cap to unlock it. Slide the lever cap upward until the larger end of the keyhole slot allows it to be lifted over the lever cap screw. The cutting unit can now be lifted out.

Loosen the cap screw (but do not remove it) and turn the cap iron until it is at right angles to the cutter. Slide it forward until the head of the cap screw clears the enlarged hole at the end of the slot in the cutter. Before turning the cap iron, it is advisable to draw it away from the edge of the cutter to avoid any possibility of any contact with the cutting edge. When a newly sharpened cutter is fitted, the process is in reverse order. Emphasis is laid on the removal (and refitting) of the cap iron, since it would be aggravating to damage it after spending time and care on sharpening the cutter.

Details and instructions concerning grinding and honing are given in Chapter 3. To reassemble the plane, hold the cap iron at right angles to the cutter (the bevelled edge of the cutter on the opposite side to the cap iron) and insert the cap screw (still fitted in the cap iron) through the enlarged hole at the end of the slot in the cutter. Slide the cap iron along the slot until it can be turned into line with the cutter without catching the cutting edge. Move the cap iron toward the edge of the cutter until its edge is about ¹⁄₁₆ inch from the edge of the cutter itself. Tighten the cap screw sufficiently to prevent it from falling out of the cap iron, and set the cap iron at the required distance from the cutting edge. This can vary with the type of work involved, but a gap of approximately ¹⁄₁₆–¹⁄₃₂ inch will cover most types of general work. When a very fine cut is required for finishing off, or use on hardwood, the closer the cap iron is to the cutting edge the finer the shaving and the smoother the finish.

Having obtained the desired setting, securely tighten the cap screw. The "double iron" (this being the cap iron and cutter combined) is now seated on the frog, cap iron uppermost. Check that the small rectangular hole in the cap iron fits cleanly over the "Y" adjusting level and that the hardened steel roller at the bottom of the lateral

A Body

B Frog with Parts M, N, O, Q

C Cutter

D Cap Iron

E Lever Cap

F Cap Iron Screw

G Lever Cap Screw

H Nut and Screw for Knob

J Knob

K Nut and Screw for Handle

L Handle (and Toe Screw 04½-08, 010 & T5)

M Lateral Adjusting Lever

N "Y" Adjusting Lever

O Cutter Adjusting Nut

P Frog Screw with Washer

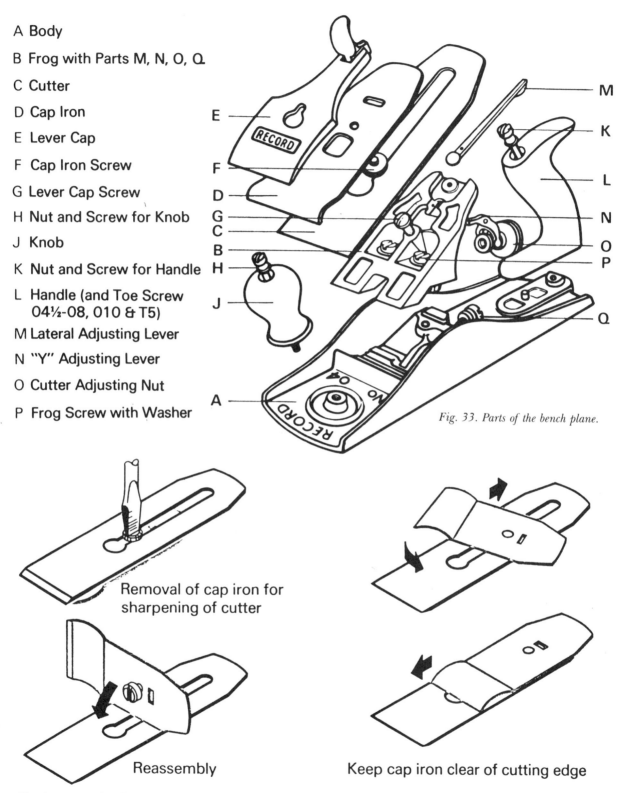

Fig. 33. Parts of the bench plane.

Removal of cap iron for sharpening of cutter

Reassembly

Keep cap iron clear of cutting edge

Fig. 34. Removal and replacement of the cap iron.

adjusting level is housed in the slot of the cutter. Finally, place the lever cap over the lever cap screw and slide it forward until the narrow part of the hole is under the head of the lever cap screw. Press down the trigger of the lever cap to lock it in place. The lever cap screw may need unscrewing or tightening, depending whether the trigger is too loose or too tight. It is important to have the lever cap secure, but it should not be necessary to exert undue pressure on the trigger to lock it.

Some users have wondered why the cap iron screw hole is placed at the bottom of the slot rather than at the top, as it is in the old-fashioned wooden plane, where fewer movements of the cap iron are needed before it can be screwed tight. If the hole were made at the top of the slot, there would be a danger, when the blade was nearly worn out, that the hole would rest opposite the roller of the lateral adjustment, which would then become ineffective. So, in order that the blade can be used right to the end, the hole is put at the bottom.

The cutter must now be accurately adjusted. Holding the plane as in Fig. 35, look carefully along the body to check whether or not the cutter is projecting through the mouth. The amount of cut is regulated by the adjusting nut. An almost hairline of protrusion should be visible. The cutter must also be brought parallel with the mouth by using the lateral adjusting lever.

Try the plane on a piece of waste wood. Adjust if necessary to bring on the type of cut needed for the particular job. Always look along the plane sole when adjusting. A further check on the wood will reveal the truth of the lateral setting, which again should be checked by sighting along the sole. Always let the last adjustment be a forward one, i.e., one that pushes the blade down. This will take up any backlash which may develop in adjustment.

Fig. 35. Sighting the cutter.

Frog Adjustment

The metal plane offers a major advantage over any of the earlier wooden planes in that the effective width of the mouth can be varied to suit the particular type of work which is being undertaken. Thus, when coarse "hogging" work (rough planing to remove saw marks) is the order of the day, a wide mouth can be used. When fine, accurate, finished work on hardwoods or softwoods with awkward grain has to be done, the closest mouth can be used, giving a mere tissue shaving. The width of the mouth is adjusted by loosening the two frog screws (A, Fig. 36) and by turning the adjusting screw (B) until the desired setting is obtained. Then tighten up the two frog screws (A). A fine mouth in conjunction with a close-set cap iron will give the very finest shaving. A coarse shaving can be removed by a combination of a wide mouth and a coarsely set cap iron.

Users generally do not make enough use of this frog adjustment to get the full use they might out

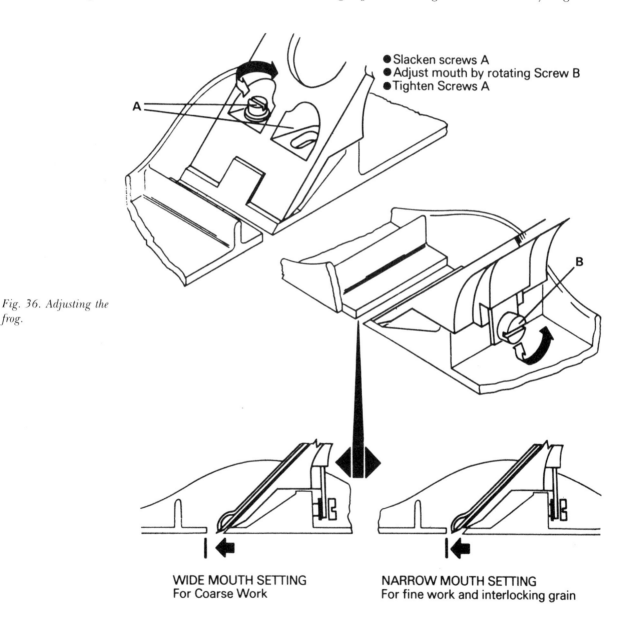

- Slacken screws A
- Adjust mouth by rotating Screw B
- Tighten Screws A

A

B

Fig. 36. Adjusting the frog.

WIDE MOUTH SETTING
For Coarse Work

NARROW MOUTH SETTING
For fine work and interlocking grain

Fig. 37. Cut-away plane, to show action of the cap iron.

the cutter may be honed many times and the deflector put back in exactly the same place as it occupied before. There is no need to remove the upper portion, even for grinding.

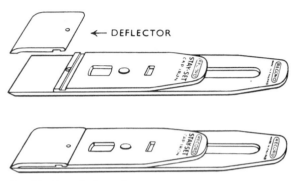

Fig. 38. "Stay-Set" cap iron.

of the planes. When adjusting a fine-set cap iron to a very narrow mouth, it must be remembered that the plane is set for the finest shaving, and consequently it will not do to have too thick a cut. On a slightly uneven surface, it is quite possible, bearing in mind the accuracy of the plane sole, that a fine-set plane will take off a shaving in one place and refuse to do so in another; this can happen when the unevenness is very slight indeed.

The remedy to this problem is not an increase in cut, but the planing off of the high spots until all is true. If a coarse shaving is required, then the mouth must be adjusted accordingly. A fine mouth and a closely set cap iron will give a fine shaving, but if the cutter is adjusted too far out at the same time, there will not be room for the shavings to get away, and choking will result. The frog adjustment is a very delicate one. A small turn of the screw has a large effect. It is important that the screw (A) be tightened after every adjustment.

Record "Stay-Set" Cap Iron

An Improvement in plane development was the Record "Stay-Set" cap iron (Fig. 38), which was made in two parts, the upper, or main part, and the lower, or deflector. In adjusting this cap iron, the sequence shown in Fig. 34 is quite unnecessary, as the deflector is merely lifted off and it will seldom be necessary to move the upper part. Once the deflector is set at the required distance,

The "Stay-Set" cap iron is a great time-saver. (Woodworkers generally do not appreciate the total time taken up in sharpening and setting tools.) The saving of time, however important, is not the main advantage of the "Stay-Set" cap iron. The one flaw in fine work with planes was the tendency some of them had to chatter. Chattering with the "Stay-Set" cap iron is an impossibility. With the "Stay-Set" cap iron the following occurs:
1. The cutting iron can be honed or sharpened without removing the cap iron.
2. The Record "Stay-Set" cap iron remains set. The deflector, which fits into a slot on the cap iron, can be lifted clear when released from the plane. After honing, it is only necessary to replace the deflector in the slot. No unscrewing or tightening is required.
3. The cutting iron can be honed many times before resetting the cap iron. When resetting is necessary, the operation is identical with that of resetting the old type.
4. The application of pressure at three points (instead of two, as in the old type) has at last eliminated all possibility of chatter; the "Stay-Set" cap iron is guaranteed chatter-proof.
5. The "Stay-Set" cap iron is increased in thickness and in close pressure contact with the cutting iron for the whole of its length. This greatly increases the rigidity of the entire cutting unit.
6. The extra thickness of the cap iron and deflector not only increases rigidity, but it also allows

a longer thread for the cap screw, lessening the need for complete removal of cap screw with possible loss in the shavings on the floor.

7. On account of the parallelism of the top face of the deflector with the cutting iron, the pressure exerted by the lever cap is always constant throughout the entire length of adjustment of the cutter. In the old type, the convexity of the cap iron caused a variation of pressure of the lever cap, according to the position of the latter on the cap iron.

Record planes with "Stay-Set" cap irons can be recognized by the letters SS, i.e., Record jack plane 05½-SS.

3

Maintenance of Plane Cutters

All plane cutters (still called "irons" by many companies and users) are manufactured with accurately ground bevels. Most will need to be sharpened or honed before the plane can be used. In use, the cutters can be misused in various ways and the bevel become mis-shapen or out of square. The solution must be to regrind them to the original angle.

Fig. 39 shows several cutters in various stages of wear. The edge of the cutter at A is damaged either by a nail or some other metallic obstruction. B indicates frequent honing at a greater angle than 30° so that several angles have been formed. C is due to bad stance and movement of the body, i.e., rocking when sharpening has brought about a sharply rolled bevel with no clear angle. All are cases where regrinding is vitally necessary.

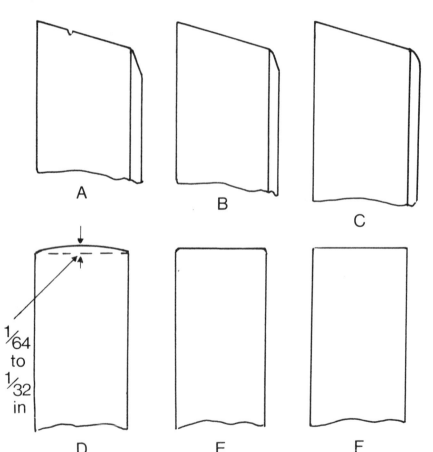

Fig. 39. A, B and C: Cutters in various stages of wear. D, E and F: Cutter shapes.

The bench plane irons are shaped for particular reasons or left totally straight, depending on the type of plane and the particular use to which the plane is to be put. The correct shape of the bench plane irons are shown in Fig. 39, D, E and F. D shows the shape given to a hogging or roughing plane. This may be fine for bringing coarsely cut boards down roughly to size for accurate planing, but the cutter leaves a corrugated surface. E is to be preferred for general work, the corners slightly rounded but the edge perfectly straight. F shows the cutter for the fore, jointer and bench rebate planes. Many craftsmen prefer to have two cutters for both the jack and smooth planes, one for finishing work and one for less accurate applications.

At all times the edge must be at right angles to the side of the cutter. The sides are straight and parallel at manufacture, unlike the handmade cutters of earlier years. The cap iron edge must also be square with the sides. Carefully use the try square to check the squareness of all these items. If difficulty is found in maintaining squareness

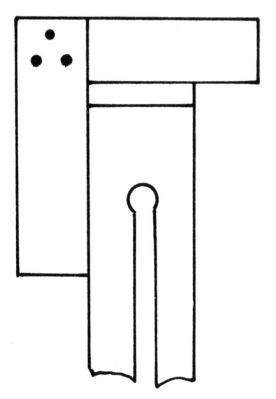

Fig. 40. Testing bench plane irons for squareness.

Fig. 41. Roughing cutter at work.

during grinding, leave the cap iron in place to act as a guide.

There are many ways and several types of grinding machines which can be used. The old-type natural sandstone wheel running in water and powered either by hand or foot treadle has largely disappeared. Fortunately, there are a number of machines having this type of wheel which have been motorized in recent years. Generally, they rotate in water or water drips with the wheel rotating towards the operator—a messy business. The wheel must not stand in water after use—this will soften the wheel. The tank must be cleaned periodically. The cutter itself can be overheated. This is the greatest disadvantage this type of wheel has when compared to wheels which run dry.

Dry wheel machines with the wheels running vertically are fast-moving. Very great care must be taken not to use excessive pressure or attempt to remove material too quickly. Otherwise, the cutter will overheat, and with the temper drawn the edge will have to be cut back. This is certainly a waste of material and money. When using a fast-moving dry grinder, keep a can of cooling water alongside for frequent dipping. The hand-operated grinders of this type leave only one hand for holding, which often results in inaccuracies of angle and shape.

One of the greatest advances in the approach to perfect grinding was made with the introduction in England of the Denford horizontal grinder.

This consists of a man-made wheel rotating slowly in an oil drip. It has an attachment for holding plane cutters and chisels at the exact angle and is the perfect answer to grinding. These machines are extremely popular in the schools in England. The angles are perfect and the cutter can be kept square. The oil passes through the stone and is filtered to return via the pump.

Fig. 42. Sharpedge oil-cooled grinder.

Almost a copy of the Sharpedge is the motorized Japanese water stone. This is, again, a man-made stone either with a cement-bonded or vitrified wheel rotating through a motor and gear train at a very slow speed. A water tank is provided which takes water into the middle of the stone. The stone moves in a tank that moves the water up the sides of the wheel and across the

stone by centrifugal force. Both the cement-bonded and vitrified wheels are fitted with tool holders. They remove metal fairly quickly, leaving a finely polished bevel. They can be fitted with several grit-size variations, as well as several different diameters of wheel.

A variation in horizontal grinding is provided by the Belshaw power hone, which has a metal disc surfaced with 600-grit diamond dust and rotates at 120 rpm. No lubricant is needed with this machine. It is ideal for plane cutters, since it remains perfectly flat and needs only infrequent cleaning, which can be done with kerosene (paraffin).

The Xenix hone is another type of dry grinder working in the horizontal. This machine offers a choice of wheels for sharpening and grinding. Probably the wheel of the greatest interest to the woodworker generally is the one of reconstituted leather mixed with rouge in a plastic bond. This wheel is shaped on the edge for curved cutting edges. The wheels can be changed over for grinding.

An increasingly popular method of grinding is the use of the abrasive belt. Several types of these are available. Perhaps the most efficient belt machine is one designed and marketed by the Woodcraft Supply Corporation of Massachusetts. It is called the Mark Two Sharpening System. Most of these belts use aluminum oxide grit No. 80, which is fine for plane cutter grinding. The Woodcraft Mark Two permits perfect holding of the tool for grinding at any angle, and the width of the belt covers most sizes of cutter.

Fig. 43. Woodcraft Mark Two.

There are a number of machines combining the abrasive belt and the wheel with either wet or dry running. ELU machinery in Germany makes a combination machine which provides this facility.

Fig. 44. Elu dry grinder.

Fig. 45. Spokeshave cutter holder.

Discs either with aluminum oxide grit or silicon carbide grit are also useful, particularly to the craftsman unable to add another machine to his workshop. These discs can be glued to wooden discs and assembled to a normal disc sander or screwed to the woodturning lathe using the faceplate, or substituted for the saw in the circular saw. They can also be screwed to an adaptor and fitted to the electric hand drill, which everyone seems to possess these days. All must have an adequate holding facility, that is, to the bench. The craftsman must also be sure of accuracy of angling and be aware of the danger of the discs burning at very high speeds, even though the discs are considered safe.

Plane cutters require far greater attention to shape and angle accuracy than most of the other cutting edge tools, and one or two holders may have to be devised. The one shown in Fig. 45 is excellent when the grinding or sharpening of spokeshave blades is necessary.

Sharpening

There are two groups of stones which can be used for sharpening: man-made or natural. The finest, best known and most expensive of the natural stones come from Arkansas. These stones are a form of quartz called novaculite.

Washita is the finest for fast sharpening. The next is soft Arkansas, then hard Arkansas and finally black Arkansas. The latter is the most difficult to obtain in the quarry and is generally the most expensive, but gives an extremely fine sharp edge suitable for planesmen. Probably the most useful would be a combination of hard Arkansas and Washita. Even the lovely boxes in which many of these stones come are fashioned from local cedar growing in Arkansas. Many of the natural stones of the past like Welsh slate, Italian marble, turkey stone, water of Ayr stone and Charnley Forest stone are now difficult or almost unobtainable.

The more commonly used stones are India® or Carborundum®, obtainable in several grades from coarse through to fine. A very fast stone is made of crystalon, again available in a number of grades. A slower cutting stone which hardly wears at all is the Ultimate Diemond, manufactured in the U.S. White in color, it almost resembles marble.

Fig. 46. Using the oilstone.

Sizes 8 × 2 × 1 inch or 6 × 2 × 1 inch will be most suitable for bench planes, while the edges of these stones can be used for smaller cutters. If difficulty is found in holding cutters at the correct angle, a number of holders have been designed which serve to assist in this.

For the sharpening of beading and other curved cutters, one or two slip stones are needed. Probably the best buy is the Arkansas Fileset, which has a number of shapes that serve to sharpen not only plane cutters but other curved edge tools.

Another useful sharpening medium is the rubberized abrasive stick, block or wheel. In this product, silicon carbide grit has been bonded in neoprene rubber. The sticks, blocks and slips can be used in the same way as other traditional sharpening stones. The wheels can be mounted in place of the vitrified wheel of the double-ended grinder. It is better to reverse the direction of the wheels to avoid any possibility of digging into the slightly softer material. A great advantage in using the rubberized abrasive is that not only is a fine edge produced, but the bevel is polished at the same time. This latter point will be more appreciated by the woodturner and the woodcarver.

Oilstone Oils

Though any thin nondrying oil will do, the old-time enthusiast will call for neat's-foot oil or a mixture of neat's-foot and sweet oil. A light machine oil like 3-in-one ® or motor oil thinned with kerosene (paraffin) will be perfect. An oil becoming very popular is Sharp'N Aid. The manufacturers of the Ultimate Diemond stone even suggest that

water be used, as, of course, do the makers of Japanese water stones. Using water helps greatly inasmuch as there is no possibility of transferring oil to the wood after sharpening since the cutters wipe clean.

It must be remembered that the oilstone has a true cutting action like that of the grindstone, but it cuts more slowly and leaves a keener edge. The edge and its fineness will depend to the degree of fineness found in the actual sharpening stone. The craftsman himself will have to make the decision as regards the quality of the stone he selects.

Sharpening the Cutting Iron

The process of honing or sharpening is simply rubbing the bevelled edge of the blade on the face of the oilstone. There are one or two things that must be observed in doing this, or the desired result will not appear.

First put a few drops of oil on the stone and wipe the stone thoroughly clean with a rag. Many craftsmen are in the habit of cleaning the stone with a handful of shavings, but this so often results in filling the pores of the stone with dust and grit that it is not a practice to be commended. A clean rag is much preferred.

Having cleaned the stone and put some fresh oil on it, take up the cutter in the hands, as indicated in Fig. 46. Bring the cutter in contact with the stone, noting Fig. 47. Feel the bevel in contact

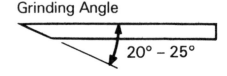

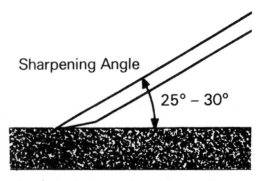

Fig. 47. Angles for grinding and sharpening.

throughout, and then raise the back slightly so that you will work on the front, i.e., the cutting edge. The best motion is to and fro, though some craftsmen use a figure eight motion. The latter in inexperienced hands is apt to produce an alteration of bevel. Its possible advantage is that there is a certain amount of oblique cut that is supposed to clear the "grindings" away and distribute stone wear more evenly. As, however, the particles of steel float on the oil and so are carried away, the advantage of the figure eight motion (see Fig. 48) is a little doubtful.

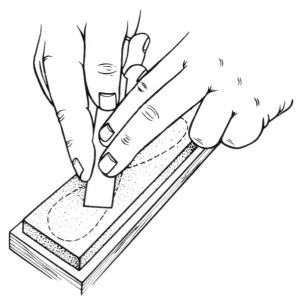

Fig. 48. Figure eight movement.

Do not be too sparing with the oil; lack of oil will result in "glazing"—i.e., the pores of the stone become clogged with steel and the stone assumes a polished appearance. When this occurs, the chances of cutting it are poor. The condition can be remedied by cleaning with kerosene (paraffin) and retruing, which will be described later on. Often the application of kerosene (paraffin) tends to make the stone cut more quickly; this is not always an advantage. A soaking with melted Vaseline ® will usually slow a stone that is too fast.

For an initial attempt, use the to and fro motion, as in Fig. 46. Use as much of the flat surface of the stone as possible, for in this way the wear on the stone is more evenly spread. You will also delay the time when your stone becomes "hollow" and needs truing up. Do not allow the cutter to

"rock," as this will inevitably result in a curved surface that cannot produce an edge that will cut well. It will almost certainly call for a regrind. Keep the angle of the cutter to the stone constant. This will mean that the wrists must be kept rigid, but it does not call for a viselike grip. Apply moderate pressure and keep on honing until the line of reflected light on the edge disappears and a black hairline of cutting edge results.

A certain amount of wire edge will be left on the edge of the cutter after honing. This amount will vary with the type of stone used and the amount of actual sharpening that has had to take place. To remove the wire edge, lay the cutter down perfectly flat on the stone, bevel side uppermost, and rub gently—preferably in a circular motion. This will remove the wire edge, but it is important that the cutter is kept perfectly flat during the process, as any tendency to lift it will start a second bevel on the opposite side to the ground edge.

Fig. 49. Removing the wire edge.

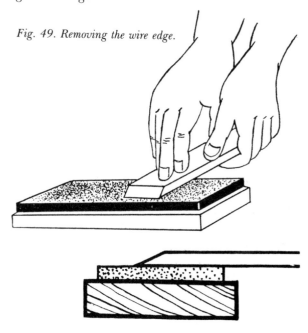

When there is a second bevel on the opposite side to the ground edge, very small shavings wedge between the cap iron and the cutter, subsequently causing choking in the mouth of the plane, especially if the cap iron is set for a very fine cut. Rubbing the thumb or finger on the flat side towards the cutting edge will denote the presence of such a wire edge. If the edge cannot be felt, a final check is to use the thumb or finger in the same way on the bevel itself. If the wire edge has been pushed over, it will be detected on this side. Rub the bevel once again very lightly on the stone until it disappears, but repeat the check on the flat side. A good-quality stone will leave only a very small wire edge which, after one or two rubs, will disappear almost entirely, denoting that the edge is ready for use. A coarse stone will create a rougher wire edge which will take longer to remove. Also, the actual cutting edge will not be as keen or as fine as that obtained with the smooth, hard stone. It cannot be overemphasized that no matter how many times you have to change sides when removing the wire edge, the cutter must always be perfectly flat on the stone when the flat side is in contact.

The effectiveness of the edge will depend upon the accuracy with which you have kept the two faces truly flat and free from curve, as well as the meeting of these two faces in a sharp keen angle and the "polish" which you will have put on with the oilstone. A coarse stone will not give this polish—the surface will be covered with scratches: It is these scratches which must be removed. That is why an Arkansas stone or a very fine artificial stone gives an edge that is better. Moreover, a scratch-free sharpening will have a longer working life than a sharpening which is indifferently finished.

Cutters are not only made of the finest steel for their particular purpose, but the face side of the iron is finished smoothly so that the operator can work up the type of surface required in a reasonable time. Good honing is an art worth taking considerable trouble to perfect, and it goes a long way towards explaining the old craftsman's belief that you don't really get the best out of a cutter until you have been using it some time.

Much can be said in favor of the method of honing employed by many experienced craftsmen, in which the whole of the surface of the 25° bevel is honed to a keen edge, thus using one bevel instead of two. For fine finishing work this method gives a very pleasing and satisfactory cut, and in fact with most woods the cut is better than with two bevels. The time taken up in honing is not very much more than that taken up in the two-bevel method, owing to the structure of the blade.

Exponents of the two-bevel method claim that the time taken in sharpening is slightly less, and that the edge is slightly stronger because the "thicker" angle results in more metal behind the edge. The latter point may be realized more clearly by comparing a paring chisel edge with a mortise chisel edge. This advantage is not so clear when a plane cutter is used, because the action is very dissimilar to that of a mortise chisel. There is a definite advantage to the two-bevel method in that one never has a thick edge. Therefore, it is possible to get a workable, satisfactorily honed edge even when one is working on a site away from the workshop and grindstone or when one does not possess a wet grindstone (as is the case with most amateurs).

The amateur (and the younger professional) who finds difficulty in mastering the art of sharpening will find an edge tool honer of great value for honing not only plane cutters and plow (plough) cutters, but also spokeshave cutters and chisels.

Sharpening the Plow (Plough), Combination and Multi-plane Cutters

All these cutters have been accurately ground to the correct 35° bevel before leaving the factory, but all will require sharpening before they can be used. After a period of time they will require resharpening. It is suggested that the sharpening be done on the ground bevel. In other words, do not give these cutters a secondary bevel, as with plane cutters. The user will find them much easier to maintain if this rule is followed.

Use as always a good-quality flat oilstone lightly smeared with a thin machine oil. Many people prefer to use the edge of the oilstone for sharpening this type of cutter, since most of the cutters are narrow in width. Sharpen the plow (plough) cutters by placing the ground bevel firmly on the surface of the oilstone, moving it forward and back in a slight figure eight movement in order to distribute the oil and wear the stone evenly. A rounded edge must be avoided, and the cutter angle kept constant. If an edge tool honer is available, then the job can be considerably simplified and the perfect angle maintained.

When a wire edge appears on the reverse side of the cutter and extends along the full width of the cutting edge, the cutter should be laid flat on the oilstone, bevel-side up. A few strokes forward and back will remove it. If the wire edge is still turned over, a few more strokes on the bevel edge will produce a wire edge which again can be removed by reversing. Care must be taken to ensure that the cutter lies flat on the stone since any lift will round the back and render it useless. The cutter will now be sharp and ready for use.

The beading and sash cutters call for two separate sharpening operations. First, sharpen the quirks as with the plow (plough) cutter. Second, the curve of the cutter must be sharpened using an oilstone slip with an edge curve to suit the sweep of the bead. Do not make a second bevel. Sharpen to maintain the shape and prevent grinding. Remove the wire edge as before. The rubberized abrasive slip can be used for this particular exercise and is adequate for the job. This sharpening also applies to the hollows, rounds, nosing, fluting, reeding and ovolo cutters.

The spurs of the multi-plane should be sharpened on the inside only. Those on the Record 050C combination plane must be sharpened as with the ordinary cutter.

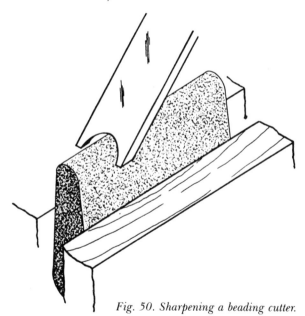

Fig. 50. Sharpening a beading cutter.

Sharpening for Plastics

Plastics, Perspex®, Formica ® and other laminates and plywoods having resin-type cements are notorious for their quick blunting of plane cutters. When only small amounts are to be undertaken or when this type of work occurs only infrequently, the ordinary sharpening can be used and the quicker blunting of the cutter is accepted as a necessary nuisance.

If the work comes frequently, however, it is worthwhile keeping a cutter especially for that work, grinding and sharpening it at a blunt angle somewhere between 80° and 85°. An edge of this type will stay sharp longer than the normally sharpened one. Special steels have been tried for this work but they are relatively expensive and cannot ordinarily be sharpened by the user. Hence, they have been ruled out. Another suggestion is that instead of sharpening all the angle from one side, sharpen the cutter at the normal angle and then take a slight grinding off the face side of the cutter, thus making a cutting angle approximate to the one previously recommended.

Storage of Oilstones

In many workshops a separate strong table is used to house the oilstones only. The table's surface is covered with zinc or some other material from which the oil can easily be wiped. The oilstone cases are screwed to the tabletop to prevent them from moving about. This practice keeps the dirty oil away from the working benches, where there is always a chance of it getting onto work in hand.

When, however, for one reason or another, a separate table is out of the question, it is a good plan to screw the oilstone boxes onto the base of a shallow box. One lid can cover all the stones. Screw a batten to the underside of the base and the whole assembly can be safely held in the vise. The oilstones must be held rigidly at all times.

Oilstones in their containers should be stored in a rack or cupboard away from the bench. Many workers prefer to have two small nails tacked into the bottom of the box to temporarily fix the oilstone to the bench top, but this is a method which could result in transferring oil to the bench, and then to the work. Japanese water stones are best stored in water. If this is not possible they should be soaked well before use.

Resurfacing the Oilstones

When the oilstone becomes hollow or out of shape in any way, it will not give efficient service for the simple reason that it will tend to mis-shape the cutters being sharpened. It can be trued-up on the flat side of the horizontal grinder if you are fortunate enough to possess one.

Another way of truing the worn stone is to grind it on a flat stone using water and some very fine sand. I have found the best method is to use a thick sheet of plate glass that one can assume to be exactly flat. Make up a mixture of oil and Carborundum ® powder about 60 to 80 grit. Rub the stone with this mixture, keeping the oil level fairly high. This will quickly arrive at a flat surface, but with the very fine stones many small scratches that will interfere with the final quality of the sharpening may well be seen on the surface of the stone. To remove these, I place a sheet of very fine wet and dry paper, that is, paper covered with a silicon carbide grit size of anything between 2 and 400. This will effectively remove any scratches and leave you with a perfect surface.

Sharpening the Cutter of the Cabinet Scraper

The cutters are supplied ground at 45°. Even a new one must be sharpened before the tool can be used. This is best carried out on a fine or medium stone maintaining the same angle. Use a light machine oil on the oilstone as before and remember to leave the stone clean and dry after use.

To sharpen, rest the ground bevel of the cutter flat on the stone. Keeping the cutter at this angle, move it forward and back across the stone. As the cutter reaches the sharpened state, a wire edge will appear on the flat face. When this extends along the full width, lay the cutter flat on the oilstone, bevel uppermost. A few light strokes up and down the stone will remove the wire edge. Great care should be taken to ensure that the back of the cutter lies flat on the oilstone. Any lift will round the back of the cutter and render it useless. A slight rounding of the corners of the cutter as with the smoothing plane cutter is an advantage if not overdone.

The cutter now requires burnishing. Place it

flat on the bench, bevel-side downwards. Using a burnisher of correct steel, draw it along the edge forward and back about 20 times, pressing quite hard but making sure all the time that the burnisher lies dead flat on the cutter.

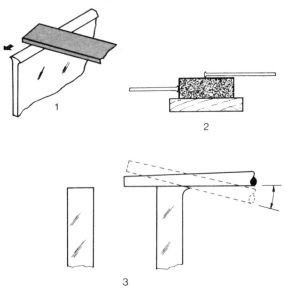

Fig. 51. Sharpening the cutter of a cabinet scraper.

This procedure consolidates the metal to give it a tougher surface. On no account must the edge be turned over. If the edge is turned at this stage, then the next operation will break the fine edge, which we need to carry out the work of scraping.

Now set the cutter up in the vise, with the ground edge towards the operator and with the burnisher lying on the 45° bevel. Burnish to and fro again, pressing quite hard. As the burnishing proceeds, raise the handle by easy stages until the burnisher makes an angle of 15° with the horizontal. Probably 30 or 40 strokes may be needed, depending on the stroke pressure. The edge will now show a definite hook and is ready for use.

Resharpening the Cutter

First of all, remove all the wire edge from the flat side of the cutter either on an oilstone or with a dead smooth file, taking care not to make any bevel. If needed, the cutter can be rubbed on the edge of an oilstone to straighten it. Grind the edge to return to the 45° angle if this should be necessary. Then proceed to sharpen it as with a new blade.

4

Using the Planes

1. Squaring a Piece of Wood

Remember to stand comfortably when planing. The left foot should be pointing forward, with the weight on the left foot at the end of the stroke. Press at the forward end of the plane at the commencement of the stroke and on the rear handle of the plane on completion of the cut.

First select the best side of the wood, then plane it free from unevenness and blemish. Carefully test this side with a straight edge in all directions by laying on the straight edge and holding it up to the light. If the side is flat, no light will appear between the straight edge and the board in any position of the straight edge. It is essential that there is no "wind" (twist). To test for this, apply two similar straight edges, as in the diagram, and sight along the line of the arrow (Fig. 53). If there is no "wind," the edges of the strips will appear as in 2, Fig. 53. If there are any deviations, they will appear as in 3, Fig. 53. The longer the winding strips, the more apparent will be the error. Winding strips should be made up as a pair—a good exercise in planing for the keen craftsman. Use a good hardwood for long service, and select it with a fairly dark color for ease when sighting.

Beginners often decide to use a smoothing plane for this accurate work, but this is a bad choice since the smoothing plane will not only work over a convexity but also in a concavity, leaving a perfectly smooth job but not a true surface. The jack plane or jointer, by reason of their long length, are unable to do this, for they plane off the hillocks and cannot work in the valleys until they are planed off.

Fig. 52. Planing stance: Squaring a piece of wood.

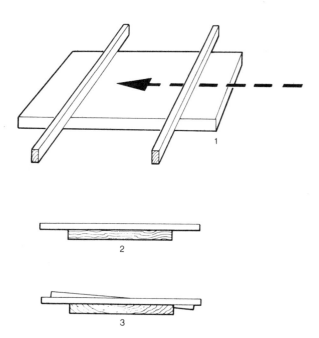

Fig. 53. Winding strips used for testing.

A short plane will not plane a long edge straight.
A long plane will bridge the hollows.

Fig. 54.

Having planed up the side, now plane an edge. This must not only be straight in length and breadth and free from winding, but must also be square, i.e., at right angles to the first or face side. Holding the plane correctly is important in this instance.

The fingers underneath the front of the plane hold it in position. At the same time, by taking a gentle bearing on the side of the work, hold the plane at right angles to the face. Test with the straight edge and try square in all positions, and when correct mark it as a face edge.

Now gauge the desired thickness of the wood, making sure that the stock of the gauge is running on the face side, as marked in Fig. 55. Plane off the waste as far as the line. The next step is to plane to width. Gauge this time with the stock against the face edge. Plane to the line. The wood will now be flat and square without winding.

2. Making Butt (Slape) Joints

Butt joints are used to join boards together to make one wide board. There are two very sound reasons why every woodworker should be able to join two or more narrow boards together:

1). Wide boards are seldom obtainable today. Even when they are, their scarcity makes them command high prices. The price per square foot or square metre is always higher for the wide boards than it is for narrower ones. Thus, a tabletop 3 feet × 18 inches would cost more as a single board than it would for 3 lengths six-inches wide, which joined together would make a board of equal size. (The scarcity of wide boards has resulted in the development of man-made boards such as plywood, laminated boards and chipboard. The quality of these boards can be seen in cabinet design.)

2). The shrinkage and warpage of wide boards is very much more apparent than that of the narrower boards, and narrower boards can always be "reversed" to minimize the tendency to warp. In the case of a tabletop it is essential that all signs of the joints are eliminated as far as possible and the boards kept level.

To make up a wide board, first lay out the boards, as in Fig. 58, putting the way of the grain as shown by the arrows, and "matching" the grain

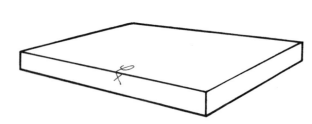

Fig. 55. Face side and face edge marks.

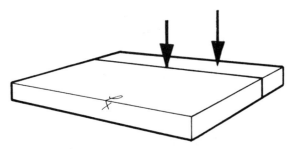

Fig. 57. Board gauged to width.

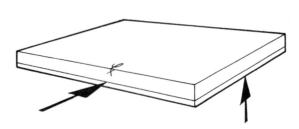

Fig. 56. Board gauged to thickness.

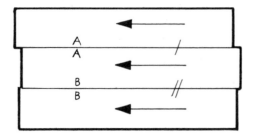

Fig. 58. Laying out the boards.

as nearly as possible for appearance's sake. Arrange the boards with heart sides alternating, as in the side view. This way, any upward pull of one board in subsequent warping will be counteracted by the downward pull of the next. Accurate planing of the faces is done after gluing, but preliminary planing will lessen distortion when the boards are glued and reduce the face finishing required. Mark the edges to be joined AA, BB or with a series of strokes (both ways are shown in Fig. 58) for instant recognition when gluing up.

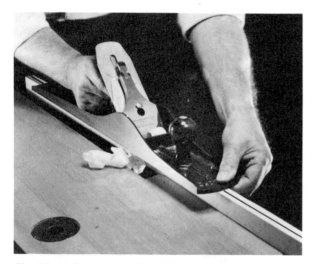

Fig. 59. Preliminary planing of boards.

Place the first two boards lengthwise in the vise, as shown in Fig. 59. If necessary, on account of their length, use C clamps (G cramps) to keep them together. The two marked edges, (AA, Fig. 58), must be on the outside. Plane straight and true. If you are slightly out of square that will not matter very much, as a slight deviation that way is compensated by the fact that you will reverse one board in fitting (see Fig. 60). However, you must plane straight in the length.

Jointing boards in this manner calls for the try or jointer plane, the long length of which is best suited for truing long lengths with extreme accuracy. Short planes cannot work accurately on a long length. The adoption of this method prevents exasperating failures such as are indicated in Fig. 61.

Proceed with the other joints in the same way until all are completed. The boards should now be glued. However, make sure before you start

this process that the glue is ready for use and that you have enough of it. (Cold glues are ideal for this purpose and are easier to use than the animal glues, which must be heated and applied hot.)

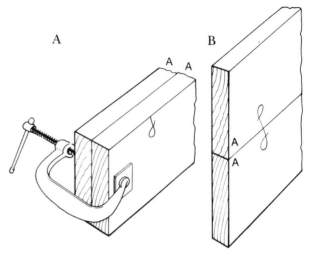

Fig. 60. A: Boards clamped together before being placed in the vise for edge planing. B: Boards together after planing.

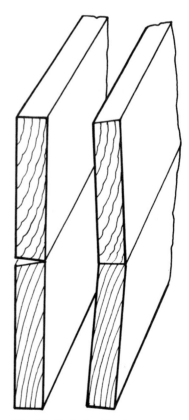

Fig. 61. Bad edge planing.

Arrange the boards on the bench in the proper order of fitting. Place the first board with edge A upwards in the vise, and lay the marked edge of the second board along it so that the marks match. Glue both edges where they are to be joined, and then place the glued edges together (the first still remaining in the vise). Rub them together until they "stick." Make sure they are in correct alignment and that the edges are not over-lapping. Leave them as such while you glue the next board in a similar manner, and so on, to the finish.

The ideal is perfectly true edges, with no line of glue showing. If the edges are planed true they will hold forever, the glued joint being stronger than the material itself. Remove surplus glue with a cloth.

When there are but two or three small pieces, they can either be left as they are for 24 hours or moved carefully and supported at the back, as in Fig. 62. Where the work is large, however, the joints should be clamped, and left in the clamps until the glue sets hard.

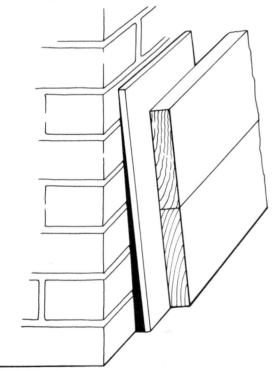

Fig. 62. Pieces supported at the back.

Another way of temporarily holding a job like this until the glue is set is by the use of carpenter's

dogs, which are much like large staples. The 2½-inch carpenter's dogs are the best. They are driven in the end grain at both ends of each joint, thus holding the two boards together. They are easily withdrawn after the glue has set.

When arranging the clamps, it is wise to have one at each end and one in the middle, the latter being placed at the opposite side from the former. Thus, any tendency the tightening of the clamps may have to spring the boards will be counteracted by the bar of the clamp on the opposite side. Protect the boards from damage by the clamps by inserting pieces of waste wood between the edge of the board and the clamp shoes. Screw the clamps up firmly, but not too hard. All surplus glue must be squeezed out, as excess glue weakens, not strengthens, the joint.

Fig. 63. Clamping boards with three clamps.

If the clamps are required for another purpose during the setting period, lightly nail a couple of splines across the boards to hold them, and then remove the clamps. In any case, allow the joints to set. Whenever possible, it is preferable to leave the clamps in their original position for that period.

With the glue set hard, proceed to square up the board. Select the better face. Clamp it face-up to the bench top with C clamps (G cramps) or between the dogs of the dog vise bench. Proceed (after removing the surplus glue) to clean up the top. If the lumber is a hardwood with cross and troublesome grain, the plane should be finely set and used across the grain until the surface is fairly true.

For final finishing, the cutter should be extremely sharp and set as fine as possible in order to obtain a very delicate shaving. Final planing should take place along the grain. Perfection can be gained only in this way. Sweetly grained softer hardwoods and softwoods will not require planing across the grain.

Gauge to thickness, and clean up the other face in a similar manner. The top or better face will possibly require a final scraping and sanding. Notes on scrapers can be found in Chapter 13.

Of late years, improvements in manufacture and length of pot life (length of time glues take to go hard when kept in a sealed pot) have made resin glues much more popular with both professionals and amateurs. Some of these glues require a separate hardener, while others are of the "one shot" type. All of them can be applied cold—which is a considerable advantage. The maker's instructions for each individual glue should be closely followed, as there are slight differences in application. All the glues, provided instructions are carefully carried out, will make a sound joint. The gap-filler type will often make a good joint where animal glue would fail.

Another advantage these modern glues have is that many are waterproof, and so can be used for joints that are exposed to the weather. One word of warning should be given: Use a somewhat light clamping, because if all the glue is squeezed out the joint will subsequently fail. Both C clamps (G cramps) and bar clamps (sash cramps) can give heavier pressures than the ones usually recommended, even when screwed up by hand. Hence, the amount of pressure given should not be excessive.

The resin glues are deservedly popular for another reason—the clamping process can be considerably shortened. The type of hardener and the temperature of the room both affect clamping times, and here again it will be necessary to refer to makers' instructions. Excess glue is preferably wiped off before it has set because when the glue is set, though it can be planed, it is not kind to plane blade edges.

3. Making Tongued Joints

The joints that have been discussed in the previous section can be strengthened by adding to the gluing surface. This can be done in a variety of ways: by putting in a "loose tongue" (which may have the grain running the same way as the boards or may have a "cross tongue"; that is, its grain running at right angles to the boards); by having a tongue on one board and a corresponding groove on the other (tongue and groove); or by a number of tongues and grooves.

The butt or rubbed joint is a perfectly sound joint which will hold up indefinitely so long as it is kept dry. It is eminently suited for cabinetwork for tops, etc., and for panels which are set in rebates or plowed grooves. There are occasions, however, as, for example, in a kitchen tabletop, where if the glue should give and shrinkage occur at some later date, it is advisable that there should not be a gap. Then we must have a tongue of some sort.

Plane up the edges exactly as if you were making a butt joint, as already shown. Then, if you are going to make a tongued joint, select a cutter that will be approximately one-third the thickness of the wood, i.e., for a tabletop a ¼-inch cutter. (Some prefer a thinner tongue than one-third.) Set your plow cutter in your plow and adjust the fence on the plane being used. This cuts the groove in the middle of the edge of the board. Keep the fence always against the face side marks placed on the wood. This is important; otherwise, the boards may be off-set.

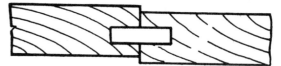

Fig. 64. Off-set boards. They are caused by failure to keep the fence against the face side of the board.

Set the depth gauge of the plane to cut the groove deeper than its width. For instance, if you are cutting a ¼-inch wide groove, your tongues should be from ¾ inch to ⅞ inch deep, and the depth of the groove should be slightly greater than half of the depth of the tongue on each board (Fig. 65). The central position can be accurately determined by fixing the fence either by measurement or by trial on the board itself.

To cut the groove, place the board, edge to be cut upwards, in the vise, face side towards you. Begin at the end farther away and take short strokes at first, each stroke beginning a little farther back than the last (Fig. 66), until you have worked back the full length of the board. Then take a stroke the full length of the board. Continue this until you can no longer cut a shaving. This will indicate that you have an even, predetermined depth—a perfectly accurate groove in both width and depth.

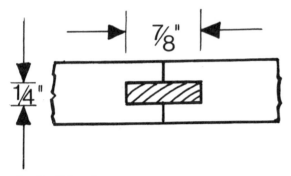

Fig. 65. Sizing the tongue.

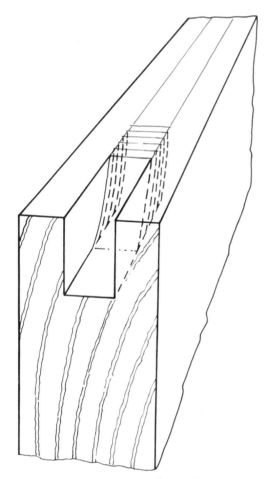

Fig. 66. Commencing to cut the groove.

It should be noted at this point that in using grooving planes there is no need whatever to bear downwards heavily. It is vitally important, however, that pressure shall be applied towards the wood, so that the fence is always in close contact with the side, particularly in the early stages of the cut. Once the groove has been started, the cutter will stay in the groove and the plane will work very well indeed. Do not use too much cutter. Two or three thin shavings are better than one thick one, produce more accurate work and are less laborious to remove. If you are "forcing" any woodworking tool, you are not getting the best out of it, out of your material or out of yourself.

Work each board the same way on each of the edges to be joined. Then prepare the tongues. Having cut the grooves, make the tongues. If you have some pieces of lumber available of a thickness equal to that of the grooves, all that is necessary is to cut pieces of the correct depth. Alternatively, plane pieces to correct width and thickness to seat perfectly in the groove. These pieces need not be as long as the boards to be joined if you are going to cross-tongue, so use up any odd pieces that are available. Saw pieces across the grain so that their width is that of the two grooves combined. They will fit along the groove end-to-end, as in Fig. 67. The fact that the grain runs opposite to that of the boards nullifies any reason for their absolute continuity.

When the boards are glued together, all the pieces, as well as the boards, become cemented into one strong whole. Loose tongues should always be crossed like this. They resist any tendency the board may have, when completed, to bend, while a long-grained tongue is weak in that very respect. Good plywood may be used for the tongue. You must, however, choose an exact size cutter that will make a groove the plywood will fit. Millimetre cutters are available to suit plywood of sizes suitable for this job. The cross-tongued joint is a very strong joint indeed.

Immediately before gluing up, it is good practice to run a thin shaving off the inside corners of the groove with a rebate or shoulder plane finely set. This assists the egress of surplus glue when clamping up. The shaving taken off must, of course, be very light.

Should the tongue need to be invisible, particularly in made-up tabletops, the tongue has to be inserted in a stopped groove. This cannot be done satisfactorily with the plow plane. A router can be used (see pages 116 and 117, Chapter 10).

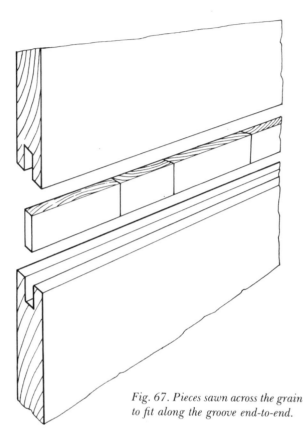

Fig. 67. Pieces sawn across the grain to fit along the groove end-to-end.

The same construction can be used for a woman's work table or a similar top where you want to give access to a recess by means of a movable panel. In the latter case, the movable panel will sit on a rebate, the depth of which will be arranged so that it just misses the tongue. Only a plain mitre appears inside the rebate.

There are times when exceptional strength is called for in a tongued joint. This strength is secured by a variation of the above method, i.e., by using two, three or even more' tongues. Cutting multiple tongues requires no more skill than cutting single ones. The thickness of the wood will dictate the number of tongues required and also their distance apart.

Set the fence to cut the first groove at the required distance, and with the fence *always* held against the face side of each board cut the first groove in each piece. Reset the fence to cut subsequent grooves. Observe the fence against the face-side rule throughout. Where a wide board is to be made up, grooves can be cut on both edges of a long board, which can then be cut to final lengths. This is probably the strongest edge-to-edge joint that can be made with hand planes.

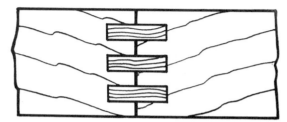

Fig. 68. Multiple tongues.

4. Making Tongued-And-Grooved Joints

A joint which is in common use and much more widely known than those mentioned is the tongued-and-grooved joint—the joint that is used on "matching" boards. Though any bending strain from side-to-side could break away the tongue in the direction of the grain, it is a joint that is eminently suited for matching boards which are not glued together, such as boards for partitions, the backs of Welsh dressers, etc. The combination plane and the multi-plane make this kind of work quite easy. For a plain tongue and groove such as is used for flooring, the edges must first be planed straight and square. The tonguing cutter is then set by means of the fence to ensure that the gap in the cutter which leaves the tongue is centered. The depth of the tongue is regulated by the small gauge on the cutter. If the thickness of the board exceeds the overall width of the tonguing cutter, the small ridges which remain on either side can be removed quite easily with a rebate plane.

Begin at the far end of the board, as when cutting a groove (Fig. 66). Make sure the fence is held securely up to the side of the work and take only light cuts. The depth gauge on the cutter will control the depth of cut to the setting made, leaving a tongue of the exact height required.

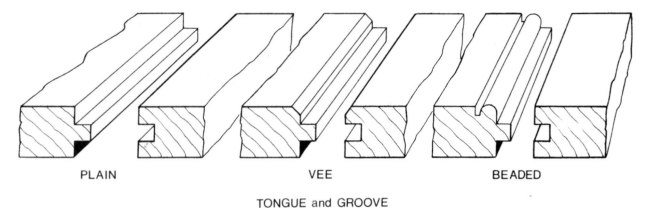

PLAIN   VEE   BEADED

TONGUE and GROOVE

Fig. 69. Tongued-and-grooved joints.

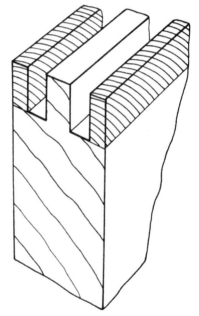

Fig. 70. Board wider than the cutter; shaded portions are removed afterwards.

Having finished the tongues, replace the cutter with a plow cutter of identical width to the tongue itself. Adjust the fence to allow the full width of the plow cutter to fit accurately over the width of the tongue. This will ensure that the groove about to be cut is in line with the tongue, and allow it to seat correctly. Replace the board in the vise, with the one now to be grooved. The depth gauge should be set to cut a groove about $\frac{1}{16}$ inch deeper than the tongue itself, which will then seat completely in the groove without leaving a gap on the outside edges.

You must plane your board true and straight first. Be sure to work from the face side when cutting both tongues and grooves or you will find that your boards join up unevenly—some farther back than others.

There is always the possibility of shrinkage and the chance of the joints opening some time after they have been in position. To improve the appearance of a tongued joint, the two front edges are occasionally chamfered, thus giving a V-shaped opening. The chamfering can easily be done with a metal jack (see Fig. 69).

A much more effective method of masking the joint is by means of a bead. The bead is planed on the side that carries the tongue. If planed on the grooved side, the quirk would so weaken the board that the bead would break away. Cutting a bead on matching boards is an easy and rapid operation either with the combination plane or multi-plane, and instructions for making it can be found in Chapters 8 and 9. As in plowing, the cut should be started at the farther end and worked backwards. The top of the bead should be slightly below the rest of the surface, so that it does not suffer in subsequent cleaning up.

5. Use of Center Beads on Beaded Tongued-and-Grooved Boards

Beaded tongued-and-grooved boards always look best when the boards are narrow, say, 3 to 4 inches wide. It may be, however, that the boards are 6 inches wide, or even of varying widths. The work entailed and the wastage of area involved in cutting the wide boards into narrow ones may not be worthwhile, or the widths available may not be suitable.

In this case, bead and tongue and groove all the boards on their edges, as already described. Then set out even (or approximately even) distances in the widths. Run a center bead down with the same cutter used for the edge beads, setting the fence suitable for the distance and the depth stop so that the bead is just below the surface. It is always wise to run the beads a little below the surface. This way, when you come to clean up and sandpaper to a finish, the beauty of the bead is not ruined by the acquisition of a flat, which has an annoying habit of catching the light and proclaiming its presence.

6. Making Dowelled Joints

Jointing two boards along their length with dowels is done very often, but it has to be admitted that a dowelled joint will often spring when a butt joint holds. However, the method of doing it is given here. Place the boards face sides together, face edges upwards in the vise, so that their face edges are in the same plane. Mark off, at intervals, the places where the dowels are to come, in such a manner that the mark appears at the intersection of face side and edge on both boards. Then release the boards and square each board on each mark from the face side, marking on the face edge.

Set a cutting gauge accurately to half the thickness of the board, and from the face side gauge across the squared marks. The crossings of the two markings will give the positions of the centers of the dowel holes. These should be approximately one-third the thickness of the boards, and care must be taken to bore at right angles to the face edge. The dowels should be slightly rounded at each end, and many workers like a slight groove along the length of the dowel, the object in each case being a means for the escape of excess glue.

Fit the boards dry to make sure all goes up well. Then take them apart and glue the dowels into one board, which is best held in the vise for this purpose. Then glue both edges and the projecting dowels, as well as the holes in the other board. Bring all together and clamp up, leaving the

clamps on until the glue sets. The operation must be done quickly. If the glue is likely to set quicker, everything required must be ready at hand before any glue is applied.

It is a good plan when jointing long lengths to plane the edges very slightly hollow. This way, the ends of the joint tend to pull together more.

A dowelled joint that embodies a rebate is a particularly strong joint. The boards are prepared as for ordinary dowelling first, and the dowels are fitted dry. A shallow rebate is then taken out of each edge, on opposite sides. The extra gluing surfaces presented, and the interlocking angles, make the joint very strong indeed. Care must be taken, of course, that the width taken out of the one side for the rebate is equal to the amount left on the other, so that when the boards are put together the faces of the two are flush. Any air space left in a joint makes a weakness.

7. Planing a Round or an Oval Rod

There is always a tendency by a beginner to solve this problem by using a spokeshave. The usual result is a keen disappointment. First, accurately square up your piece as already described. Then joint the diagonals, as at A or B (Fig. 71), and strike out accurately the circle or ellipse required. Make a pair of cradles to rest the work in against the bench stop. Now plane the corners off straight, as at D and E, leaving the piece truly octagonal. Plane off the corners now to first make it 16-sided; then again to make it 32-sided; and again to make it 64-sided. A scraper or file and sandpaper will finish off your job accurately.

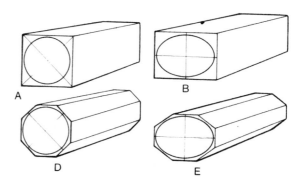

Fig. 71. Marking out for planing a round or an oval rod.

8. Cleaning Up the Edges of a Frame Too Big to Hold in the Vise

When the work cannot be secured in the vise, it can often be held between the knees, or one can sit on it, or it may be clamped to the bench end or on top of the bench. Sometimes an awkward size of frame can rest on the trestle while part of it is secured in the vise. This usually works if the planing is done towards the vise.

9. Making a Raised Panel

Square up the panel perfectly, checking each corner for squareness. Fit a ¼-inch cutter to the plane being used. Set the depth and adjust the fence so that the cut is made at the desired distance from the edge. Cut the two grooves with the grain, then set down the spurs on both the body and slide to cut just below the cutter.

Now cut the grooves across the grain. With the jack plane, remove the waste outside the grooves all around the panel. Use a finely set shoulder plane to trim the upstand edges and fine the corners. When trimming the end grain, work from the outside in to the middle. Alternatively, finish with the bench rebate plane.

Work the long way of the grain first. Make a nice, clean, straight mitre where the slopes join at the corners.

An alternative method is to use a fluting cutter with the multi-plane instead of a plow cutter. The cutter must be very sharp and finely set. In this manner, the groove is concave, so that the edge of the fielding is left quarter-round, instead of straight, as in the first case. The play of the light on this quarter-round has a very fine effect if the work is cleanly carried out.

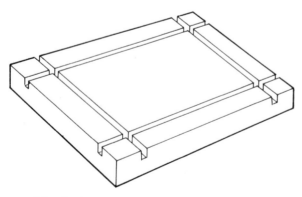

Fig. 72. Planing a groove.

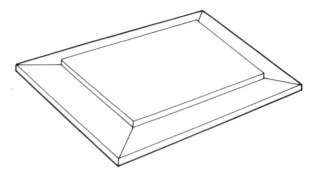

Fig. 73. Slope planed to leave raised middle.

10. Cutting a Groove or Rebate Wider Than Your Widest Cutter

The widest cutter may not be capable of cutting a groove wide enough. Work a groove of any width on the side farthest away from the face edge at the place where the edge of the required groove is to come. Now take a cutter slightly wider than the remainder and take this off at a second cut, letting the cutter make the near edge at the required distance from the face edge. Keep the depth gauge the same for both cuts (Fig. 74).

A similar method is used for cutting a wide rebate, finally removing the outside waste wood after the plow cut has been made with a jack plane.

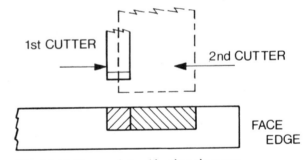

Fig. 74. Cutting a rebate wider than the cutter.

11. Starting the Mortises for Haunched Tenons

The joints of, say, a kitchen table are stronger if the tenons are haunched. The work of mortising is much lighter if the combination plane or the multi-plane is used in the preliminary cuts, working as if you were going to groove them. There is no need to mark out the width of the mortises, as the spur cutters do this for you. At the same time, the part of the haunch to fit in is brought to depth by the cutter of the plane. Any slight cut made beyond the limit of the mortise is hidden by the lower part of the rail when glued up. This is a great time-saver (Fig. 75).

The haunches and the mortises to the depth of the haunch can also be quickly and accurately cut with the Router 071. Use the straight side of the fence, as in making a stopped groove (see Fig. 206, page 114).

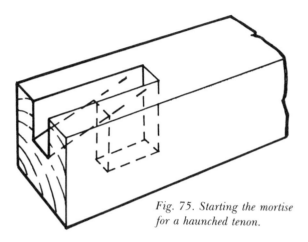

Fig. 75. Starting the mortise for a haunched tenon.

12. Making Multiple Reeds

You can make multiple reeds with the combination plane or the multi-plane when only a single bead cutter is available (Fig. 76). Start on the side farthest away from the face edge and cut the first bead. Adjust the fence to cut the next bead as

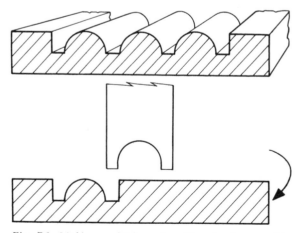

Fig. 76. Making multiple reeds with a bead cutter. The arrow is pointing to the face edge.

shown, i.e., so that the quirk of the cutter seats in the quirk cut by the first cutter. Continue this for as many beads as are required. This is a popular form of decoration for relieving any flat surface, i.e., the front face of a pilaster, or a drawer front. If the beads are cut slightly below the surface, the top round will not be flattened in the final cleanup.

Horizontally placed bolection beads as decorations for the lower parts of furniture (carcasses) can be made separately and planted in a shallow groove, as shown in Fig. 77. When neatly proportioned to the rest of the work, these can be very effective. They are more popular on modern work.

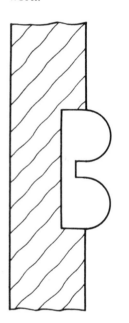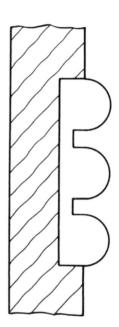

Fig. 77. Bolection beads.

13. Making a Return Bead

While this presents a difficulty with wooden beading planes, the process is simple with either the combination plane or the multi-plane. Work a bead first on the face edge. Leave just a small quirk only on the face side by setting the fence under the quirk cutter, as shown at A (Fig. 78). Then work on the face side, setting the plane in such a manner that the little quirk is just taken off, as at B (i.e., by setting the fence just level with the round of the edge).

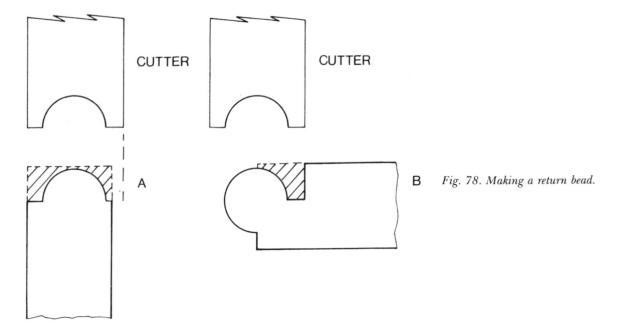

A   B   *Fig. 78. Making a return bead.*

14. Making a Torus Bead

You can make a torus bead with a combination plane or multi-plane. Choose the correct size beading cutter, set up in the plane and place the fence correctly in relation to the distance the torus bead is to be cut in from the edge. Cut the bead as in Fig. 79. Then remove the outside waste with the bench rebate plane, working on the edge or side having the plow run on the face side.

15. Making an Astragal Moulding

Work a bead on the edge of a board and then cut it off, as shown by the dotted line (Fig. 80). It can be grooved on the reverse side by plowing a groove in the edge of a board and using this as a rest, as at A.

Another way is to use wood of the same thickness as the required astragal. Plow the groove first; reverse the wood and cut the bead. Then sever with a fine saw or the slitter cutter set in the multi-plane. Trim the last edge with a block plane. Further types of rectangular astragals and the method of sticking them will be found in Fig. 162, page 97.

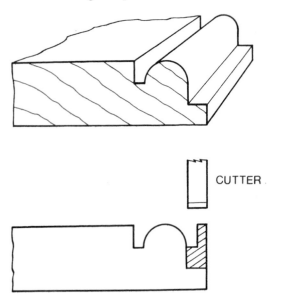

Fig. 79. Making a torus bead.

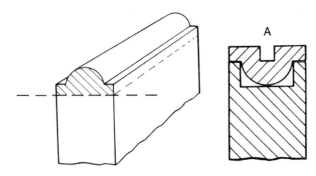

Fig. 80. Making an astragal moulding.

16. Making Round Rods

Though of limited application, this procedure is useful at times. A bead is planed on both sides of a board, which should be of the right thickness (Fig. 81). If care is taken and the board is the right thickness, good rods can be made that require very little cleaning up.

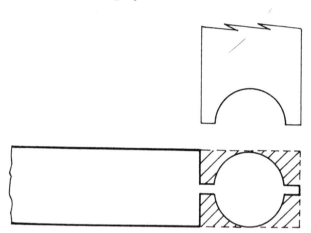

Fig. 81. Making a round rod.

17. Planing Very Small Pieces

Set the jack plane sole upwards in the vise and draw the piece along. Keep your fingers clear of the blade. When small-dimensioned fillets or keys for joints are to be planed, cut out a shallow housing in a spare piece of wood similar to that shown in Fig. 83, minus the guide. The thin piece can then be placed in the housing and planed. With this method it will not buckle, as it might if placed in the ordinary way against the bench stop.

18. Cutting a Stopped Housing for a Shelf

Mark out the housing with pencil, square and gauge. At the stopped end of the housing use a chisel to remove what in effect is a small mortise. Tack on a small fillet of wood, and with a tenon saw cut to the depth set by the gauge line. Repeat for the other side of the housing. Take out the majority of the waste with a bevel edge chisel and use the router plane 071 to finish down to the

required depth. Clean up the closed end of the housing if necessary.

Alternatively, bore a hole the width of the housing near the stopped end. Tack on a squared fillet and with a tenon saw cut to the depth required, then proceed as before.

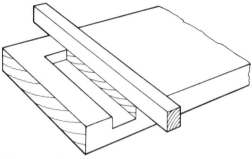

Fig. 82. Completed dado.

Should the small mortise method be used, the fillet may be dispensed with. Place the saw in the mortise, pointing down, moving the saw backwards to start the cut. As cutting proceeds, lower the handle until the saw is cutting the full length of the housing. Repeat for both sides. The small portion of wood at the far end of the housing will act as a buffer stop for the saw, and it can be cut away when all other work is complete.

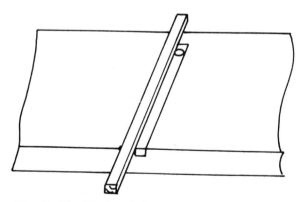

Fig. 83. The fillet is tacked on to guide the saw.

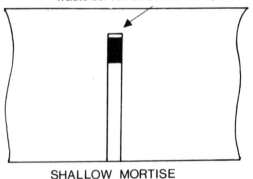

waste serves to act as a stop for the saw

SHALLOW MORTISE

Fig. 84. Alternative method of cutting a dado.

19. Chamfering

When chamfering, always set out the chamfer with a pencil. If a gauge is used, there will be ugly gauge marks and you might have to proceed further than you intended to remove them. When chamfering along the grain, proceed as for bevelling (Fig. 85), except that less is taken away. When working chamfers or bevels across the grain, it is an advantage to use a block plane, tilting the plane slightly across the chamfer so that the cutter works obliquely, as has been already described.

Both through and stopped chamfers are easily and quickly made with the chamfer spokeshave, a tool fitted with two adjustable fences which eliminate tedious marking-out. Once the fences are set, all the chamfers will finish uniformly and without waviness. Through chamfers need no marking-out at all, and for stopped chamfers only the two ends need be marked. Very effective curved entrances and exits will come after a little practice (see Chapter 12 for working with a spokeshave).

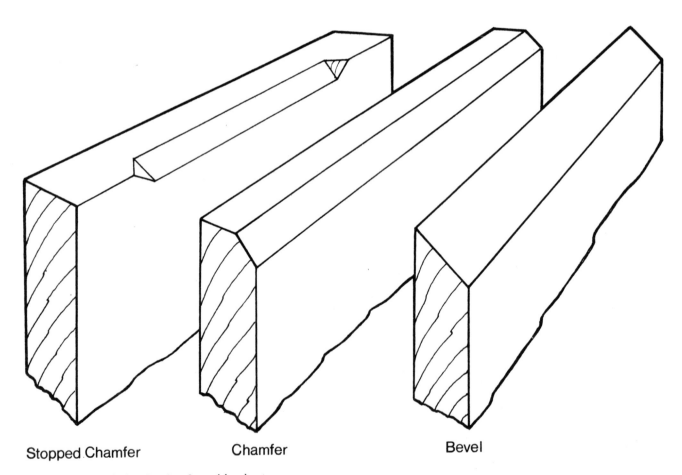

Stopped Chamfer   Chamfer   Bevel

Fig. 85. Stopped chamfer, chamfer and bevel cuts.

20. Working a Moulding on a Tabletop

First plow a groove ¼ inch wide, as shown at A (Fig. 86). Remove the shaded portion with a jack plane, rebate plane or shoulder plane, as most convenient. The ovolo at B can be done by working two grooves and by using a shoulder plane. Ovolo cutters are available with the multi-plane (see page 107, Chapter 9). For moulding end grain, see Fig. 195, Chapter 9.

21. Making a Drawer Slip

A drawer slip (Fig. 87) can easily be made from waste pieces or short ends by plowing a groove ³⁄₁₆

inch or ¼ inch wide, and ³⁄₁₆ inch deep, on the edge of a board which should be about ⅜ inch thick. After the groove is cut, the thickness of the slip is gauged. The corner is then rounded off, as has been previously described. Then the slip is sawn off (Fig. 88).

The width of the groove chosen should be in accordance with the thickness of the drawer bottoms. A center slip for drawer bottoms is made by plowing a groove the same thickness as the drawer bottom on both sides of the slip, and then rounding off the two upper corners, i.e., those which will appear inside the drawer.

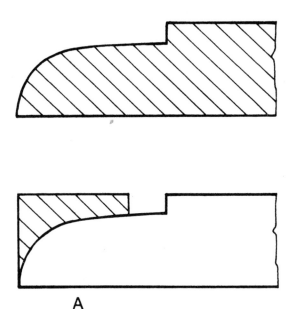

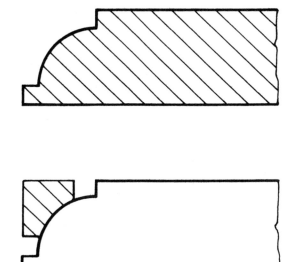

A   B

Fig. 86. Working a moulding on a tabletop.

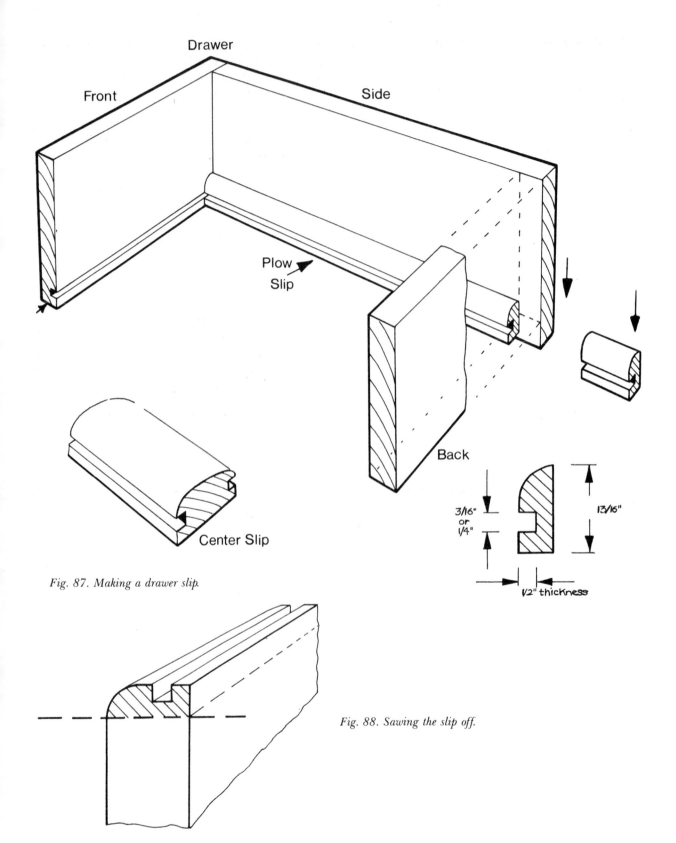

Drawer

Front

Side

Plow
Slip

Back

3/16"
or
1/4"

13/16"

1/2" thickness

Center Slip

Fig. 87. Making a drawer slip.

Fig. 88. Sawing the slip off.

22. Making a Rebated Corner Joint

A very neat corner can be quickly made by rebating one piece, as at A (Fig. 89), and nailing the second piece as indicated. If the little end grain is slightly rounded, as at B, the joint is much improved.

This joint may be used when making small cabinets of plywood, the rebate taken out being equal to all the plies but one. In this case, the planes having a spur fitted to cut across the grain should be used. If desirable, the joint may be further strengthened by glued blocks on the inside. If rounded as at B, a veneer can be laid around the complete corner.

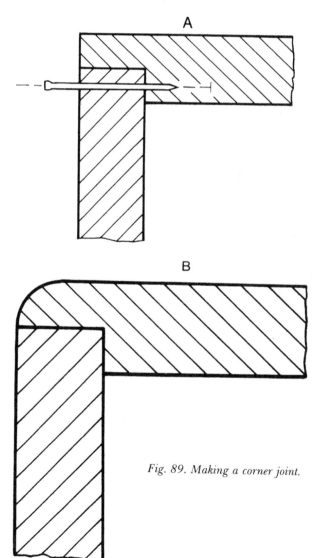

Fig. 89. Making a corner joint.

23. Making a Very Strong Corner Joint

This joint, which may be seen in much of the work of the Chippendale period, is an ingenious combination of straight forward planing and glue jointing, and is shown in detail in Fig. 90. A is the end of a bookcase or the like, and B the door. The fluted quarter-column is glued into a rebate formed in piece D, which in turn is rebated for the door, and is tongued into piece A, as shown. A, C and D, when glued up, make one very solid, yet charmingly effective corner, having a rich appearance.

The small sketch (E) will clearly show the parts which are to be rebated to form part D. The sizes, of course, depend upon the material being used. The quarter-column (C) may be made in several ways, but if only two are required they may be planed up as described for circular work. The flutings may then be cut with a scratch stock, or with a gouge, or the round may be left quite plain. Four parts may be turned up in the lathe if previously glued together with paper between, the paper facilitating the division after turning.

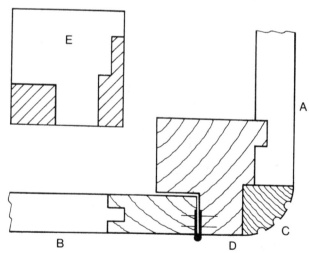

Fig. 90. Detail of a strong corner joint.

24. Simple Methods of Making Corner Joints

Simple methods are shown in Fig. 91. A offers no difficulty, being merely rebated and rounded. B is a simple variation, where a groove is first planed, as at the dotted line at D. After the rebate is cut, the corner is rounded. The rebate is cut a trifle less than the thickness of the material to butt into it, so that the ovolo is thus formed on the edge. C shows the familiar staff bead, rounded off at the back, the bead appearing on the front edge (as in a cupboard). These joints may be glued, or glued and nailed, or nailed only on commoner work.

25. Making Other Corner Joints

These can be made by the plane by introducing a little more work, and the result, particularly if the job is one for the home, well repays the extra trouble taken (see Fig. 92). The dotted line at D shows the shape before plowing the grooves for the loose tongues. The sides to be joined are plowed with the same cutter, but the groove set back about ⅛ inch. Loose tongues (as already described) are inserted. The quadrant may be rounded off with the jack plane, and the inner corner taken off similarly, finishing straight or hollow. This is a very effective corner for a wardrobe. Extra strength may be given to joints such as D, E and F by glue blocking on the inside of the corners. E offers no difficulty. The quarter-hollow is cut with the multi-plane, using the special bottom and cutter (see Chapter 9). If the concavity is troublesome because no hollow plane is available, the section may be planed straight, convex or maybe stop chamfered (see Fig. 85). Alternatively, two or three narrow beads may be used. F is a nice-looking corner calling for accurate bevelled planing, which has been described.

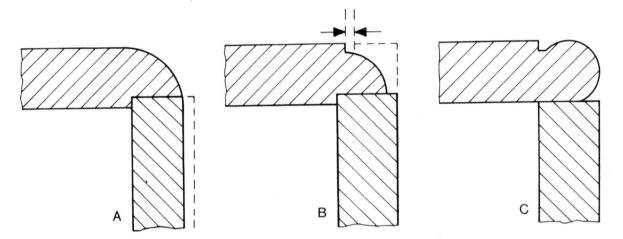

Fig. 91. Three ways of making a corner joint.

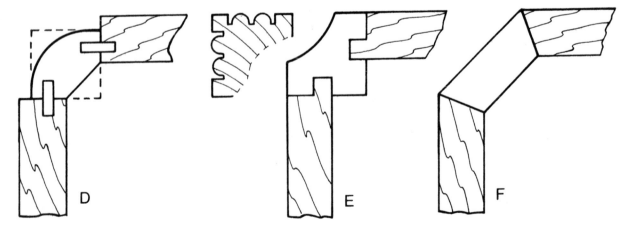

Fig. 92. More variations on corner joints.

26. Strengthening Mitred Corners

G (Fig. 93) shows a two-tongued mitre. Piece K has its edge at right angles. The groove is first plowed out the full depth, and then the side removed with the rebate plane. Piece L is planed off to the required bevel, the groove plowed and the spare rebated off. H is not so strong as G. It can be worked with the jack plane first, and the rebates cleared with the rebate plane. Extreme accuracy is called for in the corner joints described. The

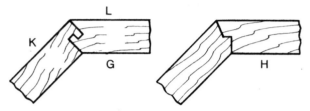

Fig. 93. Two-tongued mitre.

metal plane has made this accuracy easily attainable by anyone who will take reasonable care. The results are well worthwhile, giving an effect truly reflecting the finest traditions of craftsmanship.

27. Making Mitred Boxes

A box structure having mitred corners may be strengthened with parallel keys. The mitres can be shot on the donkey's ear (Fig. 266, Chapter 15). The two sides and the two ends should be checked for equal length, and the mitred corners should be square with the face edge. To plow the grooves, the pieces should be carefully set in the vise back-to-back, as at Fig. 95, when it's found that the fence of the plow will rest on one mitre while the other is plowed. The second groove is plowed by resting the fence on the mitre already plowed. When all the grooves are completed, slips or "keys" can be fitted, as at A. The keys not only strengthen the joint, but they are also of considerable assistance in preventing the tendency of the mitres to slip during assembly and gluing.

Small boxes such as cigarette boxes and jewel cases may be made in the manner indicated. Before the mitres are glued up, sides and ends are plowed, as at C. This is for the insertion later of a slip, on to which the lid falls. The position of this groove should be gauged on the inside of the box as shown by the dotted line in Fig. 94. Any groove for the fitting of the bottom or top should also be plowed at this stage.

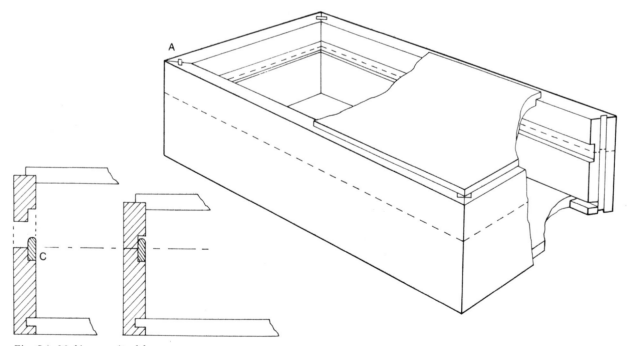

Fig. 94. Making a mitred box.

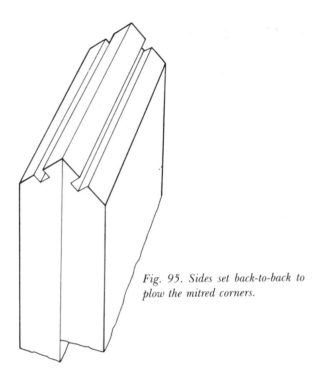

Fig. 95. Sides set back-to-back to plow the mitred corners.

The box is now assembled and glued, top and bottom being fitted. After the glue has set, a saw cut is made through the gauged line, thus separating the lid from the box. The sawn surfaces are then trued-up with a smooth or jack plane with a finely set cutter. A thin slip is now fitted flush with the inside of the box into what will now be the lower part of the groove (C), letting it project about ⅛ inch or ³⁄₁₆ inch to suit the other part of the groove (C), which is left in the lid.

While for a quick job the bottom may be nailed or screwed on, a better method is indicated in, Fig. 94, where the sides and ends are plowed with a cutter approximately half the thickness of the bottom, and the bottom rebated to suit. In assembling, only the mitres (with their keys) should be glued, and the bottom left dry, thus leaving allowance for any subsequent shrinkage of the bottom. Similar allowance could be made for the top; in this case the sides and ends would be plowed suitably and the top treated as a bolection panel (see Fig. 96). This method of box construction is much more speedy than might appear from the description, and very effective boxes can be made. Smaller boxes can be constructed using odd pieces of exotic woods, which will also present the opportunity to inlay strips and lines.

Further variation is possible in the treatment of top and bottom. Recessing the bottom slightly can give a pleasing shadow. The top may be fielded in many ways. The edges can also be chamfered or rounded over, or they can carry a simple ovolo or ogee moulding.

Serviceable boxes for the storage of special tools, i.e., bullnose, shoulder plane, etc., can be made by this method. With a slight variation of the design, which will suggest itself, the lid may be made to slide. A thumb notch can be made with gouge and chisel.

28. Framing the Panels of Doors

A to M (Fig. 96) show various methods of framing the panels of doors. A shows a plain plowed groove. The tenons for the door frame are often made the same thickness as the width of the grooves, so that their entry is through the groove into the mortise (A, Fig. 97). Make the mortise-and-tenon joints first, and plow last. Don't forget to leave a haunch on the tenon that will fill that part of the groove that comes on the end of the stile, or the result will be a nasty gap. For better convenience when cutting the mortise, it is best to leave a horn about an inch long on the ends of the stiles. These horns will be cleaned off after the frame is glued up.

B shows a plain door, which has the advantage that the panel can be left out until polishing is finished, and then the loose bead can be tacked in. The mortises and tenons should be made first, and the rebate taken out afterwards. Don't forget the long and short shoulder of the tenon, due to the rebate being taken out later.

C offers a little more complication, though in principle it is like B. If care be taken to make the rebate (H) the same depth as the moulding (K), the shoulders of the tenons can be made equal and the mouldings mitred at the corners. For carpentry work, the mouldings should be scribed at the corners. D is the same as C, but shows the panelling bevelled at the back. E has the addition of an astragal fixed on the front.

F, for a heavier door, has a bolection (i.e., protruding) moulding on the front, while G, for a heavy door, has the addition of a cocked bead on the front of the raised panel. This is a fine finish to a heavy door. The groove should be carefully plowed out with a router plane, using the fence provided, after accurately marking its limits on both sides with a cutting gauge. It requires careful workmanship, but is a joy to see when finished. When using the router, plane into each corner. Set in the groove for the cock bead first and later take the bevel off. The panels in a large door such as this are frequently bevelled on both back and front.

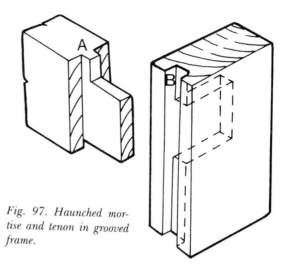

Fig. 97. *Haunched mortise and tenon in grooved frame.*

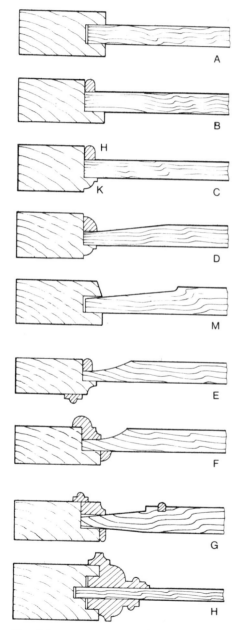

Fig. 96. *Various methods of framing door panels.*

H shows a method of inserting a panel by means of which the use of nails, with their consequent disfigurement, is obviated. The patterns of the mould may be varied a good deal, it being the tonguing that is important. Another variant of this method is by using one mould only having multiple tongues to fit into corresponding grooves in the frame, and one other groove into which the panel fits. In the latter case, of course, the panel does not run through the moulding as it does at H, but sits, as it were, on top of it, in a groove. These last two methods are only used on very high-class work where labor charges are not a primary consideration.

The slight bevel shown on the frame at M gives a very interesting play of highlights on the door when completed, and has a more chaste appearance than has a stop-chamfered frame, besides being easier to dust. When setting-out, notice that the rail has a long and short shoulder, the front shoulder being undercut to fit in with the chamfer of the stile. The hollowed part of the fielding of the panel here shown may be done with a narrow fluting cutter of the multi-plane before the bevel is planed off. The refined appearance of a pair of four panel doors made in this manner has to be seen to be appreciated.

The door shown in Fig. 98 indicates a modern method of panelling, and may be used singly or in multipanelled doors. It is very strong, as a thick panel can be used. It does not collect dust and it has a fine appearance. While needing accurate workmanship it is not really difficult if a plow plane is used.

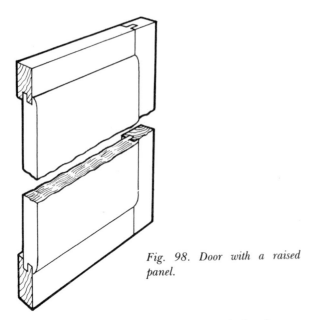

Fig. 98. Door with a raised panel.

In arranging the construction of the frame, make the grooves the same distance from the edge of the frame (i.e., ¼ inch). Then when plowing the panel you can use the same distance. Before the panel is grooved, it should be shot square and accurately to the size of the rectangle at the bottom of the groove in the frame (i.e., if the frame is 18 inches × 15 inches and the frame grooves ⅜ inch deep, the panel must be accurately squared to 18¾ inches × 15¾ inches). The Record plows will plane the groove across the grain of the panel as easily as they will plane with the grain. Before fitting the panel, slightly chamfer the "tongue" that enters the frame groove. If a slight easement has to be made in fitting the panel, the side rabbet plane is most useful. The bolection edge of the panel may be treated as indicated, or it may be fielded, or finished with two small rebates stepped, etc.

The variety of door constructions shown is indicative of many, and by no means exhaustive. There is sometimes a doubt in the mind of the worker of limited experience as to whether he should groove the panel in or fit it with a rebate and bead. The grooved door is undoubtedly stronger, but the method of finish will frequently be a deciding factor. If a grooved door is to be French polished, the panel must be polished or nearly so before the door is glued up. It is impossible to get a good finish in the corners of the panels after the door is assembled. If the door is to be painted and varnished, there is no difficulty. When French polishing is to follow, it is usually best to rebate the frames. The panel can then be polished apart from the glued-up door, and the bead can be tacked in after finishing. The inner edges of the frame are also easier to polish before fitting.

29. Making Simple Flush Doors

The variety of ways in which flush doors can be constructed are many, and only three simple ways will be shown. The quickest way, of course, is to use ready-made laminated boards when available, merely cutting to size. A quick method for ordinary work is shown at A (Fig. 99) where two pieces of plywood are glued to the front and back of a mortised frame. If need be, lock rail and muntins may be set in to strengthen this. On account of the enclosed air space a small hole is often bored from the edge for ventilation.

At B, a better method is shown. The splines are planed true on their edges (planed in pairs as in Fig. 58, so that when butt glued-up the surfaces are flat). When dry, the whole is toothed, and the inside face of the plywood toothed (see Toothing, Chapter 13) and then glued together under pressure.

Record C clamps (G cramps) are used in cases like this. The faces of the battens that contact the work are very slightly rounded from end-to-end. The center portion will then be the first to make contact when the battens are placed in position. Subsequent tightening at the ends using the C clamps (G cramps) will ensure the batten is in contact along its full length, and give a good secure hold pending the setting of the glue. At C (Fig. 99), a variation of this is shown which reduces the amount of core wood required and reduces the weight of the door. The shorter pieces are trued-up in longer lengths and then cut off.

When veneering the edges of flush doors, let in a piece of solid long grain, as at D, on the end grain. A groove is first plowed and the bevels shaped with a shoulder plane, the shaped fillet being similarly worked to a fit and then glued-in. This fillet may be wood of the same kind as the veneer used or it may be of a cheaper wood, and afterwards veneered.

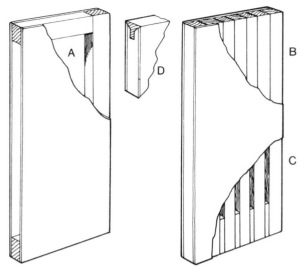

Fig. 99. Construction of flush doors.

30. Meeting Edges of Doors

The problem of breaking the joint between two doors is overcome by the carpenter by making each door wider to allow for the overlap. A rebate is cut on the left-hand door, a bead on the right, and a rebate behind the bead, as at A (Fig. 100). The cabinetmaker in cheap work plants an astragal with glue and pins, as at B. In better work, C and D are used. At C a rebated slip is prepared with the edge rounded at the front. This slip is then glued on to the right-hand door as shown, a gap being left for the purpose.

In the best class work, the slip has an astragal on the front, and besides being rebated itself it is glued into a rebate in the right-hand door. The slip is easily made on the edge of a board by making the rebate first, and then the bead. Last, either cut the whole slip from the board with the saw, or sever the slip easily from the board by using a 1/8-inch plow cutter in the combination plane, or the slitting cutter in the multi-plane. A modern rectangular method of breaking the joint of two meeting doors is shown in Fig. 101.

The advantage of making these slips yourself are: a), they are well-made; b), they are made of the same material as the work itself; c), they are made to the individual size required, and do not have to be "adapted" to meet standard machine-made sizes; and d), the cost of the material is negligible—you make just as much as you require and do not have to buy considerably more than you

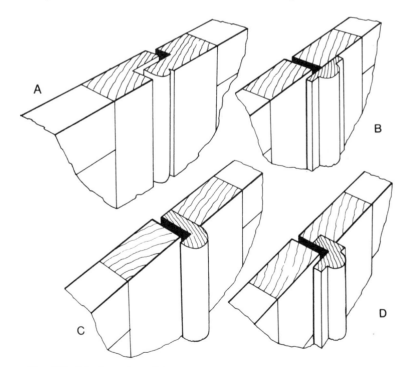

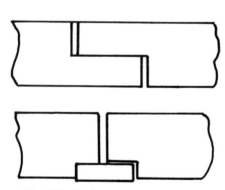

Fig. 101. Modern methods of meeting edges of doors.

Fig. 100. Meeting edges of doors.

need. In good class work, handmade mouldings of this description are always worthwhile, giving both the human touch that is so often absent from machine work and the real satisfaction that comes from work well done.

31. Panelling Backs

The back of a Welsh dresser may be done with matching by any of the methods shown in Fig. 69. Alternatively, the muntins may be thicker than the panels, as at A (Fig. 102), which enables wide, thin boards to be used while keeping a rigid construction.

The panel may be relieved with a bead, as at B (see Beading), or, in the case of a wardrobe, may be chamfered, as at C and D. The panelling on the back of a wardrobe door may be arranged in a simple rebate, the framing being screwed to the door in the manner shown at E.

32. Facing

If economy in lumber is a consideration, it is possible to limit the use of more expensive lumber by using only a very thin section and gluing this to the face side of a piece of cheaper lumber.

A (Fig. 103) shows a thin piece of mahogany or walnut glued to a thicker piece of pine. B shows a similar combination with the addition of a moulding, which may be of any desired section. All that is necessary is that the pieces shall be planed accurately on their abutting sides (for this purpose use the longer planes.) The abutting sides are then glued and the pieces rubbed until they "suck." They must then be left until the glue has set.

If there is any tendency for the thin piece to rise, two or three Record C clamps (G cramps) should either be placed along the length or weighted down and left under the weights.

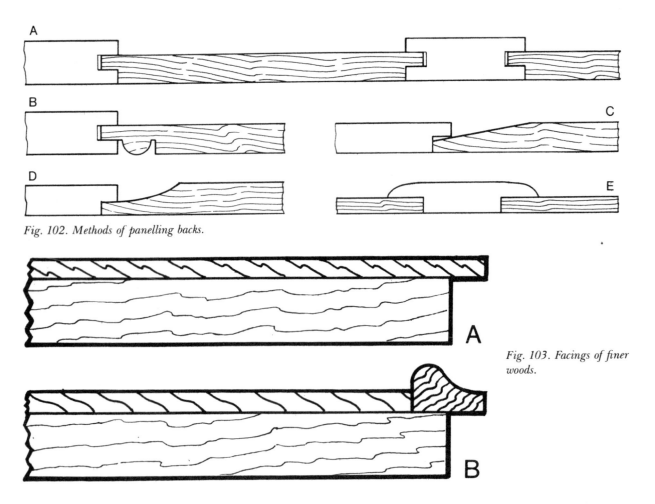

Fig. 102. *Methods of panelling backs.*

Fig. 103. *Facings of finer woods.*

Frames may be constructed in any of the orthodox manners, and the facings may be glued on with the frames complete.

33. Lipping

This is a term used for covering the edge of a piece of wood (such as a bookcase shelf) with a thin piece of better quality hardwood. The sections shown in Fig. 104 illustrate the variations in the way this can be done. At C, a plain strip is glued along the edge. D has a thicker lip that is grooved on the underside to allow a length of scalloped leather or similar material to be attached by tacking. This material prevents dust accumulation on the book edges.

When lipping a writing tabletop, the lipping should be cross-tongued and should stand higher than the middle by the thickness of the leather covering (E, Fig. 104), which should be fitted later. The outer edge may be suitably moulded or rounded, and the corners mitred. Cross tongues may be fitted in the mitred corners, as already indicated.

Facing up the members of a wardrobe cornice will reduce the need for expensive material. The "backings," while of cheaper wood, must be quite dry and of even grain. Otherwise, in time the frames will pull and twist.

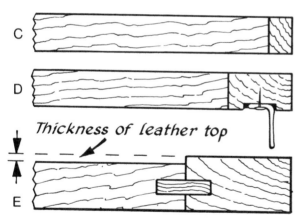

Fig. 104. Lipping or edging a top.

34. Decorative Applications of the Plane on Drawer Fronts

The appearance of a plain drawer front may be considerably enhanced by a simple, yet intel-

ligent, use of the plane. Fig. 105 suggests an infinite variety of treatments that are possible with the use of the center bead in the combination plane or the multi-plane.

Fig. 106 shows a refined effect that may be obtained by various rebates easily and quickly worked with the same planes. In cutting across the grain, use the spur cutter keenly sharpened, or there is a danger of tearing the fibre·afterwards, which will mean endless work cleaning up. If the grain is very intractable, run a cutting gauge down first, and set the plane to the cut made.

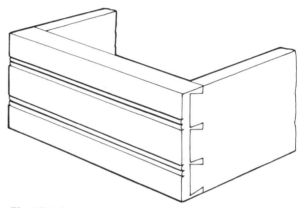

Fig. 105. Decorative beading on a drawer front.

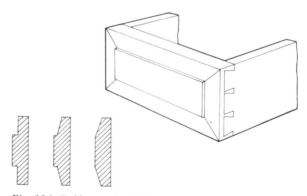

Fig. 106. Rabbets made with a combination plane or multi-plane.

The fielding may be done with a finely set bench rebate plane. As an alternative to the square-edged part of the fielding, a fluting (additional fluting cutter 3/16 inch or 1/4 inch for a multi-plane) may be used. Be careful while taking very light cuts with a very sharp cutter, and in running the fielding into the line of the fluting. It may have to be touched-up lightly with a scraper.

While calling for a somewhat high degree of skill, it has a very pleasant appearance, and it is easy to dust.

One of the richest effects of all is that given by a cock bead, as at Fig. 107, which can be quite thin (1/8 inch), and looks very good. The drawer can be completed plain and fitted. The top can then be planed away the full thickness to the depth of the bead. The sides and bottom should be finally rebated to the ends of the dovetails for width, and the thickness of the bead for depth. The bead must be mitred at the corners, keeping in mind that for the two top corners the top bead will be mitred partway only. The planing should be true, and the beads glued in position, clamping securely until dry.

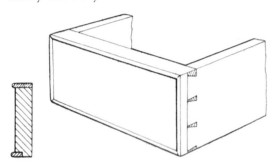

Fig. 107. Using a cock bead on a drawer.

A modern treatment (which may be varied a great deal in detail) is indicated in Fig. 108, where vertical grooves or inlays are run in the drawers, and sometimes the rails also, so that a continuous vertical line of ornament is shown throughout.

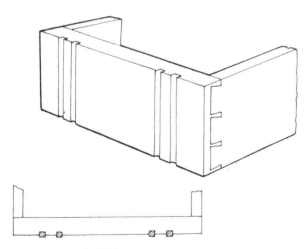

Fig. 108. Vertical inlays.

This is a case where the combination plane or multi-plane is indispensable—the cross-grained work being done as shown in Chapters 8 and 9, under Dado Work. The grooving can also be carried out expeditiously with the router plane.

Drawer fronts may also be decorated by a small moulding planed on the edge, or by having a moulding glued on, as in Jacobean work. They may be relieved by inlaid bandings or lines, or may be veneered. The fenced router has made the laying of bandings a very easy process. Fig. 109 is typical of a quartered veneered drawer front, having cross bandings around the edge, and an inlaid band which may be plain or fancy, or may be a very narrow line of box or other wood. The fitting of the edges of the veneers is simplified when they are shot with a thicker piece of wood, either in the vise or on the shooting board. Before being laid, the abutting surfaces should be toothed, an operation neatly done with the toothed cutter of the cabinet scraper (see pages 131 and 132, Chapter 13).

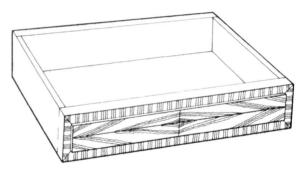

Fig. 109. Quartered veneered drawer front.

The drawer front shown in Fig. 110 is made up of a frame and three panels. The muntins are set at right angles to the drawer front, and are shaped to form handles, as indicated in the side elevation. The shape of the handles may be varied and the panels left plain, as shown, or fielded.

A panelled front drawer such as this cannot be satisfactorily dovetailed because the grain of the stiles runs the wrong way. Therefore, the sides of the drawer should be tenoned into the front, and pegged. This method is at its best in large drawers such as in wardrobes, etc. The shrinkage of the front is negligible, owing to the method of con-

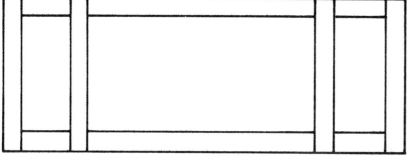

Fig. 110. Panelled drawer front with muntin handles.

struction, and the handles, being tenoned into the frame, get a sound grip on the drawer when pulled out, and will never come apart.

35. Fitting Drawers

Drawer rails and runners are traditionally worked, as at Fig. 111. The rail is tenoned into the carcass end. The runner is housed in a stopped housing (see Fig. 84) and stub-tenoned into the rail. Rail and runner are plowed on their inner edges, as shown, for the insertion of the dust board from the back.

A much less laborious method is shown in Fig. 112, where a length of angle metal (about 5/8 inch × 5/8 inch × 14 or 16 gauge) is let into a stopped housing in the carcass end and screwed home. The drawer fronts will need to be deeper than the openings by the thickness of the metal. No rails are needed, and no dust boards are fitted. The drawers glide exceptionally easily on the runners. The time and material saved is considerable, and drawer space is greater. The corner joints of the carcass must be sound, as there is no bracing by rails on the front.

Various designs of plastic rail and runner are now available. These provide smooth running facilities and are extremely strong. Similar rails in aluminum alloys will also provide the answer.

Wooden shooting boards are best made by the craftsman to his own sizes to suit his work and workshop. They should be made from selected straight-grained beech for even wear and lasting quality. The various parts are best dowelled and glued together, to avoid the possibility of work or tools being damaged by protruding screws.

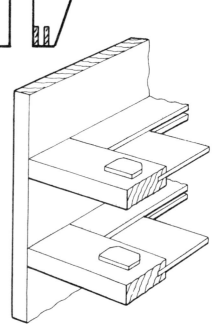

Fig. 111. Drawer fitting: Rails and runners.

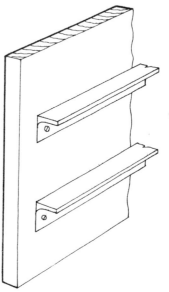

Fig. 112. Angle metal let into a stopped housing.

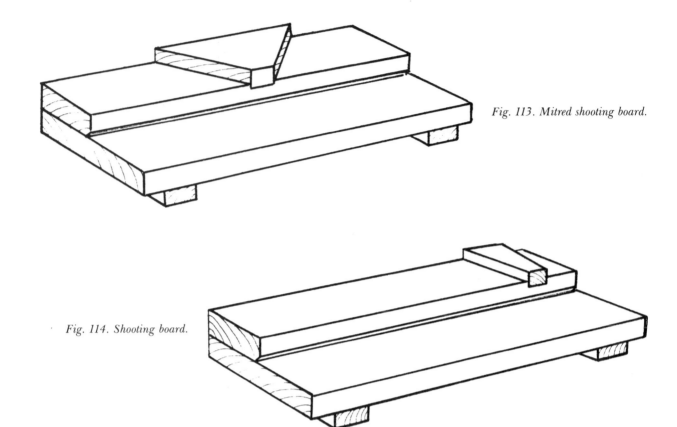

Fig. 113. *Mitred shooting board.*

Fig. 114. *Shooting board.*

5
The Block Plane

The earliest block planes in metal can be attributed to Leonard Bailey. His list of 1883 showed three styles, all in a variety of finishes. Two had adjustable mouths and one a normal bench plane handle. They were marketed under the Victor label. Two others can be seen in the Stanley list, carrying the "Defiance" brand name.

The block plane is so named because it was originally brought into being for the making and retrimming of butchers' blocks which, to better withstand the constant wear due to chopping, were made of hardwood—usually sycamore or maple, these being white in color—with the end grain upwards. The angle of the smoothing plane cutter was too high to do this work without the danger of splitting off much of the fibre, so a lower-pitched plane, made of wood, was devised for the purpose.

Lowering the pitch of the cutter naturally necessitated making the grinding angle more acute, and it became impossible to lower the pitch to any appreciable extent without making the grinding angle so acute as to make it too weak. Consequently, it was found that the only practicable way of lowering the pitch was to fit the cutter with the bevel uppermost. This eliminated the need for a cap iron on a block plane.

For a long time the only woodworker who possessed a block plane was the man engaged on butchers' blocks. In due course, with the introduction of iron planes, as with the bench planes, the wooden body was replaced with a metal casting. Today, with the variations in design, the use of the block plane is almost universal. Yet it is quite certain that only a small proportion of those used ever come into contact with a butcher's block.

To understand how the block plane evolved, it will be necessary to digress a little and to examine a part of the history of the craft. Fifteenth century woodwork owes a good deal of its charm to its simplicity and to the frankness of its construction. Its mortise-and-tenon joints were straight through and there was no attempt to hide them. Later they were still openly shown, and further secured with "trenails"—wooden round pegs. These pegs formed decorative spots by virtue of their careful placing, yet they were primarily essential parts of the construction.

However, by the end of the 18th century, the woodworker's skill had advanced so much he was able to make good and sound joints which were hidden away out of sight. His tenons were curtailed so that they did not project through. There was good enough reason for it—the shrinkage of the stiles due to the natural drying-out of the wood resulted in the ends of the tenons projecting. With a contemporary advance in the art of polishing, this projection became a very noticeable blemish. Thus, open and frank dovetail box joints gave way to secret dovetails, and it was traditional in the workshops never to leave end grain exposed if there was any possible way to prevent it.

With such conditions, it is quite easy to see that there was a grand opening for the unscrupulous worker. If a joint was hidden from sight and no one was ever to see it, why be honest about it? Good joints call for careful workmanship and time expended on them. The unscrupulous spent time only on those parts which were to be seen. The result was a very widespread decline in craftsmanship, for the honest man cannot compete under such conditions.

A return to sound ideas had to come sooner or later, and the main credit for its return must be given to Ernest Gimson and his immediate followers. He broke away boldly from the hidden constructions and the superfluous ornament of the Victorian Period, and designed and executed his work along the lines of simplicity, good proportion and decoration based mainly on the essential constructions he employed. The characteristic expression of the cabinetmaker of the present day was inspired by the school of craftsmen he founded. The secret dovetail gave way to the open box dovetail, the arrangement frequently decorative (Fig. 115). The stub tenon gave way to the through tenon, often left deliberately projecting, the edge either bevelled off as a decoration (Fig. 115) or wedged with wood of a different color from the tenon.

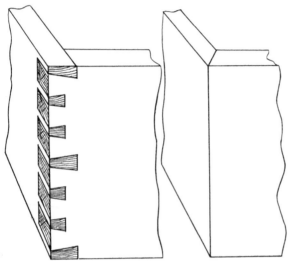

open box dovetail   secret lap dovetail

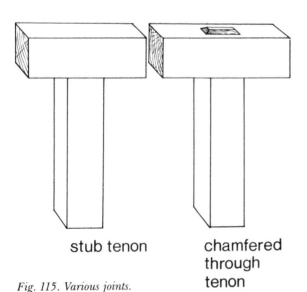

stub tenon   chamfered
                  through
                  tenon

Fig. 115. Various joints.

This extended use of end grain has increased the need for the block plane to such an extent that practically every woodworker today finds it impossible to get on satisfactorily without one. There have been so many constant improvements in the design that today some of the block planes are highly efficient precision tools. They are able in ordinary daily work to leave clean surfaces by the removal of shavings the thickness of about .001 inch.

Record block planes are designed according to the demands for both a simple and economical tool and a highly finished tool with every refinement of accurate and quick adjustment. Block planes No. 0110 and No. 0130 belong to the first category.

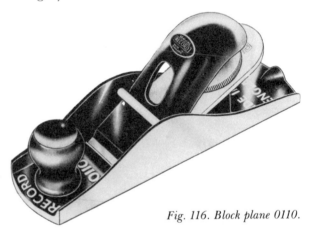

Fig. 116. Block plane 0110.

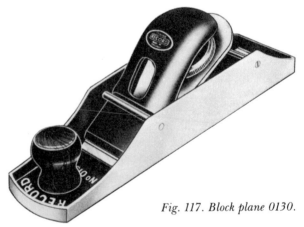

Fig. 117. Block plane 0130.

These two planes are quite efficient in practice. The cutters are rigidly held with a knurled wheel and screw. The base and sides are accurately ground and polished and square to each other. While 0110 is just a block plane pure and simple,

0130 is so designed that the cutter may be used at either end, one end positioning the cutter so that it may be used for bullnosed work. This plane is a deservedly popular one with the joiners, who find that they can use it in places difficult of access, and that it can be conveniently held in one hand.

No. 0120 is fitted with a screw adjustment for regulating the depth of the cut. This addition is well worth the little extra initial cost, as adjustment of the cut is both positive and speedy. No. 0220 is also screw-adjusted, but differs in design in that instead of the cutter being secured with a knurled wheel and screw it is held in place with a lever and cam which, being on the top, is slightly more accessible.

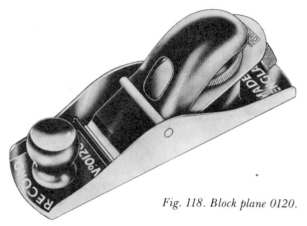

Fig. 118. Block plane 0120.

Block plane 09½ can clean up the most difficult of woods to a fine finish. Adjustment of the mouth has been fitted in addition for finer adjustment. This is made possible by fitting a separate unit to the underside of the front portion of the body. It consists of a flat metal casting seated in an accurately machined housing in which it can slide backwards or forward, so varying the width of the mouth. This metal plate is fitted in position

Fig. 119. Block plane 09½.

prior to the machining of the base, so ensuring it is perfectly flush with the remaining surface. It is secured by a knurled-headed screw inserted from the top side of the body. Backward and forward movement is effected by a "cam"-action quadrant, having a curved slot through which the tightening screw passes before it screws into the plate.

The "cam"-action quadrant is pivoted at the rear, and when the curved portion is moved sideways it moves the tightening screw which, in turn, moves the plate, so varying the width of the mouth. Tightening the screw locks the plate in the desired position. In general design, No. 09½ follows No. 0220. It is 6 inches long, with a cutter 1⅝ inch wide, and has thumb recesses. Sides and base are accurately ground and polished.

Fig. 120. Block plane 09½ in use.

Block plane 018—the most refined plane in the range of block planes—is six inches long, with a 1⅝-inch-wide cutter. The blade is secured with an ingeniously designed knuckle-joint lever cap, made of steel and plated. This enables the cutter to be firmly locked in a moment, and at the same time forms a very comfortable hold for the palm of the hand. In general design it closely follows No. 09½, as it is also fitted with the adjustable mouth. It has a screw adjustment for depth of cut and a lever for sideways adjustment of the cutter, as well as recesses for finger and thumb. Sides and base are accurately ground and polished, and the whole tool carries a high-grade finish. A craftsman possessing this tool need have no fear whatever of cleanly finishing any work from the plane, end grain or long grain, easy lumber or difficult lumber.

The 0102 is a small plane which, while not ordinarily appealing to the joiner or cabinetmaker, can be very useful to those engaged in small woodwork such as the making of models. This is a craft which can call at times for a high grade of skill—though of a different type from that of the general woodworker—and can lead to a high degree of pride of craftsmanship. Each one of the block planes mentioned has appealed in miniature form to the woodworker and model enthusiast, though its prime purpose is for full-scale work. No. 0102 is a block plane 5½ inches long, with a 1⅜-inch cutter which is reduced to bare essentials. The cutter is held in position by a knurled wheel and screw, and the base and sides are ground and polished. There is no adjustment to the cutter.

Block plane 60½ is very similar to block plane 09½, but the cutter is set at an angle of 12½°. This plane is fine for cutting plastic laminates and other man-made composite materials. It will, of course, be fine for end grain in normal lumber.

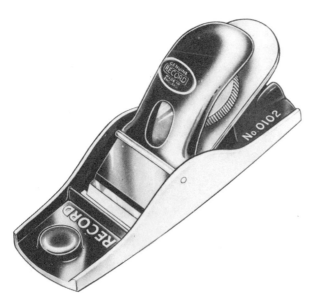

Fig. 121. Block plane 0102.

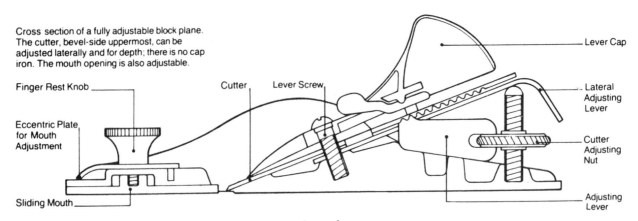

Fig. 122. Block plane 60½.

Cross section of a fully adjustable block plane. The cutter, bevel-side uppermost, can be adjusted laterally and for depth; there is no cap iron. The mouth opening is also adjustable.

Finger Rest Knob

Eccentric Plate for Mouth Adjustment

Sliding Mouth

Cutter

Lever Screw

Lever Cap

Lateral Adjusting Lever

Cutter Adjusting Nut

Adjusting Lever

Fig. 123. Section through the block plane showing construction and parts.

6
Rebate Planes

The word rabbet, in use from the late Middle English period, appears to have an Old French derivation, though there are authorities at some variance with each other over the source of the word. Some experts believe the word originated from *raboter* or *rabouter*, which means to plane, or to thrust against. Others prefer *rabat* or *rabbat*, from *rabattre*, which means to beat back or down. The word rebate appears to have crept in later, probably in the 17th century; however, when thus spelled it was pronounced rabbet, the pronunciation "rebate" being a fairly modern interpolation.

The antiquity of the name is an indication that a rabbet—a channel or slot cut along the edge or face of a piece (or surface) of wood that receives the edge or end of another piece or pieces of wood—has been known for several centuries. Indeed, the word, used in the sense of cutting a rabbet, occurs before the end of the 16th century.

In its simplest form a rebate may be seen in the open channel of a door frame, possibly its earliest appearance. This type of rebate indicates the manner in which the early craftsman surmounted the difficulties presented by the material in which he worked. No matter how carefully and accurately he made his door fit the frame, natural shrinkage was bound to occur, giving rise to drafts. A rebate was the natural solution to the problem. While a fillet nailed on would have served the same purpose, the craftsman preferred a planed rebate as being, with the means at his disposal in those days, not only more workmanlike and lasting, but actually quicker and easier. It must be remembered that the days of machine saws had not yet arrived, and the cutting of comparatively thin stock at a time when boards were cut with a pit saw was a laborious process.

The rebate is used in many other ways. Rebated boards are often used to cover a wide surface, as on the walls of outdoor wood structures, etc.,

where the boards are free to move with atmospheric variations while still remaining weather-proof. Also, certain constructions in cabinetwork and other work depend upon it, i.e., meeting stiles of doors, joints, sliding lids, etc.

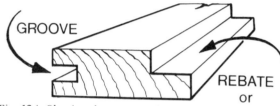

Fig. 124. Showing the groove and rebate.

There are various ways of forming a rebate, depending a good deal upon the type most frequently met with in any particular shop. In cabinetwork and in much joinery, quite a lot can be done very conveniently with the combination plane No. 050 or 050C and the multi-plane No. 405. Instructions for cutting rebates with these tools can be found in Chapters 8 and 9. Mouldings depending for their character upon the rebate may also be struck with these planes. The spur of these tools helps tremendously in making the top and bottom rebates of a flush panel, where the rebate cuts across, and not with the grain. It would indeed be difficult to find a rebate that the multi-plane could not negotiate successfully.

In most shops, however, the rebate is so frequently employed that a single purpose plane has advantages. After all, a tool designed for rebating is likely to perform its function with some superiority over a tool mainly designed for some other purpose, and having rebating as a secondary adjunct.

The Record range of rebate planes is quite a wide one, and a short examination of the various patterns will prove a profitable study. The bench rebate planes Nos. 010 and 010½ are designed for the larger work required of the joiner, cabinet-maker, shop fitter, etc. No. 010 is a jack rebate, having the proportions of a jack plane, i.e., a length of 13 inches. Its cutter is 2⅛ inches wide. The No. 010½ has the proportions of a smoothing plane, i.e., a length of 9 inches with a 2⅛-inch cutter. Neither of these planes is fitted with a fence or depth stop, so it will be necessary to gauge the limits of the rebates when using either of these tools and to use some form of guide when working, as will be explained later. The cutter is made the full width of the sole, so there is no difficulty in working from either side, or even, if necessary, working left-handed. Earlier planes were made of malleable iron, which is practically unbreakable, but the present 010 is manufactured in spheroidal graphite iron.

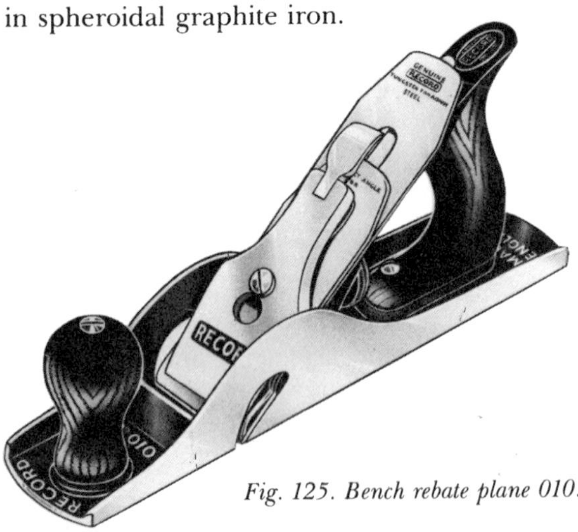

Fig. 125. Bench rebate plane 010.

The performance of these bench rebate planes is very similar. The shorter plane is lighter, and in some fingers a little "handier," whereas the longer plane is more likely to give a straighter cut on long lengths owing to its extra length. One or two methods are generally employed for this type of cut. A very good way indeed is to mark with a gauge the limits of the rebate and then make a plow cut on the inner gauge line, just inside the waste. This plow cut should be set for depth with the depth gauge of the plow plane. The remainder of the waste can then be taken away with the rebate plane, working just up to but not past the gauge line. This allows a rebate to be made either on the face edge, or on the edge opposite the face because the plow may be set to cut from the face while the rebate plane takes away the rest, whichever way the rebate lies.

It should also be noted that there is practically no limit to the depth to which the rebate may be cut, and the width of the cutter, 2⅛ inches, is wide enough for all practical cases likely to come within the scope. As these planes are similar to other bench planes, there is nothing new to be learned in the way of handling. Because the vertical and lateral adjustments are similar to those of the bench planes, these two planes are popular with skilled tradesmen.

In the second way of using the smooth and the jack rebate, Nos. 010 and 010½, it is still preferable to gauge on both side and edge of the work. Then, on the side of the work, a spline is fastened temporarily to act as both fence and guide. This spline is usually nailed on, leaving the nails projecting to ensure their easy removal when the spline has accomplished its purpose. In work which has to be polished in finish, and where nail holes would be an unpardonable blemish, the spline may be temporarily secured to the work by means of Record C clamps (G cramps). The nature of the work will suggest the size of clamp required—usually 4 or 6 inches will be used. Some thought may be required in positioning the clamps so that they do not foul either the tool or the fingers, but a little experience goes a long way in these matters, and learning by making a few mistakes is usually the best kind of learning. The spline having been attached, use the method of cutting shown in Fig. 127.

Fig. 126. Cutting the rebate with the stop planted on.

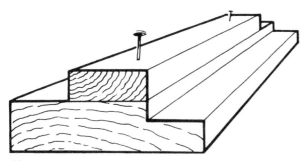

Fig. 127. Spline fitted to act as a fence and guide.

If the grain proves very difficult, turn the work about and work the other way. Often it will be found advantageous to work as with a plow plane, i.e., making short strokes at the end farther away, gradually working backwards and deeper. However, with a sweet-grained wood as used in normal joinery, the plane may take a long cut, such as is done with an ordinary jack plane.

Sometimes, as when fitting a heavy back to a wardrobe or cupboard, an obtuse-angled rebate is called for. It is easiest to work this square first, and then work to the angle—having, of course, gauged the limits before the rebate is started. An acute-angled rebate, used occasionally but not so frequently, should first be cut square, and then the undercut made with a Record side rebate No. 2506S.

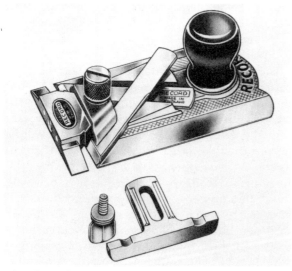

Fig. 128. Side rebate plane 2506S.

Record No. 010 and No. 010½ are sometimes erroneously referred to as "badger" planes. A badger was a wooden rebate, about the size of a jack plane, evolved to do the fielding of door panels. Its blade projected as far as the edge on one side only, and it was sometimes provided with some sort of fence. But the essential difference was that it had a skew blade, which was very advantageous in the top and bottom fielding, which were, of course, cross-grained cuts.

While it is generally preferable to gauge a rebate and work to a gauge line, it is very convenient to have a rebate plane that is fitted with a fence and a depth stop. The Record rebate and fillister No. 078 is so fitted, and for many years has been a very popular tool with both the advanced craftsman and the amateur. It is a simple tool, and will do its work very well.

Fig. 129. Rebate plane 078.

There is available an improved pattern of rebate and fillister in Record No. 778, and it is interesting to see where the difference lies. Both Record No. 078 and Record No. 778 have the same capacity—they will both cut a rebate up to 1½ inch wide. This of course is less than the larger rebates we have been discussing, but these two planes are not designed for the heavier work more suitable to the cabinetmaker than the carpenter and joiner. Both planes are 8½ inches long. Both are fitted with a fence and depth stop, the former controlling the width of the rebate, the latter the depth of it. Both are fitted with a spur so that a rebate may be cut across the grain, as for a flush panel.

On the 078, adjustment of the cutter is by means of a lever that is pivoted to the body of the

Fig. 130. Fillister plane No. 778.

plane. The lower part of the lever has segments which face upwards and seat into slots on the underside of the cutter. Raising or lowering of the adjusting lever increases or decreases the depth of cut required. The lever is also positioned conveniently for use and coincides with the position of the thumb when holding the plane handle; during use, care must be taken not to upset the setting. Positioning the thumb under the lever will overcome this possibility.

A more positive method of adjustment is used on the 778. This consists of a knurled nut on a screwed rod. A flange on the nut fits into a slot in the cutter. In addition to allowing a much finer adjustment, the cutter remains fixed when the required adjustment is obtained.

From Figs. 129 and 130 it will be seen that while No. 078 has only one arm rod for the fence, No. 778 has two arms, these passing right through the body. This results in a much more accurate setting, and allows a little more lateral adjustment. Both planes, of course, may be used to start a fillister—this being cut on the opposite side from the face. (Let me explain the difference between a rebate and a fillister. A fillister is the rebate that holds the glass and the putty. Thus, it is a rebate which is cut on the side opposite the face, but it must be cut parallel with the face.) In the case of 078, the arm rod may be screwed in from either side; with No. 778, the rods will slide right through the plane bodies. When the planes are used in this manner, the arm rods touch the wood fairly soon after the rebate (or fillister) is started. The fence must then be removed and the rebate

finished to the gauge line. No. 778 cuts this initial cut deeper than 078 does.

In Record No. 078, when the arm rod and fence are fitted, the arm rod will normally be screwed into the left-hand side of the body. A small hole is drilled in the arm rod so that a thin rod (a nail will do) may be used to screw the rod up tightly. Screws for securing the fence and depth stop should be finger-tight. The use of pliers is entirely unnecessary. Besides, they can damage the thread, which will eventually cause slipping.

The arm rods of No. 778 pass right through the body and are secured by set screws. In normal use, they are inserted from the left-hand side of the tool only and are not allowed to project on the right-hand side, as the projecting ends would be in the way. When the fence is required on the right-hand side, the arms are moved through the body and secured, ensuring that they do not project on the left-hand side.

The depth stop requires no explanation, being simply set to the depth required. There is a point to watch, however, in this simple setting. The distance should be measured from the sole of the depth stop to the edge of the cutter—and not to the sole of the plane if very accurate work is attempted. Hence, it is wise to try a cut first before finally setting the depth stop. Similarly, in setting the fence, measure from the face of the fence to the edge of the cutter rather than to the side of the plane.

In setting the cutter in the body, the side of the cutter may project very slightly on either side of the body. When grinding and sharpening the cutter, care must be taken to keep the edge square with the sides, or one side of the rebate will be deeper than the other. When adjusting, the projection of the cutter must be even all the way. Beginners always favor thicker shavings, believing this to be a time-saver, but experienced craftsmen have learned that two thin shavings are better than one thick one. This is probably even more true in rebating than in other types of planing.

Seldom will the spur be required when one is rebating along the grain. Only when the wood has a very difficult grain will this be required, and it must be noted that a score mark in the corner will be left when this is done. Should this be objectionable, the last few strokes should be done with the spur in the "off" position. Very rarely is the spur called for when rebating with the grain.

When working across the grain, however, as in the end of a shelf where the thickness of the shelf is reduced to form a shoulder, or in the fitting of a flush panel, one cannot do very well without the spur, as it dispenses with a preliminary saw cut—often not too easy to do across a wide board. It is essential that the spur is sharp, as it must make a clean cut vertically. Here let us remember that both the spur and its screw are very small, and easy to lose if dropped on the floor, so it is very wise when manipulating the spur to do all the operations over the bench.

The best way of sharpening the spur is to hold it in a pair of flat-nosed pliers, resting the spur on the end of a spline (i.e., 1 inch × 2 inches) held at a convenient height in the vise (usually the height of the elbow when one is standing up). A few strokes with a smooth file are taken on the bevelled side, swinging the file to the curve but keeping the bevel quite straight.

The slight wire edge on the flat side can then be taken off with one stroke of the file, taking care to make no bevel on this, the face side. Still holding the spur in the pliers, take a few strokes on the oilstone, making no new bevels, but working up to a keen edge. Insert the spur flat, side outward, and screw up tightly. Check that no dirt, etc., is resting on the seating. This would cause the spur to project beyond the side of the body.

A little practice with either No. 078 or No. 778 will soon enable the worker to make a clean rebate. Adjust the fence and depth stop as required, and fasten the board to the bench, either in the vise or by means of C clamps (G cramps), buttons or otherwise. The action of these planes is very similar to that of using a plow plane.

Both these planes have two positions for the cutter. For normal work the cutter is inserted in the rear position. The forward position converts the tool to a bullnosed rebate used when the tool is required to work close to an obstruction. The cutter adjustment on both planes can only be used when the cutter is in the rear position. In the bullnose position, the cutter must be set by hand.

Hold the plane level, pressing the fence against the wood. Take each and every stroke evenly and carefully. Start (as in plowing) at the front end. Gradually increase the length of the strokes until

they cover the full length of the work, then continue until the depth stop rides on the face of the work. This will prevent further cutting, and the rebate should be to the depth required.

A slight variation of this procedure is required when working across the grain. As already mentioned, the spur is required for this. Take the first few strokes at the end of the cut that is away from the worker, slowly and carefully allowing the spur to cut downwards before taking anything off with the cutter. Then proceed as you would when working with the grain.

The few preliminary spur cuts are important, as the cleanliness of that end of the rebate depends upon the skill with which they are made. If they are carelessly done, the wood will almost certainly break away at that point. To make sure, some workers will score a line with a sharp knife; however, properly used, the spur should be quite satisfactory. Don't be discouraged at initial failures. Skill can only be acquired with constant practice, but once having attained that skill there remains a very permanent sense of personal satisfaction.

At all times the fence must be kept firmly up against the lumber to ensure that the width of the rebate does not vary. The necessary pressure on the fence is made with the left hand, the plane handle being firmly held in the right hand. With a well-sharpened cutter, no downward pressure is necessary, the weight of the plane being sufficient to allow the cutter to do its work. Another aid for keeping the plane under control is the extension of the index finger of the right hand forward rather than wrapped around the handle. At first, the beginner can profitably set the cutter back (so that the plane does not cut at all) and practice "working" with the tool until the "feel" of it comes along, later making short and then longer cuts, as already described.

Removal of the fence allows these planes to be used as square planes. A square plane can be used to clean up certain work, make mouldings and oblique walls to a rebate, much in the same way as the larger rebate plane. The length and width of the square plane also make a much handier tool for a lot of smaller work. Although with care and a very fine cut it can be made to trim a shoulder (on the ends of the fibres of the wood), it is not very strongly recommended for this purpose, as the pitch of the cutter is too high. This work is better done with a low-pitched shoulder plane, which will be described later.

When the worker has become accustomed to using the rebate planes, many adaptations will suggest themselves to him. Fig. 131 shows a very strong carcass joint, the work on which can be considerably curtailed with the intelligent use of the rebate plane. The joint should be set out after the ends of the sides have been shot true, squared and accurately cut to length, and the tenons and mortises made the width of the mortise chisel. The tenon length can be cut with the rebate plane, using the spur after the tenon saw cuts have been made. The recesses can be quickly removed with the bow saw. For the leg, make the mortises first, then cut the groove (which is a stopped groove) using Record router No. 071, and the fence as described on page 114.

As with all iron planes, a little lubrication of the

sole and fence is very desirable from time to time. A rub with a paraffin wax candle—little and often—is probably the best method.

Figs. 132 and 133 show two useful adaptations of rebated work. For the cutting of the grooves, see Chapters 7, 8 and 9. Grooves are quite quickly cut across the grain as dado cuts, using two spurs with either the combination plane No. 050 or 050C or the multi-plane No. 405. For the box construction, leave a trifle extra for final cleaning up on the outside of the dado cut—the end of the box is thus left at its full thickness. In the cabinet end (Fig. 132), if the grooves only occupy part of the length of the leg, they are best cut with the router No. 071, using the fence, as in Fig. 206.

Very handy boxes can be made for the safe storage of such tools as the multi-plane, the plow, the router, etc. If a slide lid is preferred, the two sides and one end may be grooved before gluing up, and the other end made narrower to suit. The

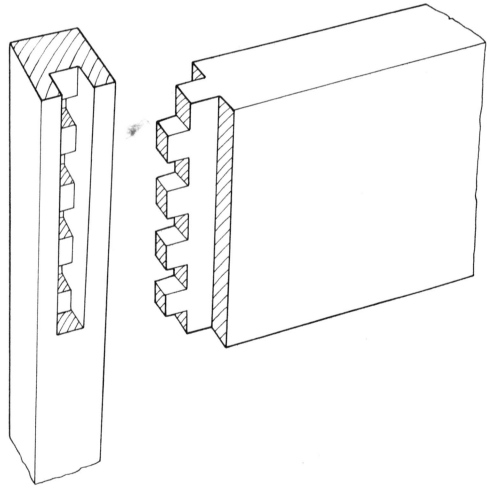

Fig. 131. Carcass joint.

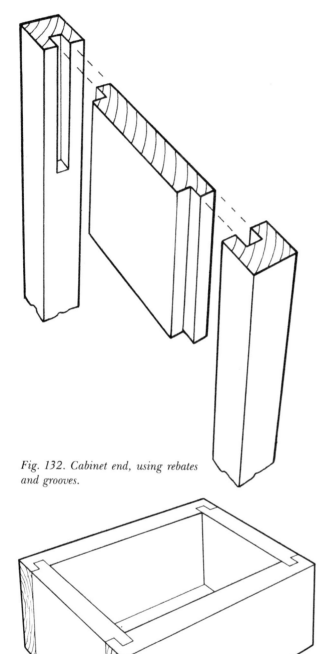

Fig. 132. Cabinet end, using rebates and grooves.

Fig. 133. Box construction, using rebates and grooves.

suited for this purpose because the joints and the end grain are weak spots on which to veneer.

If used as a base for veneer, the end grain should be first treated with a mixture of thin glue. This will prevent the end grain from showing through the veneer, but there still remains the possibility of the line of the joint showing through at some future time, owing to unequal contraction.

Another operation which calls for the use of the rebate plane is the shooting of mitred rebates, as shown in Fig. 134. This corner joint is used on small cabinets and other work, but has a special application in the fitting of rebated frames to the backs of carcasses (i.e., a wardrobe). When a fairly heavy back frame has to be fitted into a rebate, if it is fitted as at C it will frequently result in the narrow slip curling outward, as shown. To prevent this, the rebate should be mitred as at A and the framing shot to a corresponding mitre, as shown at B. The rebate plane is used with the fence to cut the square part and then canted without the fence for the mitre part. The mitred part of B offers no difficulty, being simply shot with the jack plane.

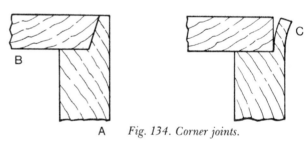

Fig. 134. Corner joints.

Shoulder Planes

The method employed in Fig. 127 and the use of a sharp spur should ensure dead accuracy of fit of the shoulders to the post, as they can be worked parallel to the edge, which has been previously shot with a jointer plane. There are cases in which this method cannot be employed, as for instance in the sloping shoulders of a gunstock stile and other shoulders, particularly when these are wide and come from the saw, as in the lock rail of a door. However skilled the workman may be, there are times when some adjustment must be made. It is for such work as this, and for the very close fitting of shoulders to the stiles, that the Rec-

bottoms may be grooved in, or maybe glued, or simply screwed or nailed on. This construction is often used for veneered boxes, but is not well-

ord shoulder planes Nos. 041, 042 and 073 were designed.

No. 041 is a short and narrow tool, 5 inches long, ⅝ inch wide. No. 042 is slightly larger, 8 inches long and ¾ inch wide. Both planes are of great service on smaller shoulder work and in general accurate fitting. They are used by many as small rebate planes. Planes such as these are very useful in such operations as the cleaning up of the edges of shaped small brackets, i.e., the two brackets of a towel roller.

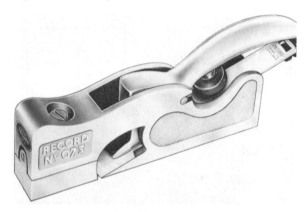

Fig. 135. Shoulder plane 042.

Fig. 136. Shoulder plane 073.

Fig. 137. Cutting a shoulder with the 042.

Often, the terminal members of the curves are awkward to clean up, but if the two pieces are placed together in the vise, and the square and curved portions planed crosswise with Nos. 041 and 042, the process is much simplified. The brackets will be exactly similar in shape and the finish of the smaller parts that the spokeshave cannot reach will be quite clean. Along mouldings they are equally useful, and for small work they will generally be found a great asset.

Shoulder work proper (Figs. 137 and 138) calls for extreme accuracy of cut on short grain. Since the plane must "run through," leaving a dead true surface, it needs a very sharp iron and a mouth which can be adjusted to varying conditions of wood, grain, etc. A break of grain at the end of the cut would be fatal, so, in addition to the adjustable mouth, the blade must be set at as low an angle as possible and the adjustment of the cutter must be of micrometre fineness. All these exacting conditions must be combined with the utmost rigidity in the plane itself, so that the tool may work with smoothness and regularity throughout. Finally, the tool must have a correct "balance" and a comfortable "feel."

Fig. 138. Trimming the mitre on a secret-mitre lap dovetail.

The most fastidious and meticulous of craftsmen will find in shoulder plane No. 073 the answer to his every demand. No cutter will take a sharper edge and retain it longer than the ones fitted to these planes. The adjustment of the mouth—from 0 (completely closed) to ³⁄₁₆ inch (fully opened)—securely locked in any intermediate position is not only ingenious but also has an accuracy that can be found in engineering. The adjustment of the cutter is quick and positive, yet extremely fine, and the ease of handling may be judged from the two examples in Figs. 137 and 138.

Adjustment of the Cutter

The cutter is adjusted by means of the knurled nut engaged in the slot at the top end of the cutter. To remove the cutter, loosen the tightening screw, which screws into the underside of the lever cap, when the lever cap itself can then be removed. Lift the top end of the cutter from engagement with the adjusting nut. Tilt the cutter to allow the cutting edge to clear the inside of the plane body and withdraw it.

Reverse the operation when replacing the cutter, taking care not to catch the cutting edge on the inside of the body and seating with the bevelled side uppermost. Ensure the slot in the cutter engages correctly with the cutter adjusting nut and that the cutter itself seats perfectly. When making any adjustment of the cutter, slightly slacken the tightening screw of the lever cap and tighten this when adjustment is complete.

To adjust the mouth on the 073, first slacken the locking screw, which is fitted vertically inside the front end of the body, subsequently engaging with the adjustable mouth and locking it in the position required. It is only necessary to loosen this screw sufficiently to allow the mouth to slide easily when being adjusted. The screw in the front end of the plane adjusts the mouth, opening when turned right and closing when turned left. Having obtained the width of mouth required, tighten the locking screw on top of the plane.

Experts argue as to whether shoulders should be shot or not. It should be noted, however, that some of the best craftsmen of recent years make a regular practice of shooting their shoulders. It is suggested to those who do not do so that they compare the final appearance of work—in which the shoulders have been shot with that left from the saw—with or without deep knife cuts. Correctly shot shoulders contribute something to that feeling of joy that a true craftsman experiences in a job well done.

Bullnose Planes

The values of these planes is immediately apparent both to the cabinetmaker and to the carpenter. In fact, to both they are indispensable in fine fitting and in the construction of diminished (gunstock) stile work, etc., and in the trimming of such mouldings as ovolos, when slight adjustments must be made. No. 076, while possessing the advantage of a receding nose, cannot have the depth of its cutter adjusted by the screw. The blade is removed by slackening the tightening screw under the lever. A slight cant sideways allows the blade to be easily withdrawn for sharpening, etc.

As for all low-pitched planes, the blade is used with the bevelled side upward. The cutter is quite rigidly held when the screw is tightening. The lever cap provides a convenient hold, fitting nicely to the hollow of the hand.

No. 077 has the great advantage that the blade is adjustable by means of the milled nut at the upper end of the cutter. When removing the blade for sharpening, etc., slacken the tightening screw under the lever and remove the lever. A slight cant of the cutter will enable you to withdraw the cutter.

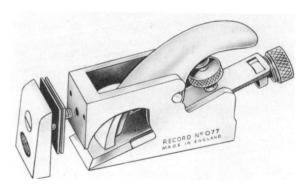

Fig. 139. Bullnose rebate plane 077A.

When replacing, return the cutter, bevelled-side up, in the same way, i.e., by canting the projections through the aperture (alternatively, you may "feed" the cutter from the bottom). See that the slot in the cutter engages with the washer on the feed nut and that the cutter beds down nicely. Replace the lever. Feed the cutter by means of the milled nut in the rear, either back or forward, as required, and tighten all by means of the tightening screw under the lever. Always slacken the tightening screw before altering the adjustment and tighten it when adjustment is complete.

This plane is capable of very fine and accurate work. It also has the very desirable feature of an adjustable mouth in addition to the cutter adjustment. It can further be used when the front is completely removed, as a chisel plane.

Adjusting the Width of the Mouth

The front of the plane is removable by undoing the middle screw in front. When this is removed you will find two "shims" or spacing pieces, one 1/64 inch thick and the other 1/32 inch thick. These give four distinct effective widths of mouth:

(a). When the front or nose is screwed down without any spacing pieces, a very close mouth is formed. This will give, with a fine-set iron, a shaving less than 1/1000 inch thick.

(b). A slightly wider mouth is obtained by inserting the 1/64-inch spacing piece alone.

(c). A still wider mouth is obtained by inserting the 1/32-inch spacing piece alone.

(d). The widest mouth is obtained when both the 1/64-inch and the 1/32-inch spacing pieces are inserted.

No. 075 is a small bullnose plane, 4 inches long and an inch wide. Its mouth is adjustable by means of the screw at the top, but there is no fine screw adjustment of the cutter. Properly sharpened and set, it is capable of quite good work in spite of its low price. However, it is somewhat tedious to set. As the blade is not low-set, as in the other bullnose planes, the bevel side of the blade is fitted downwards.

The No. 311 bullnose, shoulder rebate plane is a three-in-one plane that will appeal to many am-

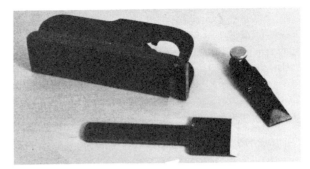

Fig. 141. Stanley 75 bullnose plane with cutter and level cap.

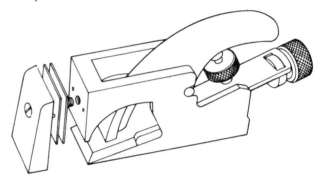

Fig. 142. Bullnose plane with shims for mouth adjustment.

ateurs. Through an ingenious interchange of the fore end, effected by a single screw, which is apparent in Fig. 143, it may be used as a shoulder plane, a bullnose plane and a chisel plane. The cutter is adjustable for depth of cut in the same way as 077A (Fig. 139) and the plane is quite efficient in working in any of its forms. No shims are provided for varying the width of the mouth.

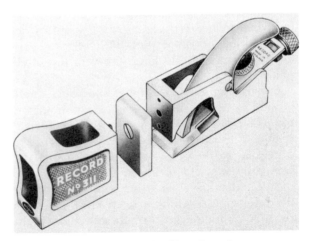

Fig. 143. No. 311 bullnose shoulder rebate plane.

Fig. 140. Stanley 75 bullnose rebate plane.

Care in sharpening the cutters of all rebate, bullnose and shoulder planes amply repays the worker. The edge must be kept true and square, as it is when it leaves the factory, and a hollow stone will achieve this. When extra fine work is attempted, the grindstone and oilstone must also be quite true. Adjusting the cutter requires that it lie evenly to the sides of the plane. With these simple and obvious precautions, there will be no difficulty in doing the finest and most exacting work with any of the planes in this section.

Side Rebates

It so happens sometimes that the wall of a rebate or a groove requires some adjustment. It is not always possible to do this with a rebate plane. For instance, a panel may be slightly too thick to enter the groove of a frame. If the panel is of wood and unpolished, it may of course be thinned down; if it is polished or veneered this may not be advisable or possible; if it is a glass or mirror, it is obviously quite impossible—one must widen the groove. For this purpose, the side rebate plane No. 2506S can be used. It has two cutters and can therefore be used either left- or right-handed. It can also accommodate itself, as in a groove, to the lie of the grain. Should the work demand planing right up into a corner, this may be done by removing the nose, which is held in place by a screw at the front.

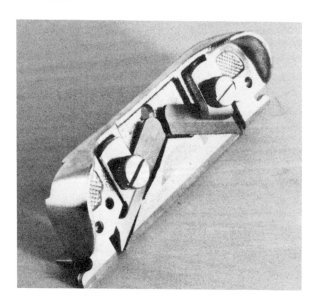

Fig. 144. Stanley 79 side rebate plane.

The plane is also of great value in the adjustment of mouldings, as for instance where there is a slight discrepancy at a mitre, and also for trimming a damaged moulding, etc. Fig. 145 shows how the side rebate may be used in easing the rebate of a door frame without the necessity of removing the door. A further refinement is in the

Fig. 145. Easing a rebate in a door frame with the side rebate plane.

form of a depth stop, adjustable and reversible, which is fitted to the base.

Regarding the working of these planes, little explanation is called for. The plane fits naturally to the worker's hand, and even with very little practice it is quite easy to take off a continuous shaving from the wall of a groove or to make a slight local adjustment as required. The blades should be kept quite sharp. Naturally, the set should be fine and not coarse. Work can be accurately done in a few moments with a side rebate plane that would be a puzzle with any other tool. No kit can be considered complete without a side rebate plane.

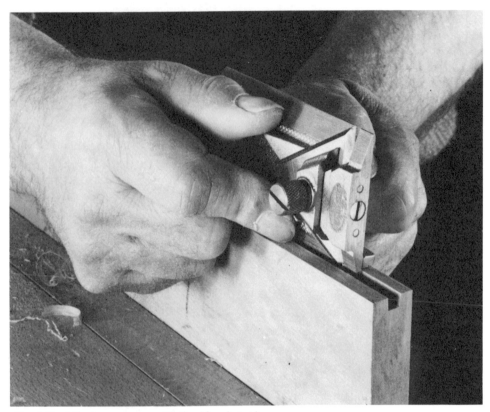

Fig. 146. Adjusting a groove with the side rebate plane.

7

Plow Planes

The modern joiner and cabinetmaker accept the plow plane as an essential tool in the kit, for without a tool that will make a groove of some sort all work would be very limited. Yet there was a time when woodworkers had no such tool. Constructions prior to the 15th century were without grooves. How is it then that the plow has become so necessary a tool since that time?

Probably in no better way is this question answered than in the evolution of the chest—that simple box-like structure from which practically all our modern furniture can trace its ancestry. Chests can be traced back to the 13th century, many of the earlier ones being laboriously "dug out" from a solid balk of lumber, and strongly bound with iron bands.

A natural progression from this type of chest was a chest nailed up from boards. A few such chests are still preserved in some of our churches and museums. If an examination of these is made, it will be found that as a rule: the front and back and the bottom are single boards with the grain running horizontally; the two ends are single boards with the grain running vertically; and in most cases the front and back boards are split. This, of course, is to be expected, for wood naturally shrinks across the grain, but very little along the grain, and as the boards of the front are nailed across the vertical long grain of the ends, when shrinkage occurs something has to give way. Hence, the carpenter sought a way of preventing this damage.

The practical outcome was the invention of a panelled construction, a construction which is standard practice to this day. If the wood could be free to shrink (and, for that matter, to expand also—as in a moist atmosphere) the problem was solved. A frame grooved for a panel offered the solution. So in the 16th century, we find chests with panelled backs and fronts while the ends remained solid. Both frames and panels were often elaborately carved, as indeed had been many of the "planked" chests.

The first grooves were probably made with a scratch tool, for the ancestry of this tool goes far back (it was used for mouldings long before moulding planes were common). Yet a scratch tool has its limitations, and is a difficult tool to use. Therefore, the need for a tool that can easily cut grooves led to the creation of a plow plane.

It is not easy to say just when the plow plane came into existence or what the early plow planes were like, as none are now in existence. However, they were known well enough in 1678 for their name to appear in the literature of that time. In principle, they were probably not unlike the wood-wedged plows later improved by screws and nuts of hardwood, many examples of which are still seen. Major improvement in the plow planes did not come until the introduction of iron plows much later. This introduction can probably be attributed to Russel Philips of Boston, Massachusetts. He patented a plow and fillister plane in 1867.

The metal plow planes have many advantages over the wooden ones. The material of which they are made does not warp and shrink like wood. Neither is the wear on any part comparable with that of wood. No periodical truing up, with its consequent reduction of material, is necessary. The adjustments are much more rapid, and at the same time more accurate. The handling is far more easily mastered, for they are less cumbersome than the earlier wooden ones.

The metal plow planes such as the Record Nos. 044, 044C, 050, 050C and 043 also pack into less space, so they are easier to carry about and store. The tungsten steel cutters of the Record plow planes are much more efficient than those of the wooden ones.

Fig. 147. No. 044 plow plane.

In order to understand the function of a plow plane, we must first consider what is required from it. We expect a plow plane to: (a), plow a groove that is constant in width, though this width may not be identical for all projects; (b), plow that groove at a constant and predetermined distance from the face side (this distance must be variable and under the control of the worker); and (c), plow the groove so that its depth shall be constant (as in b, the distance should be variable, yet under control).

(a). The width of the groove is determined by the width of the cutter. That cutter is held in the body in such a way that it is rigid, but the thickness of the shaving is controllable. In Record Nos. 043, 044 and 044C plow planes, the cutter is held in the body by means of a lever cap. While in No. 043 the thickness of the shaving is regulated manually by setting the cutter to project the required amount below the body, in Nos. 044 and 044C a screw adjustment is provided which gives a quick, easy and critical setting. No. 044 has a further refinement in that a side screw is provided to ensure the cutter seats flush up to the body; this also eases the pressure on the lever cap and adjusts as required. The cutter in the 044C is held in position with a clamp.

(b). The distance of the groove from the face side is determined by the setting of the fence. The body is provided with two fence arms on which the fence may slide easily, parallel and square. The fence arms are themselves adjustable in that they pass through holes carefully drilled in the body and are secured in position by set screws. A position for the fence arms approximately halfway through the body will usually give the best balance.

When the groove is to be farther away, the fence arms can be moved quite easily. The fence can now be passed towards or away from the body and secured by means of the two knurled screws in any predetermined position. In setting up the fence, the cutter must be in working position. Measure between the edge of the cutter and the fence, not the body and the fence.

The fence has two holes drilled in the face. These are provided to permit a deeper fence to be made, with a fillet of hardwood screwed to it with No. 8 roundhead screws. The size of the fillet will be chosen to suit the particular job, but it must be planed parallel and square and a recess will have to be cut (continuing the recess of the fence) in order to allow the egress of shavings. The deeper fence, taking a bigger bearing on the face side of the work, tends to make the operation easier, but it seriously limits the amount of work which can be done in the vise (the vise jaw is in the way of the deeper fence).

It cannot be too strongly emphasized that there is no need whatever to use any tool to tighten the knurled screws. The adjusting screw for the cutter and the set screws holding the fence arms will call for a screwdriver, but finger tightness on all the knurled screws is all that is required. Any excessive weight may damage the threads.

To ease the working of the plow, a wax candle may be drawn from time to time along the fence and the runner. This will provide a lubrication superior to that provided by oil.

(c). The depth of the cut is controlled by the depth gauge. The required setting is made by measuring from the underneath face of the gauge to the cutting edge of the cutter.

Having considered the essential features of this type of plane, the variations of the 043 and 044 may be of interest. No. 043 is a smaller plow plane and is provided with three cutters only: ⅛ inch, ³⁄₁₆ inch and ¼ inch. These sizes are the ones most usually required by the skilled amateur. It does not follow that a wider groove cannot be cut, for if the limits of the groove are first marked on the wood then it can be done by making a number of cuts while progressively increasing the setting of the fence.

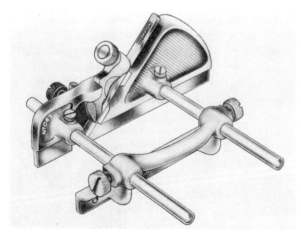

Fig. 148. No. 043 plow plane.

Thus the joiner or cabinetmaker who has no time for double cuts when single ones will suffice requires a plane with enough cutters to do any-

thing in the way of plowing that ever arises. Record No. 044 with its ten cutters is the tool such craftsmen prefer. Indeed, this plane was regarded as the standard one for many years. Where millimetre grooves were required (as for some types of plywood) 4, 6, 9 and 12 millimetre cutters were available as extras. (When a groove has been cut to receive plywood, particularly veneered plywood, it may be necessary to widen it using the side rebate plane No. 2506.)

For the serious home craftsman, the 043 is an ideal plane, capable of cutting grooves and rebates within the limits of the three cutters: ⅛ inch, ³⁄₁₆ inch and ¼ inch. (Though they are no longer being manufactured, there are thousands of Record plow planes Nos. 043 and 044 in existence.) It is an excellent tool for young people who are first learning cutting techniques. For the more demanding craftsman, the 044 is perfect with its better handling and its bigger range of cutters.

Fig. 149. Plowing a groove with the 043 plane.

From its introduction, the Record plow plane No. 044 was immensely popular with woodworkers in all parts of the world. Because of its usefulness, accuracy and ease of operation it was universally adopted in woodworking classes and technical colleges. Its range of eight cutters enables it to plow grooves from ⅛ inch to ⁹⁄₁₆ inch by sixteenths, with wider grooves making two cuts. It will plow ⅝ inch deep at any distance from the edge up to 5 inches. Narrow rebates can be made by moving the fence up to the cutter. Wider rebates are best made by first plowing a groove and then removing the rest with a bench rebate plane.

Check the cutter for sharpness. Ensure that the fence is always in contact with the face side of the work. Little or no downward pressure is required with the right hand as the sharp cutter will ensure a satisfactory cut. Slight pressure with the left hand will nevertheless keep the cut parallel with the edge of the work. Uneven grain will often tend to pull the plane out of parallel. Care must also be taken to keep the plane upright.

Grooves should be started at the end of the wood that is farthest away, and gradually deepened backwards as the work proceeds. The work is much easier if the fence and the runner are occasionally lubricated either with a spot of oil or with a wax candle. The wax candle, used little and often, is strongly recommended.

The worker should not find much difficulty in sharpening the cutters, this being in keeping with the sharpening of other plane cutters, but it should be noted that in the case of a plow plane the angle of 35° is desirable. It is better to keep to the one bevel rather than make two bevels. The flat side should be kept flat—no bevel on this side. Beginners who have not enough confidence in sharpening should use a tool honer.

The constant pressure of the woodwork vise tends to hollow out the wood facing of the back jaw (the one on the bench), particularly when this is of softwood. As a result, the stile or rail being plowed can bend to a slight curve when gripped in the vise. In such a case, the plow binds in the groove. The straight fence, of course, cannot accommodate itself to the curvature the wood assumes. A temporary remedy is to pack up from the back with a piece of wood that will keep the stile being plowed straight.

However, the real and lasting remedy to this problem is to cut away the worn and bruised jaw facing and replace it with another piece of hardwood. Indeed, when bench tops are made of softwood, as many are because of the need to economize, it is a good practice to face up the whole of the front edge with a 2-inch piece of beech or similar hardwood. This problem is mentioned because it is common with a much-used bench, and often enough it has escaped observation. Nowadays the use of the shallow fence is almost universal, and only those workers who have been used to an old-fashioned plow plane will feel the need to deepen the fence.

While the plow plane will most often be called upon to make the grooves for panelling, this does not by any means represent the full measure of the work the plow plane may be called upon to do. As will be seen from Fig. 150, the plow plane may also be used for constructional and decorative work. The decorative detail is modern in spirit and sound in taste, and springs directly from the use of the tool used in a natural manner. These are suggestions only. Much leeway is given to the imagination, ingenuity and experience of the craftsman.

The craftsman should remember that in the majority of this work the disposition of the proportions of the components of his decoration and the proportion of this decoration to the whole will be the deciding factors in the success or failure of his efforts. An extra rebate on the fielding of a panel may make or mar the whole appearance by being $\frac{1}{16}$ inch too big or too little. This will not always be apparent from a drawing which has a two-dimension limitation; the flat drawing cannot show the subtleties of the light and shade of the finished work in the solid. It is best to experiment a bit with spare pieces. In any case, unless the workmanship is of the first class, any attempt at this kind of decoration will certainly be a dead failure.

The cross sections illustrated in Fig. 150 are examples of what may be done with Record plow plane No. 043. If the occasion arises, the fence may be used left- or right-handed, and with a little care a groove may be planed on the end of a board as well as along the grain. Neither of these plows is recommended for cutting housings or dados (i.e., grooves across a board) since they are not fitted, as are Record planes Nos. 050, 050C and 405, with spurs for this purpose.

The 044 was finally superseded by the 044C, an entirely new design. It is capable of carrying out a variety of plowing and rebating work. It has a double arm-bridged fence, an improved adjustable depth gauge of unique new design and ten cutters which, except for the $\frac{1}{8}$-inch and $\frac{3}{16}$-inch cutters, are screw-adjusted. The handle is of shock-proof material, with other parts of plated grey iron and steel.

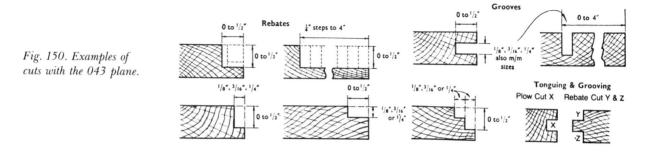

Fig. 150. Examples of cuts with the 043 plane.

Grooves

Rebates

Tonguing & Grooving
Plow Cut X   Rebate Cut Y & Z

Parts of the Plow Plane 044C

Parts List

A Body and Cutter Adjusting Screw
B Cutter Clamping Bracket and Cutter Clamping Screw
C Fence
D Fence Knurled Screws (2)
E Fence Arms (2)
G Depth Gauge and Stem
H Cutter
*J Cutter Adjusting Nut
K Depth Gauge Locking Screw
L Depth Gauge Expander
T Fence Arm Set Screws (2)
*W Cutter Clamping Nut
Y Handle
Z Handle Fixing Screw
   Cutters (set of 10)
   Cutters' Wallet
   Packing Arms (")

*These parts are identically paired and are freely interchangeable.

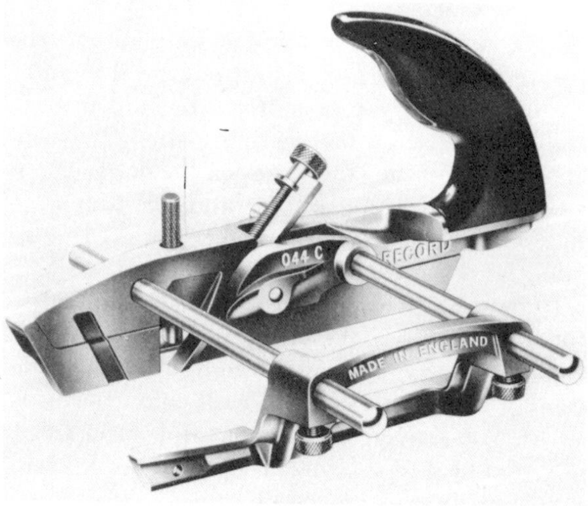

Fig. 151. No. 044C plow plane.

Fig. 152. Parts of the 044C plow plane.

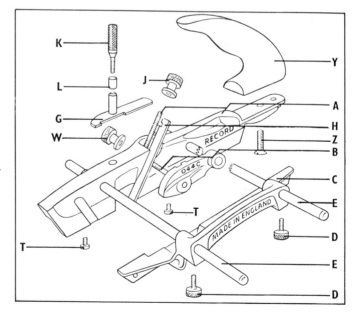

Assembling The Plane

For packing purposes the plane is fitted with two black plastic arms. These must be replaced with fence arms (E) by slackening the fence arm set screws (T) and positioning the arms (E) approximately midway through the holes. (On no account should the plane be used with the black plastic arms.) Tighten the screws and only change the fence arm position when the full fence capacity is required. Fit cutter clamping bracket (B) onto the fence arms.

Place cutter (H) in position by sliding it into the groove from underneath and engage the cutter slot onto the collar of cutter adjusting nut (J). Lightly tighten cutter clamping nut (W) sufficiently to hold the cutter. Adjust for depth of cut with cutter adjusting nut (J) and firmly tighten nut (W). Slide fence (C) onto fence arms (E), tightening fence knurled screws (D).

To increase the depth of the fence, fit an additional hardwood fence using the holes provided. Prepare a piece of long, straight-grained hardwood accurately to size and with edges perfectly square. Cut shaving escapement and cutter clearance identical to that in the metal fence and assemble as shown in Fig. 153.

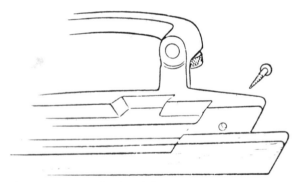

Fig. 153. Fitting a hardwood fence.

Setting Up the Plane

For Plowing

To set the cutter, slacken off the cutter clamping nut (W) and operate the cutter adjusting nut (J) until the cutter edge shows slightly forward of the body skate. Fully tighten the cutter clamping nut (W). To set the fence, slacken the fence knurled screws (D) and use a ruler, as in diagram "A," to measure the required inside distance between cutter and fence. To control depth of groove or rebate, set the depth gauge (G) by slackening the depth gauge locking screw (K). Use a ruler to push down on the depth gauge, which will be held in position by the nylon depth gauge expander (L), until the locking screw (K) is tightened down. By removing the depth gauge, you can obtain an extra ⅛ inch depth of groove or rebate.

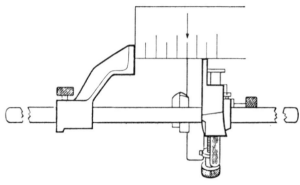

Fig. 154. Setting the fence for grooving.

For Rebating

Always keep the fence firmly against the face side or face edge of the wood. Keep the plane upright and make sure that the cutter is removing the shavings. A little paraffin wax applied to the fence will make for easier working. Always start cutting at the end farthest away from the operator, gradually moving backwards as the work proceeds until the plane is cutting the full length of the wood.

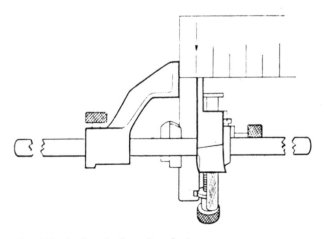

Fig. 155. Setting the fence for rebating.

The fence can be set on either side of the body, which allows the plane to be used either left-handed or right-handed. When the plane is used in the left hand, however, the depth gauge cannot be set for grooves less than ¼ inch deep, since they will prevent the fence from being brought closer than ⅜ inch to the body skate. For left-hand work when cutting rebates, the depth gauge must be removed. If, however, an additional wooden fence at least ⁵⁄₁₆ inch thick is screwed on, these restrictions will not apply. The depth gauge locking screw locks the depth gauge expander in the hole in the body. In the out-of-use position, it should be just possible to move the gauge with medium thumb pressure. To lock firmly, apply a further half turn.

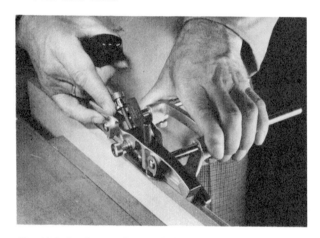

Fig. 156. Cutting a rebate with the 044C plow plane.

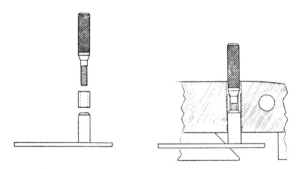

Fig. 157. Construction of the depth gauge: At left, exploded view; at right, depth gauge set in the body.

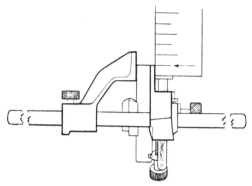

Fig. 158. Setting the depth gauge.

Care in Use

The body is of high-quality grey iron and, although robust, care should be taken never to drop it. Make sure that fence arm set screws (T) and fence knurled screws (D) are tight before use; otherwise the plane may be subjected to undue strain and inaccuracies in working may result. The plane will require a minimum of maintenance other than a little light machine oil on the screw threads.

When making adjustments, keep the plane over the bench to avoid losing small screws and parts in the shavings. Thin shavings give more accurate results than thick ones and a better finish. The cutters must be kept in first-class condition and keenly sharp at all times.

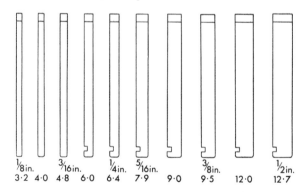

Fig. 159. Cutters for the 044C plow plane. Sizes shown include both inches and, underneath them, the millimetre equivalent.

8

Combination Planes Nos. 050 and 050C

The first metal combination plane was designed by Charles G. Miller of Brattleboro, Vermont. This design was marketed by the Stanley Rule and Level Company in 1870. It was from this early design that later developments came.

The Record combination planes are capable of a wide range of operations, including plowing, cutting rebates, fillisters and dadoes (housings), edge beading, center beading and matching (tongues and grooves, with or without beads).

All the above operations are common to carpenters, joiners, cabinetmakers and other crafts-men. At first sight, it would appear that a claim to do all of them well with a single tool would be hard to sustain, and to do them with precision and good finish with a single tool almost impossible. A close examination of the combination plane and a consideration of its design will, however, soon dispel any doubts, since many of the operations are actually very closely related.

A comparison with the plow planes will show that although the plow planes have a mainstock and a sliding fence, the combination planes have both these and also a sliding section (Fig. 160), the

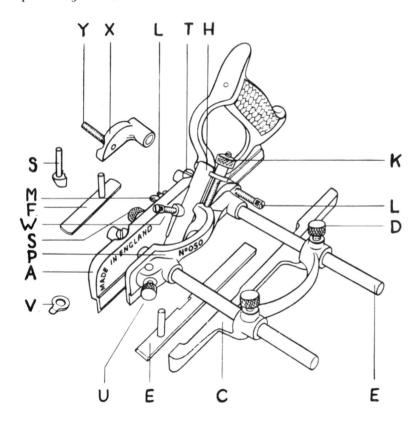

Fig. 160. Parts of the 050 combination plane.

sole of which bears on the wood in the same plane as the body. This allows the cutter to rest in parallel machined grooves, providing with the cutter bolt and nut a rigid seating for the cutter. The sliding section does not in any way interfere with the function of the plane as a plow, but allows the use of a bead-shaped cutter, of which seven sizes are provided, ranging from ⅛ inch to ½ inch. With any of these cutters used in the same manner as a plow, a center bead can be cut. As the sliding section is provided with a beading stop (E, Fig. 160), so arranged that it cuts out one quirk of the bead, any of the beading cutters may be used for edge beading. This arrangement provides the equivalent of seven center bead planes and seven ordinary bead planes, which, with the plow, represents 15 separate planes.

The fence is so designed that it can slide under the sliding section. As a result, rebate and fillister work may be undertaken at one cut up to a width of ⅞ inch (or wider, of course, taking two cuts). Adding a rebate and fillister provides the equivalent of 16 planes.

Both the sliding section and the body are fitted with spurs which, by cutting through the fibres in advance of the cutter, allow cutting across the grain. This operation may be done with any of the seven plow and rebate cutters. Thus, the equivalent of seven dado planes is added, bringing the total to 23.

Any plow plane, of course, will make a groove on the edge of a board, and with careful handling may be used to make the tongues. The combination plane, however, carries a special tonguing cutter which will make a ¼-inch tongue of predetermined height at one setting (an adjustable depth stop is provided on the cutter). This adds a pair of matching planes to the list, bringing the total plane equivalent to 25.

Planted ovolos and astragals may be made with any of the seven beading cutters. Therefore, a further plane equivalent of 14 planes can be added, which leaves a grand total, excluding extra cutters, of 39 planes in one. Yet this combination plane, a precision tool in every sense of the word, was packed in a compact box taking less space than that taken up by an old-fashioned wooden plow plane and its cutters.

Millimetre cutters are also available as extras for the combination plane in the usual millimetre plywood sizes where these are at variance with inch sizes, i.e., 4, 6, 9 and 12 millimetres. Also, additional tonguing cutters for ⅛-inch and ³⁄₁₆-inch tongues are obtainable.

Handling the Plane

Hold the plane firmly. The main thing to remember is to apply the slight pressure required in the right place, i.e., on the fence, with the left hand. The fence must be kept well up to the edge of the work, and care must then be taken not to cant the plane over. If a lubricant should be desired on the fence, a rub with the side of a wax candle will do the trick.

A great deal can be done with the work held in the vise, as the fence is not too deep on the face. Where work cannot be held in the vise, it may be clamped on the bench, "tacked" to the bench or held with dogs. When similar operations are often called for, as in some repetition work, the worker will find that a suitably plowed board or strip will be useful—a "sticking" board. Thus, strips could be held in a plowed groove while they were planed into astragals.

The advantage of the narrow fence is that so much work can be done in the vise. There are some workers who prefer a deeper fence, maintaining that this is helpful in keeping the fence vertical and close to the work. Should a deeper fence be desired, screw a parallel fillet of wood as deep as desired to the face of the fence. Screw holes for this purpose are drilled in the fence. Any well-seasoned hardwood will do for this.

Sizes of Cuts

Plowing Cuts

Any plowing can be done from ⅛ inch to ½ inch, ranging by sixteenths of an inch. It can also be done at ⅝ inch and ⅞ inch at one cut with standard cutters. Extra cutters will plow 4, 6, 9 or 12 millimetres at one operation. By a simple expedient (see Fig. 74, Chapter 4), any wider groove may be cut.

Dado Cuts (i.e., Grooves across the grain)

Any dado or through housing may be cut the same size as for plowing.

Bead and Center Bead Cuts

Any bead or center bead can be cut from ⅛ inch to ½ inch, ranging by sixteenths of an inch. The bead may be on the edge of a board (plain or tongued) or in any position on the board up to 7½ inches from, and parallel to, the edge. (With the fence in the ordinary position, center beads may be made up to 5 inches from the edge. When the fence is reversed, a further 2½ inches may be spanned.)

Rebate and Fillister Cuts

Using the fence, rebates may be accurately cut ⅛ inch to ⅞ inch wide at one cut. Wider rebates are made by two cuts, a plow cut coming first. In this way, practically any width rebate may be cut without fatigue.

Matching Cuts

Tongues may be cut ¼ inch wide; grooves are made with the ¼-inch plow cutter.

Assembly of the Combination Plane

There will be no difficulty in assembling the plane. Slacken the screws in the mainstock (A, Fig. 160), which secures the short arms. Replace the latter with the long arms, locating them normally approximately halfway through, and tighten up the screws. (When working a long distance from the edge, the arms can be located farther to the right.) Slide the section (B) on the arms as shown until the cutter-bolt (L) projects through the hole in the mainstock. Slip on the washer and the wing nut (M) loosely.

Insert the cutter from below. See that the notch in the upper part of the cutter engages with the collar (O) of the adjusting nut (K). Draw L up nearly tight by means of the wing nut (M), seeing that the cutter is properly bedded in the slots in both body and sliding section.

The projection of the cutter below the edges of A and B controls the thickness of the shavings and can be accurately adjusted to very fine limits by means of the adjusting nut (K).

When adjusting the cutter, always slacken the wing nut (M), tightening again after adjustment is made. The adjustment of the depth of the cutter is worth more than passing notice, for while it is possible to obtain any desired setting with a mo-

ment's manipulation, that adjustment is positive. When any adjustment is made to the depth of the cutter by means of the screw feed, it is impossible for any sideways displacement of the cutting edge to take place, as may occur when the cutter is held by a taper bolt. In the combination plane, the cutter sits inside the two accurately machined grooves which, when the cutter is screwed up tightly, always maintain a permanent lateral position of the cutter.

For Plowing

Insert cutter of desired size and tighten up. Use depth stop (F at P [forward of the wing nut on mainstock A]) and adjust to depth of required groove.

Slide fence (C) to required distance from edge and tighten up thumbscrews, which hold the fence to the arms.

For Rebating

Proceed as for plowing. When possible, it is advantageous to use a cutter wider than the width of the rebate and slide the fence (C) under the near edge of the cutter. Otherwise, use a cutter the width of the rebate and slide C to edge of cutter.

For Beading

(a). On edge of board.

Insert the beading cutter and tighten up after adjusting. Use beading stop (E) and depth gauge (F). In this manner, tongued boards can also be beaded.

(b). Center beading.

Select the beading cutter and proceed as for plowing. It is not necessary to use the spurs for beading.

For Cutting a Dado (Housing)

Nail a 3/16-inch-thick batten (plywood is excellent for this purpose) on the edge of the dado to be cut. Use the spurs, but not the fence (C). The batten acts as a guide. When the shoulder of the main body casting reaches the batten, if it is desired that the dado should go deeper, remove the batten. The depth of cut already made will keep the remainder of the cut straight and square. The depth stop (F) will limit the depth to be cut. Dadoes of all the usual depths can be easily cut in this way with great speed.

To cut a groove or a rebate deeper than ⅜ inch remove the depth stop. When the cutter reaches its natural limit and can proceed no farther on account of the shoulder on the mainstock (A), slacken the wing nut half a turn, screw the cutter a little forward by turning the adjusting nut (K) and tighten the wing nut. Then take off a shaving. Repeat this forward feeding of the cutter in the same manner until the required depth is cut. A groove or rebate may thus be cut to a depth of ¹⁵/₁₆ inch, and will be even in depth.

When cutting dadoes, cut a number of cross housings in a number of parallel strips. Space out the housings evenly. Arrange the strips in order and clamp them together with a bar clamp (sash cramp).

Everything should be held on the bench with a C clamp (G cramp). Insert the required cutter and set the spurs down. Tack a plywood strip at the position of the first groove. When this is completed, move the strip into position for the second groove, and so on. Housings for shop shelving and other situations can be very speedily done across the grain as quickly as plowing can be done with the grain. All shelves will fit fair and square, provided that the precaution is taken to use a cutter the same width as the thickness of the shelves and partitions that are to be inserted.

It should be carefully noted that there is need for very little marking-out. All that is necessary is that the position of one side of each dado shall be indicated. The strip of plywood gives the straight line, the cutter gives the width. There is no need to do either sawing or chiselling. The number of strips that can be worked at a time is limited only by the length of clamp available.

When a large number of strips are worked, there may be a tendency for the middle ones to work up when the clamp is tightened, but this can be overcome by tacking on temporarily a spline. If there is any possibility of the top fibres tearing, the plane should be drawn backwards several times with a slight downward pressure. The effect of this is that the spur makes a clean cut before the cutter takes its shaving. When this is done, no matter how rough the grain of the wood, the dado will have clean edges on both sides.

The spurs can be put in or out of action by means of the retaining screws. Spurs are used in dado work and sometimes in plowing or rebating, especially when the grain is at all crossed. When adjusting the spurs, take care to work well over the bench, as both spurs and screws are very tiny and can be lost among the shavings.

When sharpening the spurs (and they must be sharp if good, clean work is to be done), hold them in a pair of flat-nosed pliers on a piece of odd wood held in the vise. File the bevelled edge with a fine saw file, but do not file the flat side—merely wipe off the wire edge with one light wipe of the file.

Using the ⅛-inch and ³/₁₆-inch Plow Cutters

A valuable improvement to the Record combination plane No. 050 was introduced, enabling the plane to be used with ⅛-inch and ³/₁₆-inch cutters for plowing, rebate and dado work. The No. 050 plane had this improvement fitted as standard. The parts improved are labeled X and Y in Fig. 160. They are the narrow cutter clamping bracket, complete with plow cutters, ⅛ inch and ³/₁₆ inch.

When using these cutters, the sliding section (C) is not required. For these two cutters, the cutter clamping bracket is used in place of the sliding section. Otherwise, the operations are as previously described. The ⅛-inch and ³/₁₆-inch cutters will be found extremely advantageous when framing up plywood of these thicknesses, and in cutting the grooves for tongued clamps on thin tops, as for radio or record cabinets, etc.

Another useful application of the ⅛-inch cutter to the cabinetmaker is in the fitting of inlaid black or box lines on corners. The fence is run up to the edge of the cutter and the depth stop set to the thickness of the line to be inlaid. When working across the grain, the spur should be used, or a cutting gauge run down first, to get a clean edge. The rebate being cut, and the line fitted to length, a little thin glue is applied.

To clamp up, bind a half inch or so wide cotton tape around the box, wrapping the tape as one would do when bandaging. Stretch the tape as tightly as possible. This should be left until the glue is completely set. It is a wise precaution to cover the line with a strip of newspaper before the tape is bound, as this facilitates the removal afterwards of the tape. If the newspaper is stuck, it can be easily scraped or damped off in cleaning up.

For Tonguing and Grooving

For grooving, as already indicated, the ¼-inch plow cutter is used; there is no essential difference between this operation and plowing. The tongues should be cut first. The grooving cutter (i.e., ¼-inch plow) should then be set for the grooves at the appropriate distance from the edge; use the fence (C) and regulate the depth with the depth stop (F).

For tonguing, use the tonguing cutter. The height of the tongue is regulated by the screw stop on the tonguing cutter itself. There is no need for either a depth stop (F) or beading stop (E). The distance of the tongue from the edge of the board is regulated by the fence (C). The cutter will cut a ¼-inch tongue in the middle of boards ⅝ inch to 1⅛ inch wide. Double tongues may be cut on boards from 1¼ inch thick and upwards by taking two cuts. By a similar method, triple tongues can be cut on wider boards.

The Shaving Deflector

When tonguing under certain conditions, you may notice shavings clear themselves from the right-hand prong. There may be a tendency for them to fail to clear themselves from the other prong. Should this be experienced, the shaving deflector provided can be attached. The shaving deflector (S) is inserted loosely in the hole (P) before the cutter is inserted from underneath. When both deflector and cutter are in position, the deflector is set so that its squared recess fits the side of the cutter closely before it is secured by the thumbscrew. The cutter is then adjusted for cut in the usual way and secured by its wing nut. When the cutter is properly ground and sharpened, and correctly set for depth, the operation of tonguing can generally be performed quite satisfactorily without the aid of the deflector.

The edges of matching boards can be "Veed" or beaded. The bead should be on the face of the tongued board, and is cut as previously indicated.

Mouldings

An ovolo for planting can be made by sliding the fence under a beading cutter of suitable size so that only half the cutter is in action. The depth gauge should be set to correct depth as required. Choose wood of suitable thickness. After planing

the half bead, saw off on the line XX (Fig. 161), later trimming off the sawn edge with the jack or smooth plane. The moulding can then be planted the depth of the quirk, as at Z, for panelled work in doors and framings, finally being glued and pinned. The panel should neither be glued nor pinned, being left free to shrink. Thus only one of the flats should be glued, i.e., the one that fits to the frame, and the pins should be through the moulding to the frame only. If the panel is pinned, it may crack.

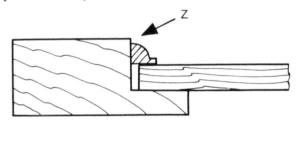

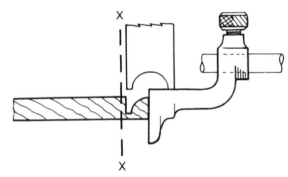

Fig. 161. Cutting an ovolo moulding.

A suggestion of further mouldings is shown in Fig. 162, the manner of cutting them being indicated with the drawings. Many rectilinear mouldings can also be made with the combination plane. Any work that can be done with the plow planes can, of course, be done equally well with the combination plane.

The cross sections (Fig. 162) illustrate various cuts that can be made with the No. 050 plane and also indicate the methods. In addition, all cuts made by the No. 044 and smaller plow planes can be made with these combination planes.

The 050 plane has now been superseded by the 050C, an entirely new design, created to eliminate some of the faults inherent in previous designs. The redesign also presented an opportunity to work on many of the parts so that they became

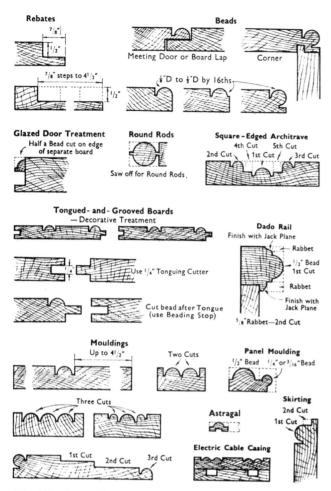

Fig. 162. Cuts with the 050 combination plane.

Parts of the Combination Plane 050C

Parts List

A Body and Cutter Adjusting Screw
B Sliding Section and Cutter Clamping Screw
C Fence
D Fence Knurled Screws (2)
E Fence Arms (2)
F Beading Stop and Stem
G Depth Gauge and Stem
J Cutter Adjusting Nut
K Depth Gauge Locking Screw
L Depth Gauge Expander
M Body Spur
N Body Spur Clamp
O Body Spur Screw
P Sliding Section Spur
Q Sliding Section Spur Clamp
R Sliding Section Spur Screw
S Beading Stop Locking Screw
T Fence Arm Set Screws (2)
U Beading Stop Expander
W Cutter Clamping Nut
Y Handle
Z Handle Fixing Screw

Cutters (set of 18). Cutters' Wallet. Packing Arms (2). The following parts are identically paired and are freely interchangeable: (JW), (KS), (LU), (MP), (NQ) and (OR)

interchangeable with those of the 044C. The 405 cutters are now standard for the 044C and 050C within the capacities and capabilities of the planes.

The Record combination plane 050C is a multipurpose plane designed to perform a considerable number of planing operations with a minimum of adjustments and additional parts. Plowing, rebating, tonguing, beading and housing can all be carried out working with and across the grain. It has a double-arm bridged fence and an improved adjustable depth gauge and beading stop of unique new design. It is fitted with adjustable easily sharpened spurs for across-the-grain work and 18 cutters which, except for the ⅛-inch cutter, are screw-adjusted. The handle is of shockproof material with other parts of plated grey iron and steel.

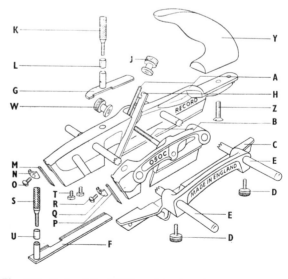

Fig. 163. Parts of the 050C combination plane.

97

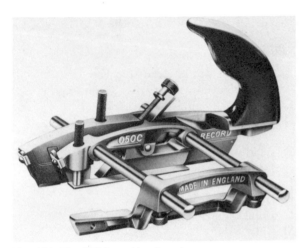

Fig. 164. No. 050C combination plane.

Assembling the Plane

For packing purposes, the plane is fitted with two black plastic arms. These must be replaced with the fence arms (E) by slackening the fence arm set screws (T), positioning the arms (E) approximately midway through the holes. (Do *not* use the plane with the black plastic arms.)

Tighten the screws and only change the fence arm position when full fence capacity is required. Fit the sliding section (B) onto the fence arms. Place the cutter (H) in position by sliding it into the groove from underneath and engage the cutter slot onto the collar of the cutter adjusting nut (J).

Lightly tighten the cutter clamping nut (W) sufficiently to hold the cutter. Adjust for depth of cut with the cutter adjusting nut (J) and firmly tighten the nut (W). Slide the fence (C) onto the fence arms (E), tightening the fence knurled screws (D).

To increase the depth of the fence, fit an additional hardwood fence using the holes provided.

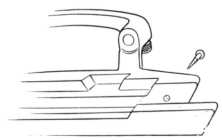

Fig. 165. Fitting a hardwood fence.

Prepare a piece of long, straight hardwood accurately to size and with edges perfectly square. Cut the shaving escapement and the cutter clearance and assemble as shown in Fig. 165.

Setting Up the Plane

For Plowing

To set the cutter, slacken off the cutter clamping nut (W) and operate the cutter adjusting nut (J) until the cutter edge shows slightly forward of the body skate. Fully tighten the cutter clamping nut (W). To set the fence, slacken the fence knurled screws (D) and use a rule to measure the required inside distance between the cutter and fence. To control the depth of groove or rebate, set the depth gauge (G) by slackening the depth gauge locking screw (K). Use a rule to push down on the depth gauge, which will remain in position by being held down by the nylon depth gauge expander (L) until the locking screw

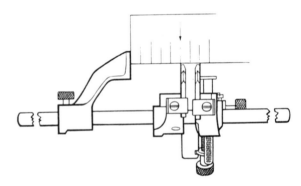

Fig. 166. Setting the fence for plowing.

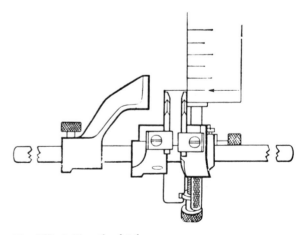

Fig. 167. Setting the depth gauge.

Fig. 168. Plowing.

Fig. 169. Grooving across the end of a board.

(K) is tightened down. By removing the depth gauge, an extra ⅛-inch depth of groove or rebate may be obtained.

Rebating

Set the cutter and the depth gauge as for plowing. Fit a cutter slightly wider than the rebate required and set the width of rebate by adjusting the distance between the fence and the outside edge of the cutter. If the rebate required is wider than the widest cutter, first cut a groove away from the face and remove the surplus with a bench rebate plane.

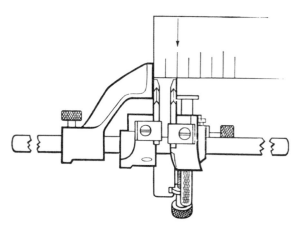

Fig. 170. Setting the fence for rebating.

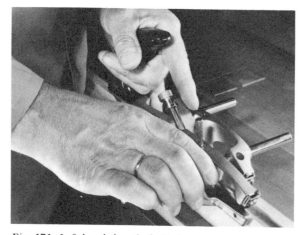

Fig. 171. Left-handed method of rebating.

General

Always keep the fence firmly against the face side or face edge of the wood. Keep the plane upright and make sure that the cutter is removing

99

thin shavings. A little paraffin wax applied to the fence will make for easier working. Cutting should always start at the end farthest away from the operator, gradually moving backwards as the work proceeds until the plane is cutting the full length of the wood. When cutting end grain, to avoid splitting the lumber on the far corner make a small chamfer or support the lumber with an additional piece.

The fence can be set on either side of the body, which allows the plane to be used in either the right or left hand. However, when used in the left hand the depth gauge cannot be set for grooves less than ¼-inch deep, since it will prevent the fence from being brought closer than ⅜-inch to the body skate and the cutter. For left-hand working, when cutting rebates, the depth gauge must be removed. If, however, an additional wooden fence at least ⁵⁄₁₆ inch thick is screwed on, these restrictions will not apply. The screw on the depth gauge, which serves to open the nylon depth gauge expander (L), must only be tightened a quarter turn. The expander spreads into the threaded body housing, preventing the depth gauge from moving. This also applies to the beading stop.

When using the ⅛-inch or ³⁄₁₆-inch cutters for grooving, it is necessary to remove the sliding section. Invert it and use it as a clamping bracket to firmly hold these small cutters in position.

Note: These cutters are not adjustable by means of the cutter adjusting nut.

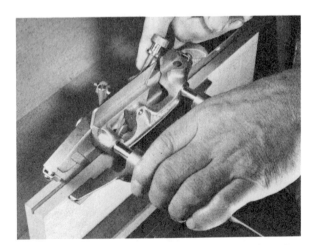

Fig. 172. Inverting sliding sections to accommodate the smallest cutters.

Housing

To cut grooves (housing) or rebates across the grain, it is necessary to sever the top fibres before the cutter itself comes into use. For this purpose, spurs are provided in front of the body and sliding section.

For cutting rebates, set the body spur (M) so that it projects slightly below the body slide, tightening down firmly on the spur screw (O). For plowing or housing, similarly set the sliding section spur (P). Remember to keep the flat face of the spur in line with the outside of the skate.

Fig. 173. Cutting a dado across the grain.

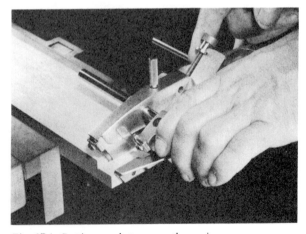

Fig. 174. Cutting a rebate across the grain.

Start the cut by drawing back the plane from the edge farthest away from you. The spurs will sever the top fibres the way a cutting gauge does, and when the plane is pushed forward the cutter will then plow without tearing the wood. A fine cutter setting is desirable when cutting across the grain.

When a housing is required at a distance from the edge beyond the limit of the fence arms, it is necessary to use a strip of wood as a guide. This strip can be either nailed or held with C clamps (G cramps). Remove the fence before starting the cut. Once cutting of the housing is under way, the guide can be removed. The depth gauge will indicate the required depth.

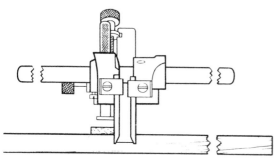

Fig. 175. Cutting a dado without the fence, using a stop planted on.

Edge Beading

Select the beading cutter required and set the plane as for plowing, but with the fence just masking the quirk of the cutter.

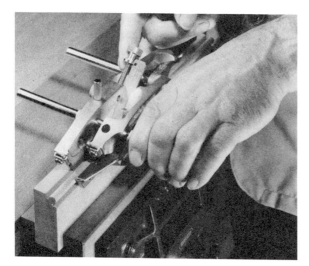

Fig. 176. Cutting a bead.

Center Beading

Set up as before, but with the fence at the required distance from the cutter.

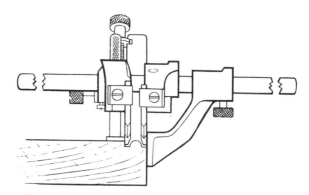

Fig. 177. Beading.

Fig. 178. Multiple beads.

Beading on a Tongued Board

Remove the fence and insert the beading stop (F) in the hole in the sliding section (B). Tighten down on the screw to expand the nylon beading stop expander (U). This stop prevents the outside quirk from being cut and also acts as a fence. Set the depth gauge as before.

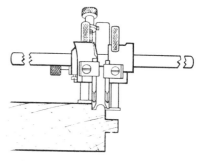

Fig. 179. Beading on a tongued board.

Tonguing and Grooving

Select the tonguing cutter and set the stop on the cutter to the depth of tongue required. Fit the cutter to the plane and set the fence so that the tongue is cut correctly in relation to the thickness of the board (there is no need to set the depth gauge when tonguing). Adjust the cutter as necessary to give a thin shaving and tighten the cutter clamping nut. Use the plane as for plowing and cut the groove to receive the tongue in the same way.

Care in Use

The body is of high-quality grey iron and al-though sturdy, care should be taken never to drop it. Make sure that the fence arm set screws (T) and the fence knurled screws (D) are tight before use; otherwise the plane may be subjected to undue strain and inaccuracies in working may result. The plane will require a minimum of maintenance other than a little light machine oil on the screw threads. When making adjustments, keep the plane over the bench to avoid losing small screws and parts in the shavings.

A little paraffin wax applied to the fence will make for easier working. Thin shavings give more accurate results than thick ones and a better finish. The cutters must be kept in first-class condition and keenly sharp at all times.

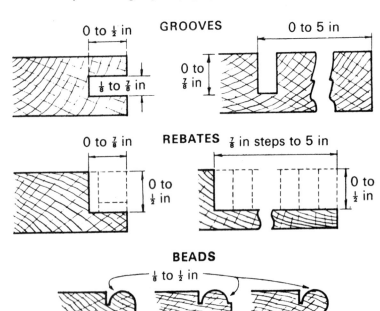

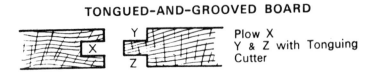

Fig. 180. Cuts that can be made with the No. 050C combination plane.

9

The Multi-Plane

The earliest form of metal multi-plane can probably be credited to Thomas Worral of Massachusetts. His plane had a wooden body with interchangeable soles and cutters. Certainly, it was Leonard Bailey in 1867 who introduced metal planes, but the credit for the first metal combination plane must go to another American, Charles Miller of Vermont. As mentioned earlier, his design was taken up by the Stanley Rule and Level Company.

In 1873, Justin Traut patented an adjustable plow plane that gained a place in the Stanley Catalogue of 1879. This was followed by the development of the Stanley 45 plane. Traut was a prolific designer, and many craftsmen as well as serious home craftsmen have a great deal to thank him for. This plane was followed by the Stanley 50 and the 55.

The Record 405 is the last survivor of this breed of superb multi-purpose tools. It combines seven planes in one and covers all plowing and beading described in previous chapters. It also includes ovolo cutting, slitting and tonguing. In addition to the cutters provided as standard, fluting, reeding and sash cutters can be obtained. Special bases and cutters make possible the making of hollows and rounds, as well as step nosings.

There are three main parts to this plane: the body, the sliding section and the fence. For packing purposes, the body (A, Fig. 182) and sliding section (B) are assembled in the box by means of two short-length arms (X). While these are suitable for work of small dimensions, the long arms (W) clipped to the bottom of the box are the ones for general use.

Removal of the screw driver allows the fence (C) to slide out. The body and sliding section can then be removed. Detach the cam steady (S) and leave in the box until required. Replace the short fence arms with the long ones. The beading stop

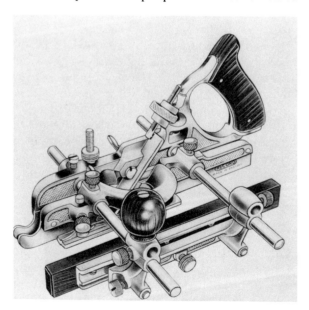

Fig. 181. No. 405 multi-plane.

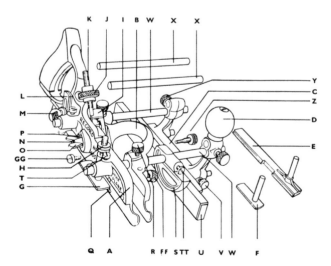

Fig. 182. Exploded view of No. 405 multi-plane.

(E) and slitting cutter stop (L) can also be removed and left in the box until required. A place is reserved for the slitting cutter in the packet containing the other cutters. The beading cutter already fitted to the body can also be transferred to the packet.

The fence has two pairs of holes for the arms. The upper pair allow the fence slide (U) to be positioned *under* the cutter, when the work involved requires this, or to give the fence slide a firmer seating (if the face of the work has sufficient depth). The lower holes permit the fence to fit flush up to the side of the cutter, but not to go underneath.

The adjustable depth gauge (G) is positioned with the adjusting nut (H) and locked by the slotted screw (GG). Clipped to the back of the box is the depth gauge for the sliding section (F). When required, it is fitted to the sliding section using the hole from which the beading stop was taken. More details of the functions of the various components are given in other sections of this book.

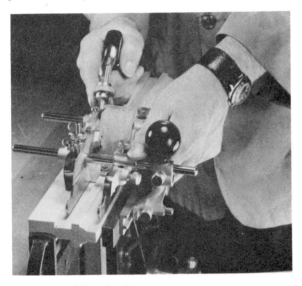

Fig. 183. Holding the plane.

Plowing and Dadoing (Cross-Grain Grooving)

The plow cutters range from ⅛ inch to ⅞ inch in width (including millimetre sizes 4, 6, 9, 12), the large sizes being used for rebating. All cutters are already correctly ground but must be honed before use.

Loosen the cutter bolt (N) by unscrewing the wing nut (O). Insert the required cutter (bevel on the underside) into the housing in the body, ensuring it is correctly seated. Clamp it lightly in position with the wing nut (O). The small peg at the bottom end of the cutter adjusting screw (K) fits into the slot at the top of the cutter.

Turn the adjusting nut (J) until the cutter edge almost reaches the mouth of the body, leaving the final setting until the plane is completely assembled and ready for use. The ⅛-inch and 3/16-inch plow cutters do not require the use of the sliding section (B), but with the other sizes it must be moved along the fence arms (W) to support the left side of the cutter. This ensures that the thin underpart of the sliding section (generally referred to as the skate) is within the overall width of the cutter, and has room to sink into the groove being plowed. Lock the sliding section in position with the screws (R) and position the fence. The distance between the wooden face of the fence and the left side of the cutter will determine the position of the groove being cut.

Secure the fence with the knurled screws (Y). An extra-fine adjustment of the fence can be obtained by loosening the locking screw (V) and turning the fence slide adjusting screw (Z). This moves the fence slide without having to reposition the fence itself. Retighten the screw (V) when the correct setting is obtained. The depth gauge on the body is adjusted with the nut (H) and locked in position by the screw (GG).

Hold the fence firmly up to the face of the wood and run the plane lightly along the front inch or so of the work. If the cutter has been fitted as advised, the cut will be made at first. Turn the cutter adjusting nut (J) about half a turn and run the plane down the work again. One or two turns of the adjusting nut (J) may be required before cutting commences. When it does, tighten the wing nut (O) to secure the cutter in position. Finer shavings ensure more accuracy and give a better finish to the work.

Cutting will cease when the depth gauge rides on the wood. Always commence at the front end of the work, gradually lengthening the stroke until the full length is covered. Keep the plane upright, firm side pressure on the fence but little or no downward pressure on the handle. The sliding section depth gauge (F) can be used when convenient to control the depth of cut on the left side of the cutter, so assisting in keeping the groove vertical.

When a housing is required, it generally calls for cutting across the grain. When following the grain, the cutter leaves the sides and edges of the groove quite clean. Planing across the grain tears the strands of the lumber, as they are not completely severed by the plane cutter. To overcome this, the spurs (Q) are brought into use, both the body and sliding section having one fitted.

Detach the spurs and sharpen the bevelled edge with a fine file, finishing with a few rubs on an oilstone. The spurs should be held in a pair of pliers to do this. Refit them to the plane with the sharpened edge pointing downwards.

Set the plane to the required dimensions and place it in position at the front of the work. Draw it backwards over the full length of the housing when the spurs will sever the lumber strands. Depending on the nature of the lumber, it may be necessary to do this once or twice before starting to make the normal forward cut. When the top surface of the housing has been removed by the cutter, the work can be continued without the spurs, which can be returned to their original position. A fine cut and a sharp cutter will ensure a good finish.

If the housing is too far from the edge of the wood to permit the use of the fence, nail or clamp a strip of wood to the work to allow the right-hand side of the body skate to ride against it. Once the housing has any depth this strip can be removed, as the groove itself will guide the cutter.

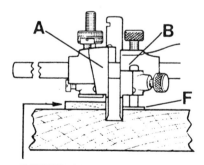

BATTEN AS GUIDE

Fig. 184. Cutting a dado some distance beyond the fence arm capacity, using a batten as a guide.

Rebating

The cutter used must be wider than the rebate required. Using the upper arm hole, position the fence under the cutter to allow the required width of the cutter to do its work. The sliding section should be placed in such a position as to allow the skate to ride on the outer edge of the rebate, which will ensure the plane remains upright. The depth of the rebate is controlled by the adjusting depth gauge. Commence cutting at the front, lengthening the stroke as previously advised.

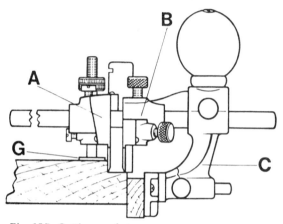

Fig. 185. Cutting a rebate.

Beading

When the cutter is fitted to the plane body, the right-hand tongue or "quirk" will be in line with the skate. The sliding section must be fitted to position its skate directly in line with the left "quirk" of the cutter. Set the fence to the required dimensions. If the bead is some distance from the edge of the wood, fix the cam steady (S) to the front arm, between the fence and sliding section. This will provide an additional bearing to assist in keeping the plane steady. If the required position is beyond the reach of the fence arms, fasten a strip of wood to the work, as described in the previous section on plowing and dadoing.

The fence can be used with the upper arm holes, if the depth of the work permits, allowing the fence slide a larger bearing surface which assists in maintaining a correct upright position. The sliding section depth gauge gives this assistance when the plane is used away from the edge and the fence cannot be used.

When edge beading, use the upper arm holes and set the fence slide under the left quirk of the cutter to prevent it from cutting. This will allow the round portion of the bead to blend into the edge down the side, eliminating the left-hand ledge. When this is being done, the sliding section will have no bearing on the wood, and care must be taken to keep the plane upright.

If the board is already tongued, preventing use of the fence, remove the fence and fit the beading stop (E, Fig. 182) in the same hole used by the sliding section depth gauge (F, Fig. 182). This gives a small bearing on the work and also eliminates the left quirk of the cutter.

Set the adjusting depth gauge to allow the top of the bead to be slightly below the surface of the work, when cutting ceases. This permits the surface to be cleaned up with a smoothing plane if desired, without marking the top of the bead.

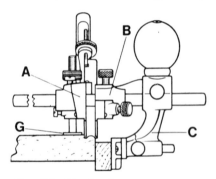

Fig. 186. Edge beading.

Beading Matched Boards

The sliding section (B) is used for ordinary beading, but instead of using the fence, use the beading stop (E) as a bearing on the edge of the

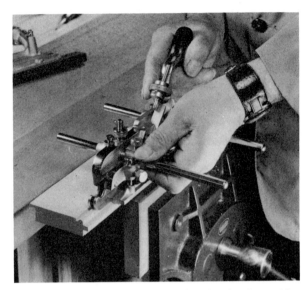

Fig. 188. Beading a matched board with a bead stop. No fence is required.

board. This prevents the left-hand quirk from being cut and has ample bearing above the tongue. The depth of cut is regulated by the gauge (G). The fence is not required.

Tonguing

As the tonguing cutters are fitted with their own depth gauges, the one on the plane is not required and can be moved out of the way. Secure the cutter in the plane and position the sliding section (B), with the skate in the middle of the left tongue of the cutter. Using the upper arm holes, position the fence under the left tongue of the cutter and make final adjustments with the fence slide. The depth gauge on the cutter is set before fitting it to the plane, but variations to the depth can be made while the cutter is in position.

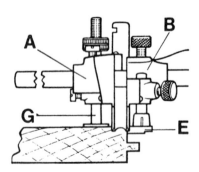

Fig. 187. Beading a matched board.

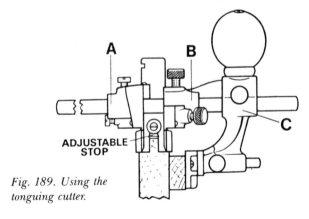

Fig. 189. Using the tonguing cutter.

Cutting the Grooves

When cutting matched boards, choose the same size cutter as the width of the tongue. Set the depth gauge to regulate the depth, which should be slightly deeper than the length of the tongue. The fence must be set to exactly match the tongue. The spurs will not be needed. When cutters of less than ¼-inch width are used, the sliding section must be removed.

Plowing the Grooves

The procedure is exactly as in cutting the matched groove.

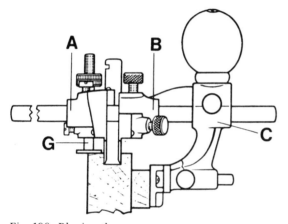

Fig. 190. Plowing the groove.

Ovolos

The sliding section is not used with the ovolo cutters. When fitting, the lower part of the cutter containing the curve projects to the right-hand side of the skate on the plane body. With the fence arms in the upper holes, slide the fence under the flat edge of the cutter until the small ledge is of the required width. Set the depth gauge to allow the right-hand side of the curved portion of the cutter to sink to a depth equal to the width of the small ledge on the left. This ensures that the shape of the ovolo is symmetrical.

The ovolo can be cut in two ways. If the width of the wood exceeds 6 or 7 inches, it should be secured to the bench by clamps with the edge overhanging the bench top. This allows normal use of the fence, which bears up against the overhanging edge. Wood of lesser width can be clamped vertically in the vise and the cut made

along the edge itself. If done this way, it is advantageous to reverse the fence and fit it to the right-hand side of the plane by moving the fence arms over and projecting them to the right.

The knob on the fence will be at the rear, but this is no handicap. The advantage gained is that the fence will be unable to "pull away" from the wood, as can easily happen when using an edge which is shaped quarter-round. The ovolo will retain its shape, and any tendency for it to taper towards the front is eliminated.

Slitting

Thin boards can be conveniently severed with the slitting cutter, which seats in a special housing on the right side of the body. The slitting cutter stop (L) enables the depth of the cut to be varied,

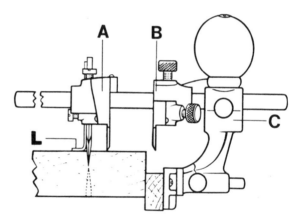

Fig. 191. Using the slitting cutter.

and both the cutter and stop are held in position by the screw (M). Slightly thicker wood can be cut by working from both sides, the fence ensuring the cuts are in alignment with one another.

Additional Cutters

These were available collectively or individually, covering a range of sizes of reedings and flutings and the varieties of sashes. The sliding section is not required when the fluting cutters are used. The reeding and sash cutters follow the methods used with the beading and tonguing cutters, respectively. Special bases with cutters, for work involving hollow and round contours, are also available, together with a nosing tool. A hollow cutter with its base, will have a rounded surface and a round cutter and base, a hollow surface, to the sizes given below.

A number of special bases were available for the multi-plane and nosing tool cutters for staircase work, for hollows and rounds. A hollow and its cutter will form a round-a-round and its cutter will form a hollow. They were in sets as such: one hollow, one round and two matching cutters.

Special Bases	Width of Cutter		Works Circles	
	in.	mm	in.	mm
No. 6 Hollow and Round	½	13	¾	19
No. 8 Hollow and Round	⅝	16	1	26
No. 10 Hollow and Round	¾	19	1¼	32
No. 12 Hollow and Round	1	26	1½	38
No. 5 Nosing Tools	1¹¹⁄₁₆	43	1¼	32

The beginner is often puzzled by moulding on end grain, as on the ends of a cabinet top or a similar top. It is really quite simple. Suppose the piece in Fig. 195 has to be moulded on all four sides. Work the end grain first, from A to B. Before starting the cut, attach a small piece of similar wood, as shown by C, to the panel at B, either

Fig. 194. Special hollow base fitted to cut a matching hollowing.

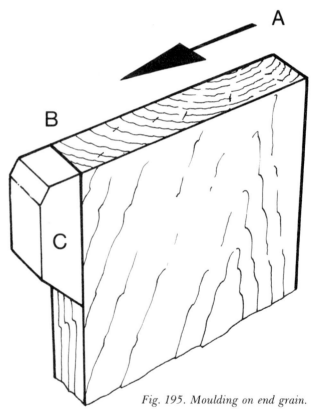

Fig. 195. Moulding on end grain.

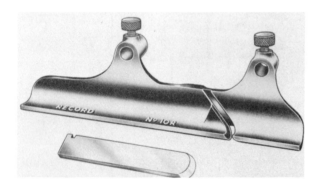

Fig. 192. Round base with cutter.

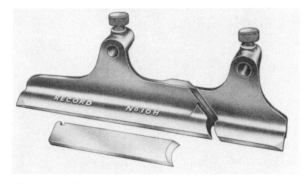

Fig. 193. Hollow base with cutter.

with glue or a bar clamp (sash cramp). This piece will allow the plane to run without breaking the corner at B, as the broken fibres will only occur on C, and even then only to a limited extent if a chamfer is taken off. The other end grain is then worked in the same way and the two long grain sides will then offer no difficulty, the plane running straight through.

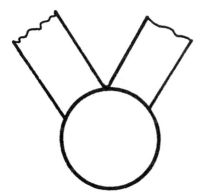

Fig. 196. Round cut greater than the actual width of the cutter.

In the case of a simple round or hollow, of course, the plane may be worked from each end, as on page 145, Fig. 261. With a fancy moulding such as an ovolo or ogee, that is obviously an im- possibility. The job is quite simply and easily done when a block is attached, as indicated. It will be clear from Fig. 196 that a 1-inch hollow or round is not confined to the ⅝ inch of its width, as it will follow any part of the curve which is 1 inch in diameter.

An example is given in Fig. 197 of a common moulding, with several members indicative of the wide scope of application of the multi-plane. First set out the section of the required moulding on the end of the wood. Much work can often be saved by running off two narrow plow grooves that meet. In Fig. 197, piece A can be cut first with a suitable plowing cutter. Piece B could be plowed away with a ⅛-inch plow cutter; piece C will then fall off. D is then cut away with the 1-inch round. Working on the opposite edge, E and F are taken away with the plane set as a fillister (see Fig. 185), and the remaining piece G worked off with the 1-

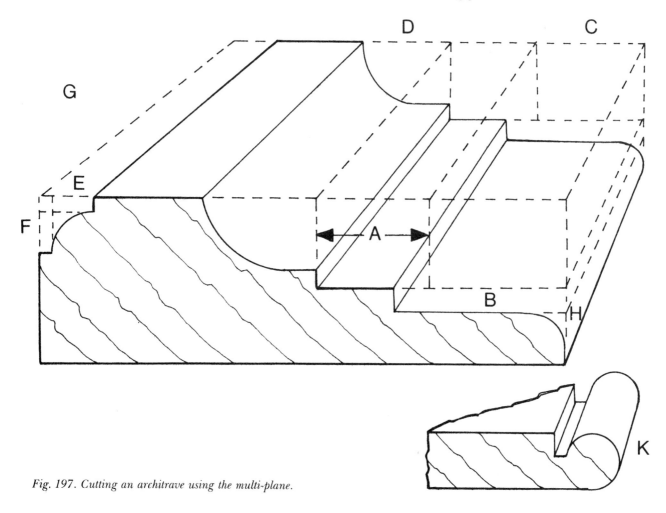

Fig. 197. Cutting an architrave using the multi-plane.

inch hollow. Alternatively, G can be worked away with a rebate plane.

It now remains to work off the edge (H), which can be a simple rounding worked with a jack plane, or more interestingly, as a bead with the 405, as at K. The ovolo at G can be made with one cut by using the special ovolo cutter of suitable size. Fig. 197 represents a moulding that appears as a door or window casing, and indicates the method by which an infinite variety of mouldings can be struck, either for new work or for matching old work in repairs.

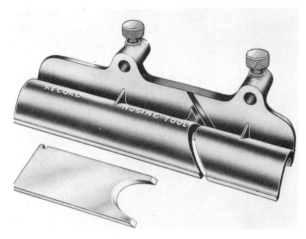

Fig. 198. Nosing tool.

The nosing tool consists of a special base and cutter which are similar to the hollows, but it is made 1¹¹⁄₁₆ inch wide, and cuts an exact 1¼-inch diameter, semi-circle or half-round. Its main application is in shaping the fronts of stair treads.

Begin a cut with a short stroke at the front end of the work, gradually increasing the length of subsequent cuts until the full length of the work is covered. The depth gauge will immediately indicate the termination of cutting when the preset depth is reached. Thin shavings will make the work easier.

When planing a hollow, cut out the first part with a gouge. With the multi-plane this may be done, if desired, but it is not necessary. The plane will cut all the hollow from the start quite quickly, and the knack of taking a steadying bearing with the fingers of the left hand is one that is very quickly learned (see Fig. 188).

Among the "special" cutters for the multi-plane that were available are: a 1½-inch sash cutter, sim-

ilar to the one supplied; a range of fluters from ³⁄₁₆ inch to ¾ inch, which are very useful for relieving pilasters, etc.; and a range of reeding cutters which cut at the one operation 2, 3, 4 or 5 beads. Ovolo cutters were made in ¼-inch, ⁵⁄₁₆-inch and ³⁄₈-inch sizes.

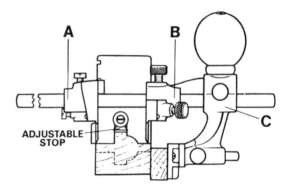

Fig. 199. Using the sash cutter for window work.

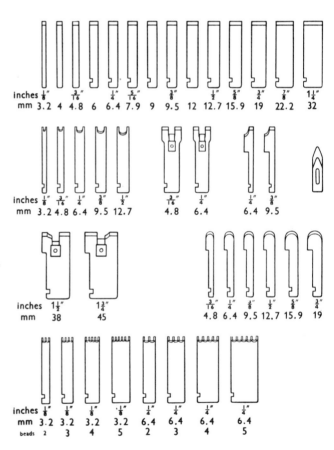

Fig. 200. Cutters for the No. 405 multi-plane.

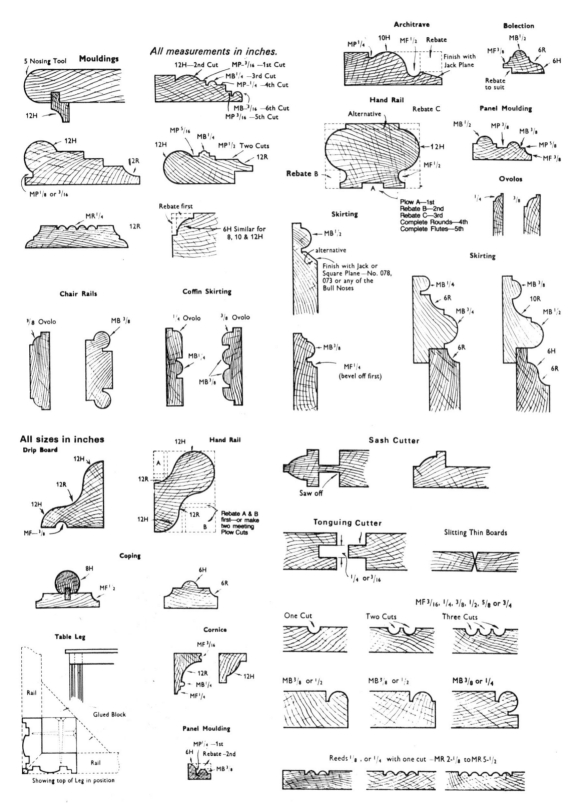

Fig. 201. *Some examples of the type of work possible with the Record 405 multi-plane.*

10
Router Planes

The earliest form of router plane arose from the need to clean up and flatten the floor of a housing or dado joint. The sides of the dado were first cut with the tenon saw, and the waste roughed out with the bevel-edge chisel. To finish the work, either a long, thin paring chisel was used or a block of wood cut to house a chisel-like blade, the blade being held in place by a wedge. The cutter in the block was set forward to the exact depth of the housing. The block was in fact acting as a stop for the chisel. These blocks were rounded over to improve handling, and became known as the "old woman's tooth." Plane makers like Marples and Mathieson standardized the shape and size of cutter, and this plane could be found in toolmakers' catalogues everywhere.

Certainly the old woman's tooth served a need, but it was difficult to set accurately and was clumsy in use. The efficiency was very largely due to the skill and experience of the operator. With the introduction of metal in the construction of planes, the modern router was designed.

The body has an open mouth (which can be converted into a closed mouth). It is fitted with three cutters, two for straightforward routering and one for smooth finishing. These cutters are controlled by screw adjustment. It has a fence which may be used either on straight or curved work.

The router is carefully shaped to provide an adequate sole, with housings for cutter and handle. Two polished wooden knobs are provided, these applying the power in just the right place for the maximum effect on the cutter with the minimum of effort by the user. The angle of the cutters is such that a clean, easy cut can be made. There is no limit to the size of the hollow it will cut.

Record router No. 071 may be used either as an open-mouth or a closed-mouth router. When the router is used closed mouth, the shoe (N) is secured as in Fig. 203. The correct setting is easily obtained by resting the plane on a level surface with the thumbscrew (L) slack. This is tightened up when the shoe is level with the face of the plane body. Experienced craftsmen may prefer to

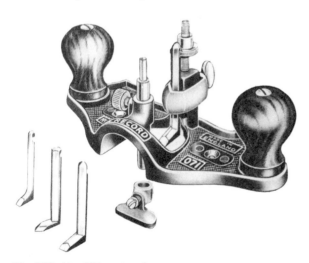

Fig. 202. No. 071 router plane.

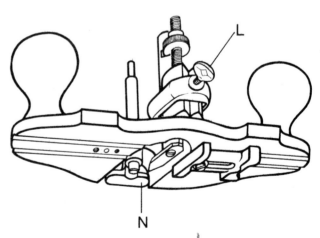

Fig. 203. Router with mouth closed and fence in position.

set the shoe one shaving thickness (about .001 inch) below the sole. When used open mouth, the shoe and depth gauge are removed from the router.

The cutters may be used for normal work in the position shown in Fig. 202, or they may be used for bullnose work, in which case they will be set in the rear slot (behind K). In the latter case, the clamping collar will be reversed, i.e., with its thumbscrew to the front.

To insert the cutter, slacken the clamping collar thumbscrew (L), raise the collar and insert the cutter from the bottom. Engage the slot of the cutter in the cutter adjusting nut (J). Lower the collar into its clamping position; tighten down the screw (L) securely after adjusting the cutter a fraction below the sole.

Insertion for bullnose work is similar, except that the cutter goes in the back groove instead of the front one. The clamping collar (K) should be set as low down as it will go, this giving a better cutting action than when it is set higher, as in Fig. 203.

When housings are recessed (Fig. 205), preliminary saw cuts (on the waste side of the line) should be made across the grain. The cutter being set, as already described, cuts are then made from the end of the housing; in the case of a through housing, from each end. The object of

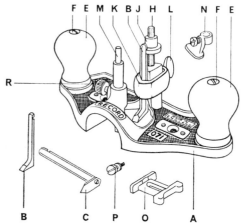

A. Body with Screws H and R
B. Cutters: ¼″ (6.4 mm)
   ½″ (12.7 mm)
C. Smoothing
E. Knobs
F. Bolt and Nut for Knob
J. Cutter Adjusting Nut
K. Clamping Collar and Screw L
M. Depth Gauge with Shoe and Screw N
O. Fence with Screw and Washer P

Fig. 204. Parts of the No. 071 router plane.

this is to avoid a breakaway at the finishing end. When the cutter has taken this portion out, the thumbscrew (L) is slackened half a turn, the nut (J) is advanced a turn and the thumbscrew (L) is tightened up.

Fig. 205. Normal work on a through housing.

The cutter is now ready for the next deeper cut, which is made as before. The knack of adjusting the two screws quickly is easily acquired and can usually be done on the return stroke. It is almost impossible to cut a housing to the full depth in one go. Gauge marks may be made on the work to indicate correct depth, or use may be made of the ¹⁄₁₆-inch divisions which are scribed on the cutters by noting their position in relation to the top of the pillar. Alternatively, use may be made of the depth gauge, as described on pages 114 and 115. The fence is not required in normal routering.

The square-ended cutters (½ inch and ¼ inch) are for normal work. The pointed cutter (C, Fig. 204) is for those occasions when the surface of the recess must be left smooth. When using this smoothing cutter, if the dimensions of the work allow it, work with a sideways, shearing cut. The smoothing cutter should not be used for roughing out.

When the recess to be cut exceeds the overall width of the plane, the body can be widened by attaching a piece of wood approximately 4 × ½ inch to increase the width. The section can be varied to suit the job in hand. The plane body has been drilled and countersunk on both sides of the mouth to enable the wooden attachment to be screwed into place with countersunk screws. Mark the position and shape of the mouth on the board, and cut with a bow saw or coping saw before finally fixing in position. The operation can be done as previously described.

The threaded holes in the sole are for the attachment of the fence (O, Fig. 204), which is fitted under the sole and may be used on either side of the cutter. The grooves which are milled on the sole will keep the fence square, and the appropriate hole is chosen which will set the fence at the desired distance from the cutter. With the aid of this fence, stopped grooves ½ inch or ¼ inch wide, according to which cutter is used, can be made.

For this operation the shoe must be secured in the "closed-mouth" position. The fence must then be set with its straight face at the desired distance from the face side of the work. Usually in this type of work, mortises are already made at the stopped ends of the proposed grooves. If not, a mortise should be cut at that end as deep as it is proposed the groove should go.

The cutter being set a little below the surface of the sole, a cut should now be made from the end of the work towards the mortise, keeping the fence well up to the work (as in plowing). On the return stroke, slacken the thumbscrew (L), advance the nut (J), tighten the thumbscrew (L) and make another cut. Repeat until the desired depth

is cut (Fig. 206). The operation is not as complicated as the description suggests, and after a little practice it becomes almost automatic.

That face of the fence which is opposite the straight face is so designed that it will follow a curve either outside or inside. It is used in a similar way to the straight face, except that it follows a curved edge instead of a straight one and the grain of the wood must be more carefully studied. In making a groove in a circular or oval base, two quarters can be done with the fence on one side of the router, and the other two quarters can be done with the fence on the opposite side of the router. This is the only plane which can be used to cut a curved groove.

Fig. 207. Using the curved fence to make a curved groove.

The depth gauge and shoe (M and N, Fig. 204) can be used in two ways. When detached from the router, they can be used as a depth gauge for testing blind mortises of the same depth. In this case, the shoe (which forms the stop) is attached so that the thinner end of the gauge can be inserted into the mortises (or similar holes or recesses).

When the plane is used as an open-mouthed router, the narrow end of the depth gauge is inserted into the top side of the hole in the plane body. It is allowed to slide down and protrude through the underside of the body to a distance equal to that of the depth of cut required. Drop

Fig. 206. Using the straight fence to make a stopped groove.

the shoe in place over the depth gauge so that it rests on top of the housing. Tighten down on the screw to secure the shoe in place. At the commencement of cutting, the depth gauge will be held in the uppermost position. As the groove deepens, it will drop until the shoe registers against the top of the housing, indicating that the groove is at the required depth.

Fig. 209 clearly shows the difference between what is usually termed a "groove" and what is known as a "dado," or more commonly a "housing." The groove, which runs the same way as the grain, is normally cut with a plow, but the "housing" (sometimes also called a "raggle"), being across the grain (as for a shelf), is cut with the router.

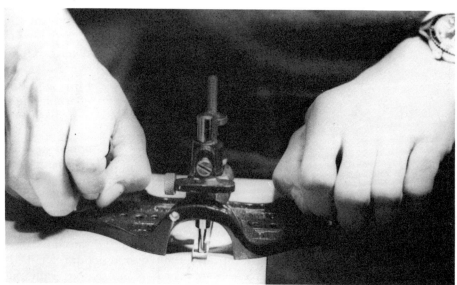

Fig. 208. Depth gauge in use, small end down.

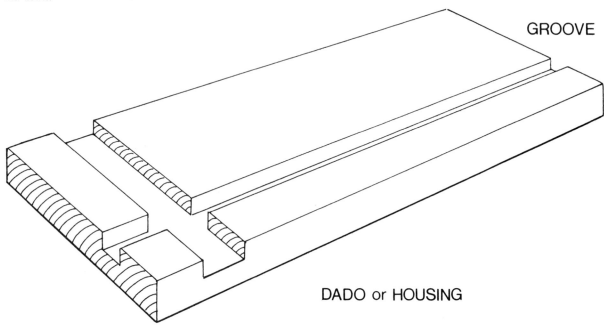

GROOVE

DADO or HOUSING

Fig. 209. Groove and housing.

Figs. 210 and 211 show two examples of stopped housings. These give a better appearance than through housings, as they cannot be seen when the other piece of wood is inserted, as in a shelf.

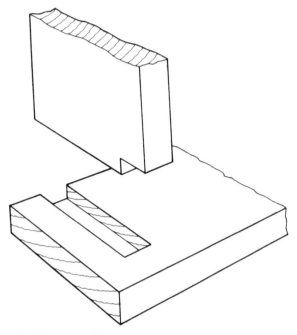

Fig. 210. Stopped housing.

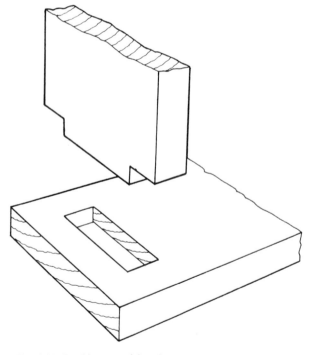

Fig. 211. Double stopped housing.

They are also stronger, as the shoulder on the shelf tends to prevent side play in the joint.

To cut a stopped housing, mark out with a square and knife. Use a chisel to remove a small mortise close to the stopped end of the housing. Leave a small portion of wood at the end to act as a cushion for the saw. Use a tenon saw to cut the sides of the housing, placing the end of the saw in the little mortise to start the cut.

This mortise will also serve to regulate the depth of the saw cut and keep the saw on the waste-wood side of the line. The router can then be used to remove the waste and flatten the bottom of the housing. In all work of this kind it is preferable to set out with a sharp marking knife after using a pencil. The limits are more positively defined.

When the housing must be stopped at both front and back, as shown on the right-hand side of Fig. 211, define the limits of the housing with a sharp chisel after marking out; tap the chisel with a mallet. A light cut can then be taken with the router, working towards each end of the housing in turn. The cutter can then be advanced for progressive cuts until the required depth is attained. Alternatively, it may be mortised-out with the chisel for the bulk of the cut, and the last ⅛ inch or so cleaned up with the router.

Recesses for locks and hinges ("gains"), can often be cut using the router, the limits of the cut being first defined with a sharp chisel. The fence can be used if necessary. The pointed (finishing) cutter will leave a very smooth face, especially if it is used at an angle where width permits and the point is useful for getting the corners clean. This cutter will cut the thinnest shaving with ease and can be used when cutting shallow recesses for inlays.

Fig. 213 shows two examples of stopped grooves using the fence as shown in Fig. 206, and as already described. Usually in work of this type, it will not be necessary to define the length of the groove with the chisel. It is advantageous, however, where there is no mortise to cut one at the closed end of the cut. The length of the runner on the plow plane prevents that tool from making a stopped groove satisfactorily, but the operation is relatively simple with the router when the fence is used. It must be noted that housings, as already described, are not done by this method.

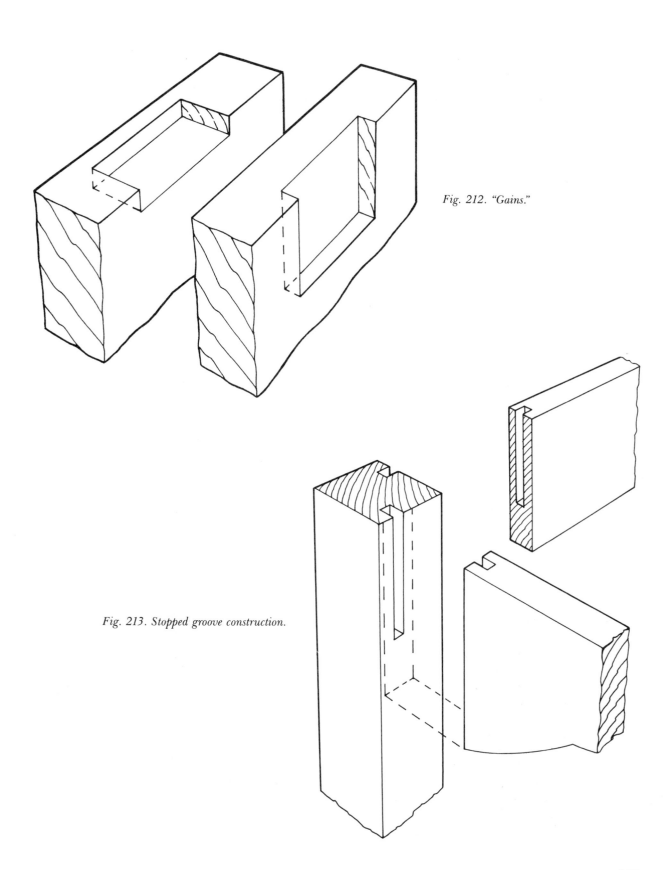

Fig. 212. "Gains."

Fig. 213. Stopped groove construction.

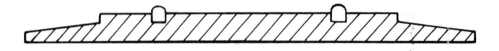

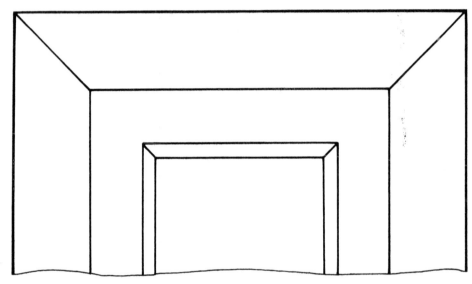

Fig. 214. Panel with a cock bead.

The fence may also be used to make the groove for a cock bead on a panel, as shown in Fig. 214. It is best to cut the groove before the fielding (i.e., the rebating) is done. On straight grain there may be no difficulty in getting a clean cut, but on cross grain the fibres should first be cut with a sharp cutting gauge, or with the slitter of the multi-plane No. 405 (see Fig. 191, Chapter 9). Some users cut long grain in a similar way. Once the groove is started the cutter will do the rest of the cut both horizontally and vertically.

Precisely the same method can be applied to cut the shallow grooves for inlaid bandings, which are later glued into the grooves. In both this case and that of cock beads, both the cutter and bead or banding should be of the same width. We have earlier mentioned the inlaying of shapes (shells, fan corners, etc., are typical examples). Both these and inlaid bands should be glued in and then pressed home with the hammer, as in laying a veneer. Allow the glue to dry.

Glue (and possibly the wetted wood) shrinks on drying, and unless the job is given time enough to dry out (say 24 hours) before scraping, the inlay is very likely to sink below the rest of the work.

Router plane No. 211 is a small but very useful router which is provided with one cutter only ¼ inch wide. Its base measures approximately 2⅞ inches × 1⅞ inch, and the cutter is very positively secured by means of a drawbolt. There is no need to screw this up more than finger-tight.

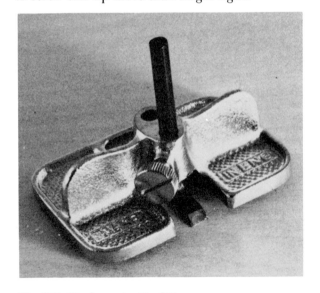

Fig. 215. Stanley router No. 211.

The cutter can be set normally or as for bull-nosed work. It will be set by sight, as required, there being no screw adjustment to the cutter as in the larger 071. Where work of a small nature is encountered, as in small grooves and in the groundings of carved work and lettering, router No. 211 will prove of inestimable value.

With the increasing scarcity of lumber and its high cost, there has been a tendency to use thinner sections of wood. Consequently, the use of the router No. 211 has increased. With the larger router, a smoother surface is left when the router cutter is used on the skew; this also applies to the smaller router. Where the groove or recess is wider than the cutter, a skew cut is fairly simple. Where groove and cutter are the same width and a skew cut impossible, a light cut is necessary.

Enough examples have been given to indicate the value of the router in overcoming not only those difficulties which gave rise to the old woman's tooth, but also many others which the old lady's dental equipment is utterly incapable of tackling. The metal router, with its screw adjustment, its cranked cutters of various sizes and shapes, its adjustable fence and its use for open or closed mouth is indeed a precision tool of the highest grade, without which no woodworker's kit can be considered complete.

Fig. 216. No. 020C circular plane.

11

The Circular Plane

The wooden compass plane was known to wheelwrights for many generations and was limited in its scope to the fixed curvature of its sole. It has long been superseded by the metal circular plane, which covers a much wider range of work and has all the advantages of adjustment that are possessed by the metal bench planes.

With the old type of wooden plane, the curvature of the sole was fixed and convex. Concave work necessitated the use of two distinct planes. The metal variety has a flexible steel sole, which can be adjusted both to a convexity and to a concavity. The adjustment of the cutter, grinding and honing, are precisely the same as for the bench planes (see Chapter 2).

The adjustment of the sole can be made quite quickly. Loosen the locking screw on the adjusting nut and turn the latter until the sole of the plane is in contact with the work taking up the correct curvature. Tighten the locking screw. The removal of the cutter for sharpening will not affect this setting.

The body of the plane is conveniently shaped at each end for a comfortable grip. The method of use is shown in Figs. 219 and 220.

There is a tendency when first using a circular plane to work the plane at an angle, as is frequently done with a jack plane. This, of course, cannot be done when working with a circular plane. The plane must be pushed forward. The direction of the grain must be carefully studied. This, in principle, is explained on page 127, in connection with spokeshaving. The same principles apply when using the circular plane. The

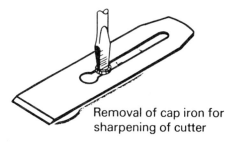

Removal of cap iron for sharpening of cutter

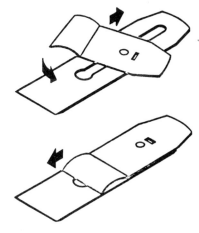

Keep cap iron clear of cutting edge

Fig. 217. Removal and replacement of cap iron.

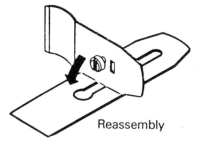

Reassembly

CAP IRON SET BACK 2mm
For coarse work and softwoods

CAP IRON SET ALMOST LEVEL
For finishing and difficult grained hardwoods

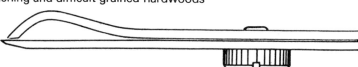

Fig. 218. Setting the cap iron.

Fig. 219. Convex cutting with the 020C circular plane.

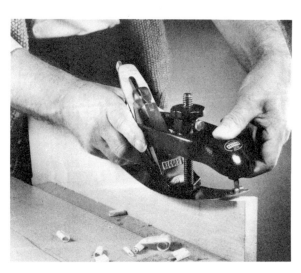

Fig. 220. Concave cutting with the 020C circular plane.

cabinetmaker will use the circular plane in the making of circular frames and serpentine work, the carpenter for window and door frames. The wheelwright will find it indispensable.

The construction of serpentine fronts (i.e., kidney-shaped table frames, bow-fronted chests, etc.) is something of a puzzle to the uninitiated. To cut them out of the solid is laborious, wasteful of material and frequently introduces short grain, which not only weakens the construction but also impoverishes the finished appearance. They are quite simply built up of short shaped pieces much in the same way as a brick wall is built.

The parts may be glued and clamped or glued and screwed, or glued and pegged. When the glue is dry, they are cleaned up and planed accurately to shape with the circular plane, toothed with the toothing plane and finally veneered. To cut the blocks, a template should be prepared from a full-size drawing and the parts marked off from the template on a trued-up board. If only a few are required, they may be cut by hand with the bow saw or coping saw. If any quantity have to

be cut, it is better to have them cut out on the nearest band saw. Patterns may be built up in a similar manner, as well as moulds for concrete castings, etc.

The Record 020C is an improved version of the 020. The body has been streamlined to give improved handling, as has the adjusting knob. The 03 smoothing plane cutting unit replaces the one used in the 020, and sits in a much improved cradle. Cutter adjustment is exactly the same as all other bench planes.

An earlier version of the circular plane was the 113. This plane has a knob at the front that serves to set the curve of the sole and doubles as a front handle. Both halves of the sole flex at the same time, through the action of a quadrant gearing marked for accurate setting.

This plane appeared as early as 1880 and has changed little since those days. Probably the earliest known compass plane is credited to George Franklin Evans, who lived in Norway, Maine. It may well be that Stanley developed its plane from this earlier one.

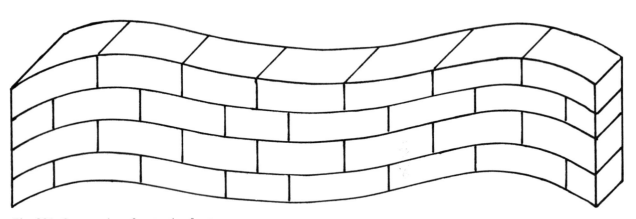

Fig. 221. Construction of serpentine front.

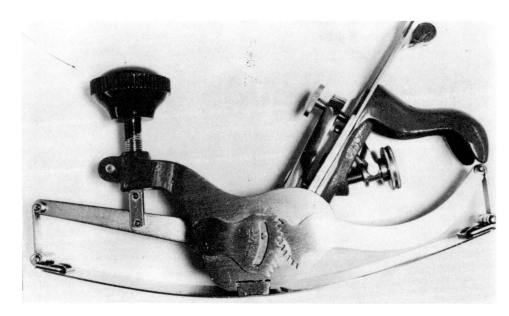

Fig. 222. Circular plane.

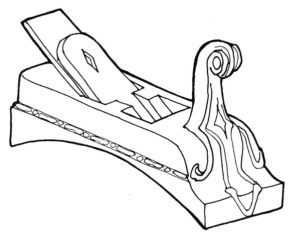

Fig. 223. Seventeenth-century wheelwright's plane.

12

Spokeshaves

While the name spokeshave is sufficiently indicative of the tool's original use, it is so useful it must have been used quite a long time ago for many purposes other than the making of wheel spokes in wood. If it was used for just the making of wheel spokes, it would now be virtually obsolete, since the wheelwright's craft itself has practically disappeared. The tool can today be found, of course, in the wheelwright's shop but the carpenter, joiner, cabinetmaker, patternmaker and chairmaker, to name only a few, also find it of inestimable value.

The older wooden spokeshave has now given way to its modern metal counterpart. The wooden stock, usually made of boxwood or beech, was very subject to wear; this occurred because the bearing surface was very small, and the constant in and out action of the tangs resulted in a slack fit of the cutter. The problem was often remedied by cutting a screw thread on the tangs, the subsequent adjustment being made by nuts. As with the very early attempts to improve the plane, the effects of wear on the sole were often minimized by the fitting of a brass sole.

Not until the advent of the metal spokeshave, however, were the disadvantages of the wooden spokeshave satisfactorily overcome. By casting the bodies in iron, production and consequently the initial cost to the user were relatively cheap. A sole, flat or round, could be easily machined. Then, for the rest of the life of the tool it would require no more thought or attention.

The blades of the metal spokeshave could be made in such a manner that sharpening on the grindstone and the oilstone was quite easy—which certainly could not be claimed for the cranked blades of the wooden spokeshaves. A fine screw adjustment of the cut was possible and a firm yet easy-to-work attachment of the cutting unit to the stock was possible. The handles could

be designed so that hand and wrist action resulted in the minimum amount of fatigue. Finally, the tool had a very long life. Initial disadvantage of the fragile nature of a cast-iron body was later eliminated by the employment of malleable castings that were virtually unbreakable.

The range of Record spokeshaves embraces both flat and round soles—the flat sole being used for working convex curves and the round sole for concave curves. Some spokeshaves are adjustable for thickness of shaving by screw adjustment, while others have no such adjustment and must be "set" by sight and experience.

Record cast-iron spokeshaves are designated with O to preface the number; the unbreakable spokeshaves are prefaced with A. Thus, Record spokeshave 0151 is a cast-iron tool, painted blue, while the Record spokeshave A151 is unbreakable and painted a bright red. (Though cast-iron spokeshaves are no longer made, Record spokeshaves 0151 and A151 are still in use.) The numbers, being identical, will indicate that the design is similar; the color of the paint will indicate the material of which each is made.

One of the simplest spokeshaves, light in weight (approximately half a pound) and very easy to handle even on long runs, is the straight-handled A63, which has a round face, and its counterpart A64, which has a flat face. Both are, of course, unbreakable. Not only are they good tools for any worker, they are eminently suited by their design and weight for use in a school workshop. The cutters are held in place by a lever cap that is secured by a single thumbscrew. The depth of cut may be set by sight or feel.

A very useful way to "set" the A64 spokeshave is to hold the sole flat on a plane surface—the wing of a jack plane 05, for instance, and then, having the blade in place with the thumbscrew quite slack, let the edge just touch the plane surface.

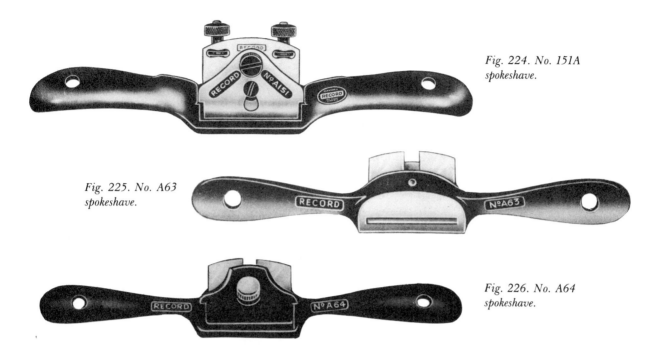

Fig. 224. No. 151A spokeshave.

Fig. 225. No. A63 spokeshave.

Fig. 226. No. A64 spokeshave.

Then tighten the screw. Ninety-nine times out of a hundred, the spokeshave will work nicely. If it doesn't, check the setting to be sure that only a hairline of cutting edge is seen below the sole; then try again. The round-faced A63 can be set similarly, but you will have to experiment a time or two to know which part of the curve to rest on the plane surface. An experienced worker will have no difficulty in setting the cutter by sight or touch. (It is remarkable how much an experienced worker "sees" with his fingertips.)

A larger, heavier (approximately 11 ounce) non-screw adjustable spokeshave is the 051, A51 series. The pattern may be obtained either in cast iron (051 flat, 051R round) or in unbreakable metal (A51 flat, A51R round)—the cast being recognizable by its blue color, the unbreakable by its red color. The cast iron is slightly cheaper in price, but the unbreakable is more strongly recommended. While the handles of A63 and A64, which were discussed earlier, are straight, the handles of the 051 and A51 are raised slightly. It is a pattern that is capable of very good work. The depth of cut must be set as for the A63 and A64.

One of the most popular spokeshaves is the Record A151, A151R; the Record 0151, 0151R is no longer manufactured. In basic design they are not very dissimilar to the A51 series we have just

discussed, but a considerable advantage lies in their screw adjustment, both vertically and laterally.

This screw adjustment is effected by means of two screws. It is advisable to loosen the lever cap thumbscrew slightly before making an adjustment, retightening when the required depth of cut is obtained. Both screws will raise or lower the cutter, each being individually adjusted to keep the cutter parallel with the sole. The lever cap acts similarly to the cap iron in a plane.

Contemporary design has favored the chamfer and the stop-chamfer to the detriment of the multimembered mouldings. As a result, this called for a tool which would minimize such work. The chamfer spokeshave, shown in Fig. 227, has a straight-handled round-faced spokeshave. Made of unbreakable metal, it is fitted with two adjustable wings that act as stops and secure a uniform depth of cut and consequent width of chamfer.

The blade of the chamfer spokeshave is not screw adjustable for thickness of shaving, but it is not difficult to set by sight or feel. The wings are quickly adjustable, and the temptation to use a pair of pliers on the adjusting screws must be stoutly resisted. A finger-tight adjustment is enough to hold them. When pliers or other me-

Fig. 227. Chamfer
spokeshave.

chanical aids are used to further "tighten" the screws, the ends of the screws cannot go any deeper. The result is a damaged thread which will never work satisfactorily.

It is usually quicker to set the wings experimentally, trying the spokeshave on a bit of spare wood rather than attempt to set the wings by measurement. A little practice with the spokeshave will soon enable the worker to get good results. When stopped chamfers are being made, a little practice of the wrist action will bring a quicker curve to the stopping. This is more pleasing to the eye than a slower curve. The shadows are more interesting.

When the chamfer is stopped at both ends, the two stoppings may be made first, then the chamfer worked out. Watch the way of the grain. When the wings have seated themselves on the work and the tool ceases to cut, the chamfer will be found to be perfect.

The face of the tool is slightly rounded, but this will not detract from its use on straight work, as the wings go a long way towards providing a bearing. When the wings are removed, the tool can be used as a normal round-faced spokeshave.

A strong recommendation has been made for Record malleable iron unbreakable spokeshaves wherever there is a choice between them and their cast-iron counterparts. They have been designed for shops where rough usage is prevalent. They will stand up to any knocks or dropping on the hardest floor without harm. They are confidently recommended for hard and lasting service under any conditions, and are deservedly popular with craftsmen and craft teachers all over.

The half-round spokeshave has a convex face and blade. It is extremely useful when working convex-shaped rails and legs. Its 2 1/16-inch blade is held in place with a single screw and is adjusted by hand. A convex spokeshave is made to exactly match the half-round.

A combined spokeshave has concave and flat cutters set alongside each other. Its overall length is 10 inches. The concave blade is 1 3/8 inch wide, and the flat blade 1 1/4 inch wide.

A throat provided on one European spokeshave can be adjusted by turning a knurled screw on the throat mechanism. This can be greatly ad-

Fig. 228. Kunz 50 half-round spokeshave.

Fig. 229. Kunz 60
combined concave and
flat spokeshave.

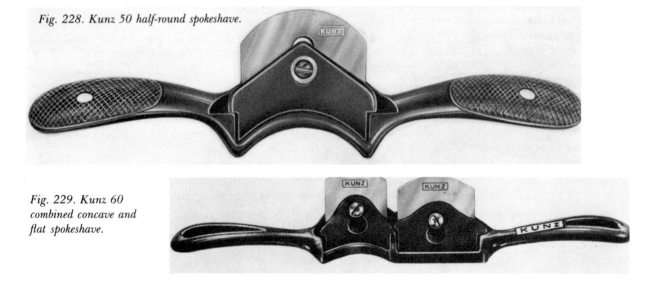

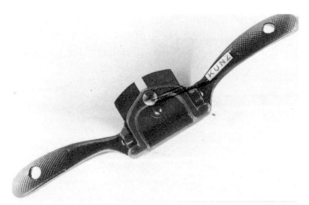

Fig. 230. Kunz 53 spokeshave with adjustable throat.

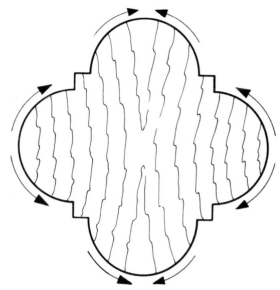

Fig. 232. Using the spokeshave, working always with the grain.

vantageous when fine work is being carried out. The flat-faced cutter is 2¹⁄₁₆ inches wide, and the spokeshave 10 inches long overall.

Using the Spokeshave

When using the spokeshave (Fig. 231), bear in mind that the tool is a plane and follow the general idea of planing. In this way, you will unconsciously acquire that light touch and wrist action that are essential to good, clean, easy working.

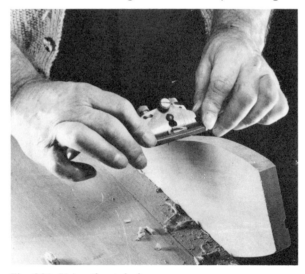

Fig. 231. Using the spokeshave.

Normally, the tool is pushed, but on occasion it may be pulled. Many beginners stumble with spokeshaving because they forget to consider the direction of the grain. Fig. 232 shows the movement of the spokeshave always working with the grain, downhill in fact.

For a convex surface use a flat face; for a concave one, a round face. Thus, in Fig. 232 a flat-face spokeshave is needed, whereas in a shaping for a bracket a flat face would prevent the cutter from coming into action; therefore, the round face must be used (Fig. 233). A round face can be used on a convex surface of large radius, but in general most convex shapes are best cut with the flat face, eliminating chattering.

Generally speaking, shapings in cabinetwork are best when of a simple nature. Elaborate curves are more laborious to produce, and are not satisfying when they are done. A simple way of drawing a free curve to fit a particular space, i.e., an apron piece, is by folding a piece of brown paper (which, when opened is the size of the opening) in half. Then strike out the half curve, as indicated in Fig. 234, by the dotted line and cut through the folded paper on the line with scissors.

On opening out, you have a symmetrical curve which you can try by placing the paper in position on the job. Pleasing and original shapes can be drawn either from squares or rectangles when the same technique is used, but the paper is folded in quarters instead of in half (Fig. 235).

Chamfers or rounds can be done with the spokeshave on curved edges. To mould a curved edge, use a scratch tool after spokeshaving to outline. Apart from curved edges, the spokeshave can also be used for reducing diameters. It can also be used where a drawknife is not available. Fig. 236 shows a number of shapings which are typical spokeshave work: Curved surfaces, which are too wide an area to be worked with a spoke-shave, are worked with an adjustable circular plane (see Chapter 11). Indeed, where the curve must be regular and geometrically accurate, the circular plane is almost a necessity.

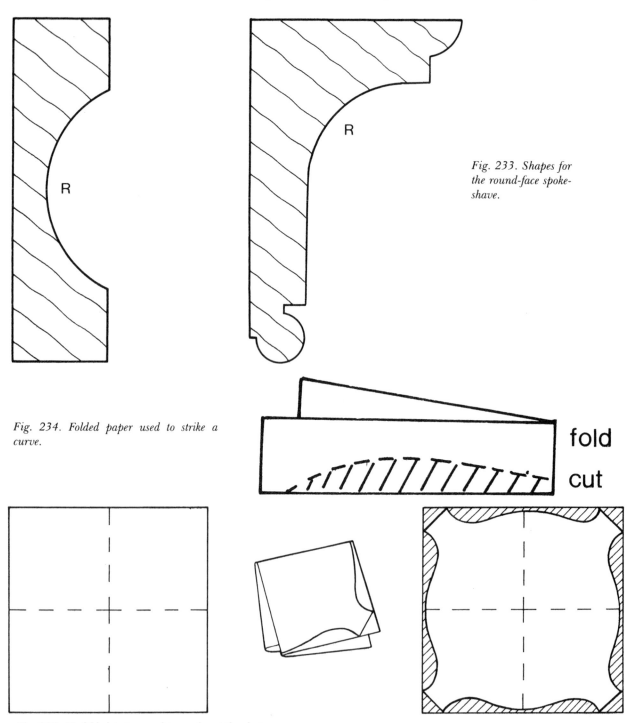

Fig. 233. Shapes for the round-face spoke-shave.

Fig. 234. Folded paper used to strike a curve.

fold

cut

Fig. 235. Unfolded paper used to mark out the shape.

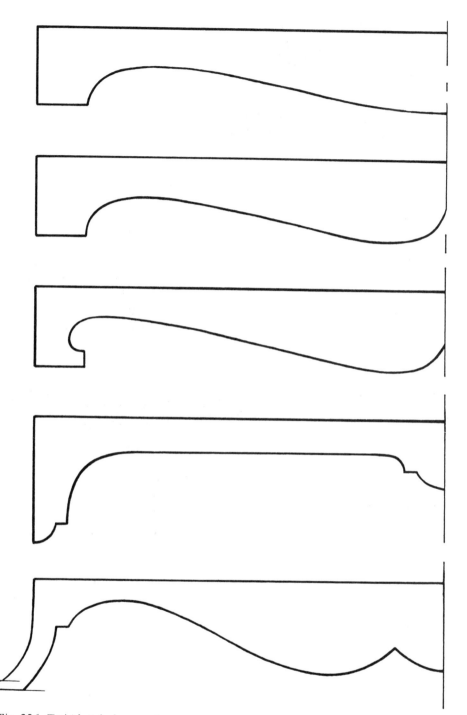

Fig. 236. Typical spokeshave work.

13
Scrapers

The careful finishing of wood was recognized more than 2,000 years ago. Work left from the plane, however well it may appear in "the white," is always apt to show variations of reflected light when highly polished. Plane strokes which show up in this manner indicate a lack of finish not consistent with good workmanship.

When articles have to be highly finished with shiny surfaces, as with French polish, cellulose, varnish or wax, the surface must be scraped clean of all marks left by the plane. Every blemish of the grain, no matter how small and insignificant it may appear before polishing, must be smoothed out. The process of polishing will intensify the character of the unevenness, owing to the play of reflected light, to such an extent as to mar the whole effect.

The need for a scraper was felt from very early times, and its use is by no means a modern invention. It has been used in one form or another throughout the ages. (A piece of glass has often been used for this purpose, but this has very obvious disadvantages.)

The early Egyptians scoured their work after the fashion of the stonemason. Old-time craftsmen used a rectangular piece of steel, upon which they formed a burred edge. The result was a very good scraper. This type of scraper can be, however, most uncomfortable in use.

In order to get the best results in a scraper it is necessary to "spring" the blade to a curve. The "springing" of the blade in the old-fashioned tool is accomplished with the thumbs, and the very action of using the scraper creates enough heat at this spot to make the thumbs uncomfortably hot. Moreover, the scraper blade always has a tendency to follow irregularities and leave a "waviness" unless a good deal of skill is employed. Some of the handled tools that have appeared from time to time have intensified rather than eradicated this defect.

The Record scraper 080 has been so designed that the disadvantages discussed have been eliminated. The design of the handles is such that a firm hold may be taken without the least suspicion of cramp or fatigue. The handles are raised away from the tool, so that a finger cut from a sharp arris—a common problem with the old type—is an impossibility. The thumbs are not required to spring the blade; this function is performed by a thumbscrew. The pressure of the screw varies curvature.

Fig. 237. Record 080 cabinet scraper.

It is practically impossible for the scraper to follow a wavy course, for the generous proportion of the sole of the tool acts the same way the sole of a plane does—and high spots are scraped off before the lower ones are touched when the tool is used with a long stroke. Also, the character of the burr, which forms the scraping edge being formed from a keen 45° edge, is considerably sharper in action than that formed in the old way from a 90° edge.

Hence, with all these factors taken into consideration it is not at all surprising to find that the Record scraper 080 works very easily and comfortably and speeds up the operation of scraping to an almost unbelievable extent. Pressure is neither advantageous nor necessary. So long as the tool is kept in contact with the work and propelled forward, the tool can be trusted to do its work—provided it is properly sharpened and set. The work with this tool is done best with a very minimum of effort on the part of the user.

Toothing cutter blades with either coarse or fine teeth can convert the scraper into a very reliable toothing plane. For veneering, a toothing plane is a necessary item in the tool kit. The Record scraper 080, used with a toothing cutter, forms a most efficient toothing plane.

Those unaccustomed to a 45° scraper edge may perhaps feel a little disconcerted at first in the sharpening of the tool, but they should not have any great difficulty. The old hand who has been used to a 90° edge should observe the following: first get a keen honed edge at 45° (without any second bevel), and then burnish and turn that edge as with a 90° edge. These procedures should be sufficient to put those unaccustomed to a 45° scraper on the right track. The edge cannot be too keenly honed on the oilstone. The beginner, or the craftsman who finds difficulty in sharpening a scraper (and there are many), should follow the instructions on sharpening given in Chapter 3.

To Remove the Blade

Slacken all three screws and lift out the blade.

To Assemble and Use

Place the body of the tool sole downwards on a flat surface. With all three screws quite slack, insert the blade, burred side to the front, i.e., the same side as the two screws, bevelled side towards the single screw. Tighten the two retaining screws, using a nail as a tommy bar. The back adjusting screw must be quite slack during this operation.

The scraper may or may not cut at this point. If it does not cut, screw the adjusting screw until it just gets a "feel," and try a cut. The harder the adjusting screw is tightened, the coarser will be the shaving produced, and vice versa. The best surface is obtained from a light cut.

Hints for Best Results

1). A little oil or paraffin wax will act as a lubricant and make for easier working.

2). The best way to use the tool is diagonally to the grain.

3). Use the tool lightly. It requires considerably less effort than ordinary scrapers, and hard work with this tool is neither advantageous nor necessary.

4). The tool properly sharpened gives a definite shaving. Dust indicates a blunt blade. Thin, silky, long and wide shavings indicate proper sharpening and working.

5). When honing, aim at a very keen edge. When burnishing, hold firmly and make firm, deliberate strokes.

6). The Record scraper 080 will give a perfectly clean finish to any hardwood, however curly the grain may be. If you are not getting such results, read the instructions and carry them out step-by-step. When properly sharpened, the scraper will clean up a panel straight from the saw if necessary.

7). The burnisher should be harder than the scraper steel so that it will turn the edge. The burnisher should be kept polished and free from rust and scratches.

Fig. 238. Using the cabinet scaper.

Toothing Cutters

The object of toothing is twofold: first, to remove any irregularity left by the plane on the ground which might result in unwanted highlights on the veneer after the polishing; second, to give a better "bite" to the glue.

The toothing cutter requires an occasional rub on the oilstone, bevelled side only, keeping the same angle. Setting and using are similar to the operations for scraping. The ground should be toothed diagonally both ways. Thin knife-cut veneers require no toothing; thicker saw-cut veneers may be toothed if desired, in the same way as the ground. Remove dust before applying glue.

The Box Scraper

This is a tool which has a great use in removing stencil marks, etc., from packing cases and the like, and will be found of service in removing the knotty unevenness of floors. It is handily constructed with a long hinged handle. Since the cutter and bottom are slightly curved, the scraper is able to cut on uneven surfaces.

The blade is sharpened on an oilstone, retaining the original curve, preferably keeping to the one bevel—which eliminates the need for grinding. There is no need to burr the edge as with the cabinet scraper 080.

The scraper plane, of which there have been a number of versions, seems to have been finalized by Bailey. His 1855 patented bronze scraper plane was certainly the first metal plane of this time. It had side handles turned in rosewood and was a beautiful piece. The modern example of this, which is basically the same design, has a fully adjustable system for the blade angle.

Another contemporary scraper plane was developed by the Stanley Rule and Level Company, and was manufactured in large numbers from 1905 onwards. The blade is fully adjustable for tilt, and the tool is handled, as the smoothing planes. The cutter is 2¾ inches wide, the sole 9½ inches long.

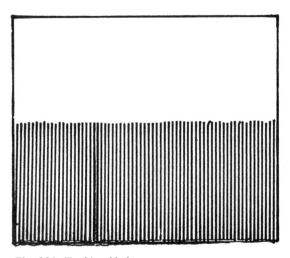

Fig. 239. Toothing blade.

Fig. 240. Record No. 070 box scraper.

Fig. 241. Kunz No. 12 side-handled scraper plane.

Fig. 242. Kunz No. 112 scraper plane.

14
Wooden Bench Planes

Several European manufacturers still make a wide variety of wooden planes. The earlier wooden planes had one great defect that the metal planes sought to eliminate. The sole became worn and needed truing up (made straight and flat) from time to time, thereby widening the mouth and thus thickening the shaving. This caused the wood to tear.

This problem could only be rectified by re-mouthing. The widening of the mouth could have been rectified if the plane had been fitted with the metal adjustable frog, as in the more modern metal plane. Worst of all, perhaps, was that the cutter had to be held by a wedge and adjusted by taps with the hammer.

William Marples in the late 1950's, when the beech planes were beginning to be withdrawn in England, designed a plane with a beech body and a metal cutter adjustment assembly similiar to the familiar, well-accepted Record metal plane adjustment. The body, of prefabricated form and made of beech, appeared in both smooth and jack plane size. Many schools in England adopted these planes in preference to the established wooden plane patterns. However, with the absorption of the company into that of Record Ridgway, these planes were withdrawn from production. One fault with the Marples plane was the fact that the frog was a fixed one, and the problem of a widening mouth was still present.

Fig. 243. Marples prefabricated plane.

The modern wooden plane, with wooden wedge and solid cutter, is still available. The scrub plane has a red beech body with a white beech or hornbeam sole machined on through an unusual modern method. Having a horn-shaped front handle with the rear body shaped to receive the hand, the cutter is held in place with a beech wedge. It has a metal strike knob.

The jack plane usually has an additional sole, with a mouth to receive a 2-inch cutter. Again, the cutter is held in place with a beech wedge, but a metal button has been substituted for the original boxwood of earlier planes.

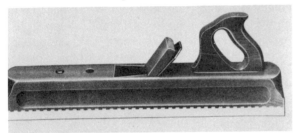
Fig. 244. No. 101S plane.

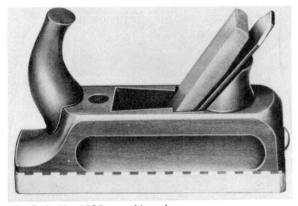
Fig. 245. No. 103S smoothing plane.

The smoothing plane has a horn-shaped front handle with double iron and wooden edge. A shaped block placed behind the cutting unit gives comfortable accommodation for the hand.

A company in Germany, E. C. Emmerich, produces a complete range of wooden planes, including a group with traditional styling but fitted with a unique, fully adjustable cutter unit. These are marketed under the tradename of Primus. Manufactured largely of hornbeam, they have the most beautiful soles made from, and machined on, lignum vitae. Those made in beech have similarly machined hornbeam soles.

All these Primus planes are fitted with the cutter assembly having an anti-backlash adjustment. This consists of a spring-loaded tensioning rod which prevents backlash. At the same time, a cross pin hooks onto the blade assembly, pulling it back and up. The depth adjustment screw presses on the rod. This clever design prevents any possibility of cutter movement or backlash. Both these adjustments are effected by knurled screw adjusters. Cutting irons are made from chrome vanadium steel. All their planes are ground and honed ready for use.

Smooth and jack planes have horn-shaped front handles, but the trying plane reverts back to the traditional rear "hand-hold" handle. A special improved smoother has a pearwood body and a lignum vitae sole.

Taking Out the Plane Iron:

1). Wind the adjusting screw backwards about $9/10$ inch.

2). Loosen the tension screw nut (do not screw it off).

3). Push the tension screw forward, and hook it out of the plane iron.

4). Take the plane iron out of the plane downwards (towards the sole), after the wood sliding block A has been moved forward.

Inserting of Plane Iron:

1). Insert the plane iron with screwed-on guide plate into the plane so that the guide plate locates in the two metal bearings.

2). Place the plane iron cutting edge approximately level with the plane sole. Hook the tension screw into the plane iron.

3). Tighten the tension screw nut until the plane iron cutting edge is $1/4$ inch (4–5 mm) above the plane sole.

4). Screw the adjusting screw forward until the plane iron is adjusted to the desired chip thickness.

Lateral Adjustment of the Plane Iron:

If necessary after reinserting the plane iron, operate the lower slotted screw to laterally adjust the plane iron.

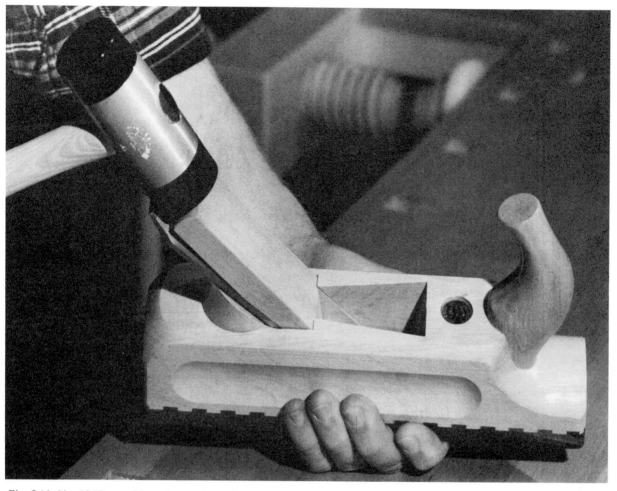

Fig. 246. No. 104S smoothing plane. It has a beech body and a sole made of lignum vitae.

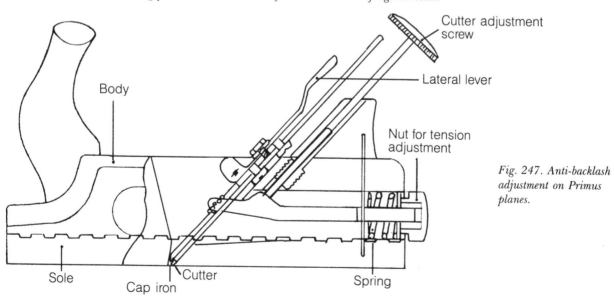

Body

Cutter adjustment screw

Lateral lever

Nut for tension adjustment

Sole

Cap iron

Cutter

Spring

Fig. 247. Anti-backlash adjustment on Primus planes.

Fig. 248. No. 701P Primus trying plane.

Another very useful plane is the stop rabbet plane No. 58 or chisel plane. It has a hornbeam body with a 7-inch sole and 1¼-inch wide cutter. It has a steep 50° pitch and the cutter must, of course, be set for extremely fine cutting. This plane is a must for finishing off that last fraction of an inch of the stopped rebate.

Many craftsmen agree that the finest of cuts can only be made with the cutter held at the skew. In the early part of the century, a number of metal shoulder and rebate planes were manufactured, but have since been withdrawn. The great difficulty with these planes is in keeping the angle of the cutter exactly correct so that the setting of the cutter in the body gives no problems of uneven shaving thickness. Primus have chosen to make a dovetail or skewed fillister plane, which has a sole and cutter edge angled at 10°. The cutter is therefore skewed in relation to both the body and fence, giving a perfect slicing action. Their moving fillister plane has a body 9½ inches long, made of beech. The sole is of hornbeam and an insert of lignum vitae to minimize wear at the corner. It is fitted with a spur for across-the-grain cutting, and an adjustable fence-and-depth stop.

The router or old woman's tooth plane is ideal for heavy routing work, and has ⁷⁄₁₆-, ⅝- and ¹³⁄₁₆-inch cutters, any of which can be housed in a sturdy beech body. The blade is securely held in a steel collar.

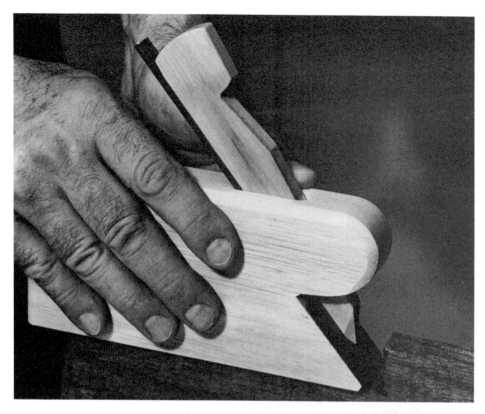

Fig. 249. No. 58S stop rebate plane, in horn-beam, with metal strike knob.

Fig. 250. No. 23S dovetail plane.

Fig. 251. No. 48S side-fillet plane.

Fig. 252. No. 20S router plane in use, finishing a dovetailed dado.

Veneering is still carried out in many home workshops. Primus and manufacturers catering to small craftsmen are almost unique in producing the toothing plane No. 108S for this work. Unlike normal planes, this plane uses a single cutter that is ridged or serrated so it can tooth-up or striate the surface and provide a grip for the glue. It is generally used after the wood has been trued-up with the jack plane. Craftsmen often use the plane to flatten lumber that is heavily burled or knotted. This plane is also made of beech, with a hornbeam sole.

Many styles of adjustable plow planes have appeared over the last century. The best of these have had threaded fence arms. Plow plane No. 30 has a beechwood body and an adjustable fence on threaded pearwood fence arms—it's a wood lover's dream! Six cutters are provided. Their sizes are as follows: $5/32$ inch (4 mm); $15/64$ inch (6 mm); $5/16$ inch (8 mm); $13/32$ inch (10 mm); $15/32$ inch (12 mm); and $35/64$ inch (14 mm).

Fig. 253. No. 108S toothing plane with serrated cutter.

Fig. 254. No. 30S plow plane.

A similar group of planes comes from another German manufacturer, Georg Ott, using the Ulmia trademark. Similar in many respects to other European planes, the Ulmia adjustable smoothing plane is very worthy of mention. The body is of pearwood, with a lignum vitae sole. It is fitted with an adjustable mouth, the adjustment being made through a block mounted in the sole of the plane. The steel wedge has a locking screw which holds in place a thin, polished cutter assembly. It has the usual horn-type handle and a metal tapping knob fitted in the rear. The handhold is dovetailed into the body behind the plane iron. It has three cutter widths: 1.8 inch, 1.9 inch and 2 inches. The Ulmia 25S plane is probably the ulti-mate in wooden smoothing planes since it not only has the cutter assembly and adjustment of the Primus previously discussed but, in addition, it also has a mouth adjustment. These planes are called reform planes, and have a movable shoe in the sole in front of the blade. Very fine adjustment of the mouth can be made so that extremely fine and perfect cuts can be made in the most awkward woods. They are 8⅞ inches long, with a blade width of 1⅞ inch.

Special planes from Primus include a fully adjustable rabbet plane. Once again, hornbeam is used for the body, and lignum vitae for the sole. The cutter is set at 52½° and the mouth is adjustable in an 11-inch sole. It can also be seen with a beech body and hornbeam sole. Fig. 256 shows the action of the cutter mechanism.

An interesting development of recent years is the use of nontraditional lumber in the construction of wooden planes. An exotic tropical hardwood known as goncalvo alves, is one of these. It has very beautiful coloring, is extremely hard and is impregnated with a waxy substance which greatly assists in the smooth movement of the plane over the lumber. One plane of this wood, called a small jointer, is 13 inches long and has a 1½-inch-wide cutter—not quite traditional, but certainly an interesting addition to the superb range of modern wooden planes.

Fig. 255. Smoothing plane.

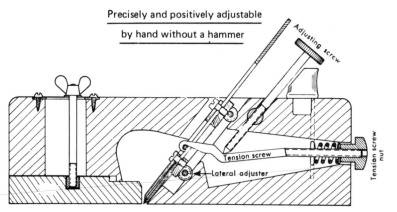

Fig. 256. Cutter mechanism action.

15

Difficulties in Planing, and Their Solutions

When planing, there are a number of problems which the beginner may meet:

1). *Sometimes, instead of leaving a smooth surface, a plane will leave a series of corrugations* (Fig. 257). This is due to incorrect grinding of the cutter, which is ground as at D, Fig. 39, Chapter 3. In very rough "hogging," this may be done deliberately to quickly plane down a surface from the rough. To remove the corrugations, work all over the board with a sharp, finely set smoothing plane, with the cutter ground as at E, Fig. 39, Chapter 3. If the board is long, use a metal jack, fore or jointer plane. Corrugation may be avoided by the use of a properly ground cutter (see Grinding, Chapter 3).

2). *Slight ridges appear in the planing* (Fig. 258). These are due to "snicking" the plane cutter. "Snicking" occurs when a piece of the cutting edge breaks because the cutter has planed over a metal object, i.e., a nail. If the cutter is examined, it will be found that a little piece has been chipped off (see A, Fig. 39, Chapter 3). Here, the cutter must be reground.

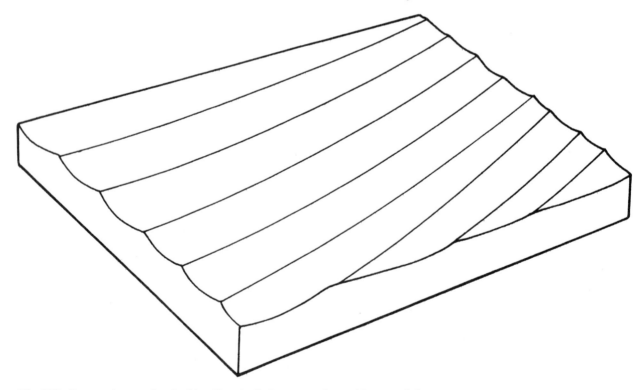

Fig. 257. Corrugations produced with a "hogging" plane or a plane with a rounded cutter.

3). *Sharp depressions* (Fig. 259) *occur in the plan-ing*. Here, the cutting iron is set more deeply on one side than the other. The cure: Use the lateral adjusting lever to bring the cutting edge in alignment with the sole of the plane (see Fig. 35, Chapter 2). This is one of the cases where the metal plane is immeasurably superior to a wood plane, accurate adjustment being made in a second.

4). *The wood tears up roughly, leaving an uneven patch of rough fibre*. The cause of this is working against the grain. Look at the grain on the edge of the board. To plane the top side of the board (Fig. 260), you must work "uphill" of the grain, i.e., from A to B, as the arrow shows. If you work from B to A you are against the grain and the wood will tear up.

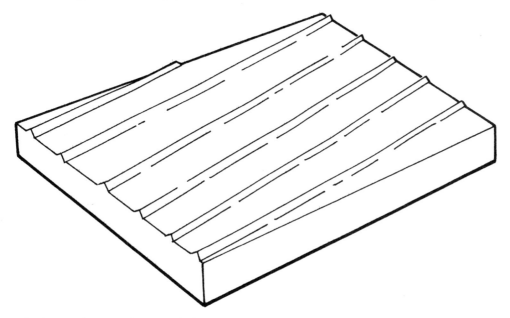

Fig. 258. Ridges caused by a "nicked" cutting iron.

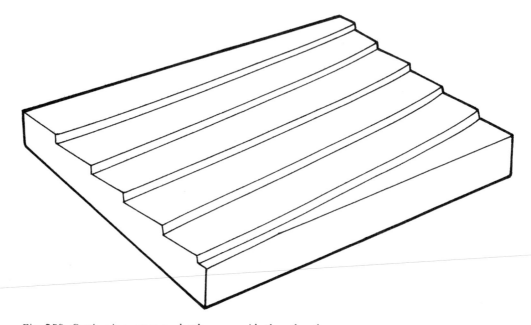

Fig. 259. Cutting iron set more deeply on one side than the other.

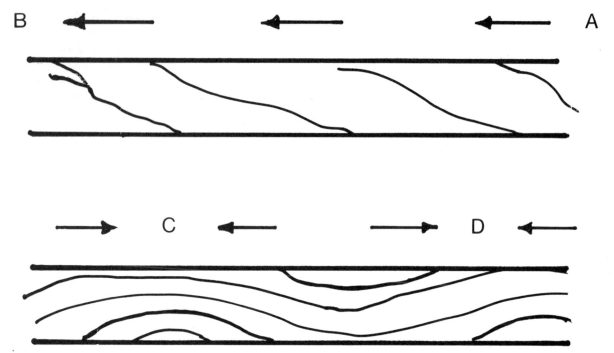

Fig. 260. Planing with the grain.

Sometimes the grain will be wavy, as shown at C and D. Here, you have an awkward grain. You must plane "uphill" of the grain, and that may mean working in several directions, as shown by the arrows. Frequently, this kind of lumber can best be cleaned up by working in a circular motion with a keenly set smoothing plane that has a very sharp cutter.

It is in this kind of work that the metal plane shows its immense superiority over the wooden plane. Its accurate and sensitive adjustments allow it to perform work that is quite impossible with a wooden wedge plane.

5). *The end grain of a board has to be planed.* This occurs when you decide to shoot the end. If the wood is planed right through from A to B (Fig. 261), the end fibres will break through, as at C.

First plane from A to D, and then from B to D, i.e., from the outer edges to the middle. This can be done in the vise. The low-set angle of the cutter of a metal plane, together with the ease with which it can be adjusted to cut a very fine shaving, makes this process quite easy and accurate. The metal block plane is most suitable for this kind of work because of the low angle of the cutter. A small bevel on the end of the board will also eliminate this.

6). *Shooting an edge on the shooting board.* (The stop may be at 90°, or at a mitre of 45°, etc.) The farther edge may be chamfered to the line with a chisel before planing. Hold the wood hard-up to the stop, as shown in Fig. 263. Lay the plane on its side in the rebate, holding it with the right hand, as shown. Slide the plane along, taking very fine cuts. The cutter must be very sharp and finely set. Three cuts are easier and more accurate than one thick one. Rub a candle lightly on the sole and on the rubbing face to give an easier movement of the plane.

Where much shooting is done, it is a great saver of time, as well as being easier to cut, if the bottom of the rebate of the shooting board forms a ramp instead of being made parallel. This way, much more of the blade is in use and the time for re-honing or whetting is postponed. When the blade is run on the ordinary shooting board to shoot ½-inch boards, only ½ inch of the edge is at work. This is dulled while the rest of the blade is still sharp. When a cant on the board is used, more of the edge is in action; the cut, being oblique, is easier, and the sharpness of the blade lasts longer.

The sides of Record planes are ground at right angles to the soles, and are therefore eminently suitable for use with a shooting board. It some-

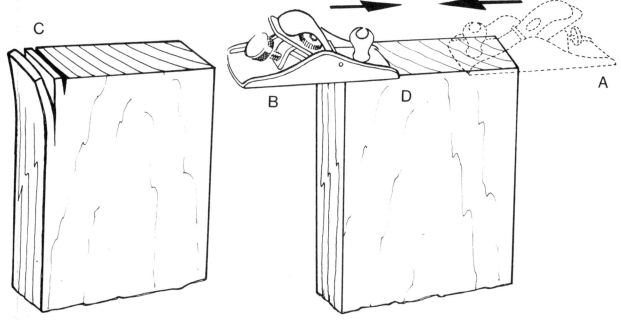

Fig. 261. Planing end grain.

Fig. 262. Planing end grain with the block plane.

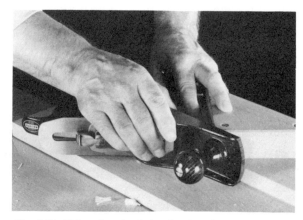

Fig. 263. Using the mitred shooting board.

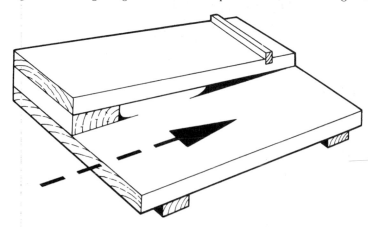

Fig. 264. Ramp shooting board.

times happens, however, that although this is so, and the shooting board is perfectly square, the cut is unaccountably out of square. The cause of this is that in setting the blade it has been set slightly out of alignment with the sole, one corner of the blade projecting farther than the other.

The remedy is to use the lateral adjusting level. Record jack plane T5 is especially suitable for use on the shooting board. It has wider wings, which have a greater bearing on the shooting board, and has an extra side handle that assists considerably in the control of the tool. (Though the Record jack plane T5 is not made anymore, there are 1000's still in use, and some are still on sale in the United States.)

Apart from the use of the shooting board in the preparation of end grain, there is an enormous advantage in its use in the preparation of pairs of boards for butt jointing. The butt joints of the parts of an occasional tabletop can be quickly prepared on a shooting board of moderate length. In using this method, shoot the first board face side up, and the next one face side down, and so on. (Heart sides should be alternated to minimize the effect of any warping.)

A typical example of the advantages of the shooting board is the making of a chessboard where, for example, sycamore and black walnut strips are edge-planed in the manner indicated and then glued together alternately. Saw cuts are then made across the face, and the new strips thus separated shot again, this time on the end grain. They will then be finally glued together with a white square opposite a black one.

When the first set of strips is made, one extra strip should be included so as to make allowance for matching up. The odd pieces not required should be discarded after the second gluing. Final support may be given by gluing the whole to a plywood base. A frame may be added or the board may be embodied in a tabletop.

7). *Shooting a mitre for a wide plinth.* When only one or two have to be done, they can be done in a vise (similar to 5 on page 144) using the plane as indicated in Fig. 261, but at the required bevel. If the job is likely to occur at all frequently, a "donkey's ear" (Fig. 266) should be constructed and the mitres shot on it, as in section 6.

An alternative way is to screw a pair of squared fillets to both cheeks of the vise at the required

Fig. 265. Record T5 jack plane in use on the shooting board.

angle to the top, in such a manner that they are exactly opposite each other. The board to be shot can then be laid on the two supports and held in the vise jaws while being shot. The two fillets are screwed to the wood facings and can easily be attached or removed. They should each project about ¼ inch or so above the cutter jaws of the vise, so that there is no danger of "snicking" the cutter on the iron vise. The same method can be used at times by setting the work in the vise by the use of a carpenter's bevel, dispensing with the use of screwed fillets.

8). *Shooting an edge cut at any other angle than 90° to the length.* A consideration of the way of the grain (Fig. 267) will show that in example 1 the plane must travel from E to F. The point at F can be saved from chipping off by clamping a small piece (G) there until the planing is finished. In example 2, B to C offers no difficulty and is planed as in section 5. The grain will show that you must plane from A to B, and then reverse the job and plane from D to C.

9). *"Warped" and "cast" boards, due to faulty seasoning, present difficulties in planing.* Warping (i.e., hollowing in width) may be straightened out by damping the hollow side and warming up the round side, but the board will probably warp again on drying-out if not fixed (after planing, etc.) by the construction, as in a groove or a rebate.

Casting (i.e., curvature in length due to bad seasoning) is difficult to cure and cast boards are seldom worth working up. There is nothing else to do in this case but to plane the high spots away, which will reduce the ultimate thickness of the board.

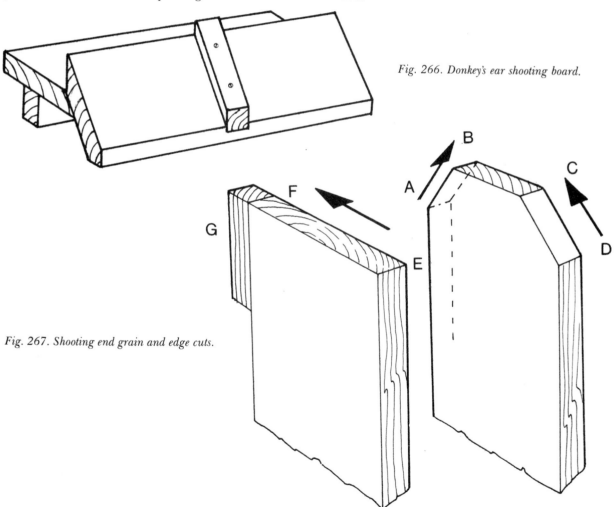

Fig. 266. *Donkey's ear shooting board.*

Fig. 267. *Shooting end grain and edge cuts.*

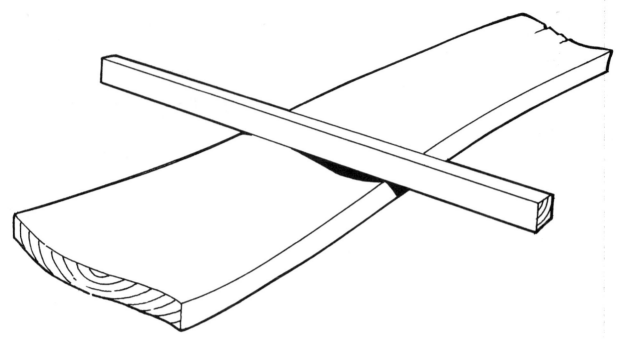

Fig. 268. Warped or cast board.

16
Contemporary Plane Makers

Jamestown Planes

Recently a number of men inspired by the British manufacturers of the past have devoted their energies and skills to the production of planes similar to the Spiers and Norris planes of the 19th century.

The Jamestown Tool Company of Jamestown, North Carolina, was pioneered by Jay Gaynor and Joseph Hutchins. They set out to produce their planes with accurately machined soles soldered to a bronze casting that was machined and hand-filled to its final perfection. The irons were made of quality-tool steel supplied ready for use. All planes were filled with mahogany, but you could have had your own choice if you wished. Each plane was supplied in a drawstring bag with an instruction sheet.

Recently the company has sold the tooling and patterns to The Mechanick's Workbench, in Marion, Massachusetts, who plan to make similar planes, not using the Jamestown name.

Fig. 269. Shoulder plane.

Fig. 270. Chariot plane.

Fig. 271. Thumb plane.

150

Fig. 272. Mitre plane.

Henley Planes

Probably the finest planes ever produced come from the Henley Plane Company of Reading, England. The Henley planes are the brainchild of Alan Beardmore, an architect by profession and a keen student of antiquity in tools. He has researched the tools of Edward Preston, on which he is an authority, and it is probably this work which has influenced and inspired him.

The shoulder plane produced in 1976 was made with a steel sole with sides of naval brass. The single iron was 1½ inches wide and the set bevel, uppermost at 20°, was fully adjustable. The infill was Indian rosewood. The plane was a joy to hold and perfect in use.

Probably one of the most sought-after planes, of any make or condition, is the mitre plane. Henley has one in its numbered collection of master tools. The mitre plane was designed with a low-cutting angle for end- and oblique-grain cutting, as well as shooting-board work. This plane not only shows perfection of workmanship, but also fine adjustment unequalled before its production.

Constructed with a steel sole and sides of naval brass, the fittings are of gunmetal, with an infill of Indian rosewood. The plane sole is 10½ inches long, and is fitted with a 2½-inch cutter. Its total weight is 6¾ pounds. The cutter is fully adjustable by means of a single lever that can move the cutter front, back and laterally. It is fitted with a wooden wedge, which only serves as a means of gripping the plane, since the cutter is fixed by a knurled screw which bears on the wedge. Thus, pressure is distributed over a large area of the cutter.

Fig. 273. Shoulder plane made with steel sole, with sides of naval brass.

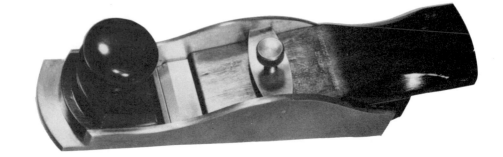

Fig. 274. Henley mitre plane.

Perfect action is secured by setting the cutter at 12° with the cutter uppermost, and sharpening at 27–28°. The cutting angle is 39–40°. This plane is infinitely superior in cutting to the normal bench plane. Chatter is practically eliminated because the cutting edge is supported by the sole almost to its tip. The perfection of construction, ensuring 90° between sole and sides, secures superb work on the shooting board.

Norris might well have envied Henley its smoothing plane, which is hand built of the very best materials to the closest tolerances ever. The sole and frog are solid steel, with handle and front grip of rosewood. The 2⅛-inch cutter, set at 50°, is fully adjustable with a single lever. The cutting unit has the double-iron system, and is of tool steel. The cutting unit is precision-ground, and its sides are parallel. The connecting screwhead is hardened to counter screwdriver wear.

A bench plane designed for finishing operations "with the grain," where a near scraping action is required, is described as a hand-block smoothing plane. Lighter in weight than the tra-

ditional-style smoothing plane, its cutter is set bevel uppermost at 27°, and secured by a pivoting lever cap and screw. Adjustment longitudinally and laterally is by an improved single-lever mechanism working on a differential screw. Shaving thickness may be regulated by 0.0015 for each quarter-turn of the screw. The plane has an extremely fine mouth that accommodates a 1¾-inch iron.

The side rebate plane is built from precision-ground, mild-steel plates with brass fittings, and has a solid rosewood knob handle. It is a combination left- and right-hand plane, whose components can be separated for individual use. It has fully adjustable irons that work by pivoting levers. The levers have differential screw action for the micro advancement of the cutters, which have a 1½-inch depth of cut. The single irons, bevel side uppermost, are set at 20° to give a precision, tear-free cut of the highest order.

The small planes include a thumb plane for small scale cleaning up and trimming work. With steel sole and sides of naval brass, the single iron, bevel uppermost, is set at 20°. The mouth width is 0.025 inch, and the iron is 1¼ inch wide. Rosewood is again used as infill.

There is a Badger version of the thumb plane, with the cutter extended to the edge of the sole on one side only. It is ideal for cleaning into a right angle on those occasions when the groundwork is dropped, or the width would preclude the use of the shoulder plane because of surface scoring by the outside corner of the iron. The plane is available both right- and left-handed.

Another version of the thumb plane is the chariot plane, 4½ inches in length, with the cutter very close to the front, bullnose style. It is ideal for finishing work and complements the other master tools.

R.H. Wood Planes

Close copies of the Norris panel plane, 14½ inches long, have recently been signed by R. H:

Wood of Grange Moor, Wakefield, England. Apparently, this plane is being manufactured on a commercial scale. The sides are dovetailed to the sole and finally cold-forged. The surface grinding is taken to a standard of 8 micro inches, tolerances throughout being better than 0.001 inch, and, in some respects, 0.0001 inch. The lever cap and screw are in gunmetal, as were the originals. The infill is of Indian rosewood. Using digitally controlled milling machines in a factory processing other highly sophisticated components, the makers have achieved an extremely high standard, far better than was possible in the Norris heyday.

The hardness of the cutting iron is 45–48° Rockwell C. (Hardness in steel is measured using either one of two systems: Brinell or Rockwell.) The material used for the iron is chrome vanadium tool steel (1% carbon, 1.3% manganese, 0.65% chromium, 0.8% tungsten, 0.15% vanadium).

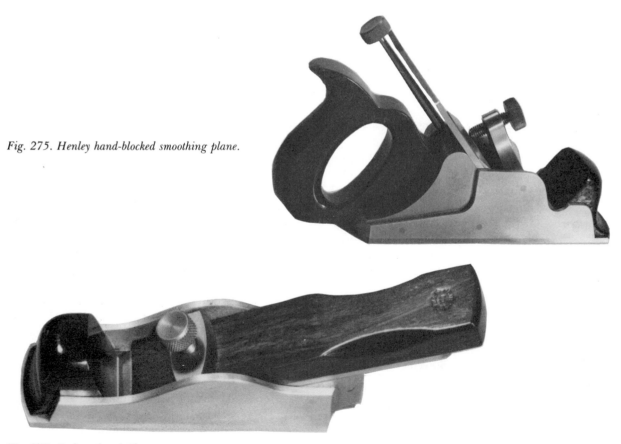

Fig. 275. *Henley hand-blocked smoothing plane.*

Fig. 276. *Badger thumb plane.*

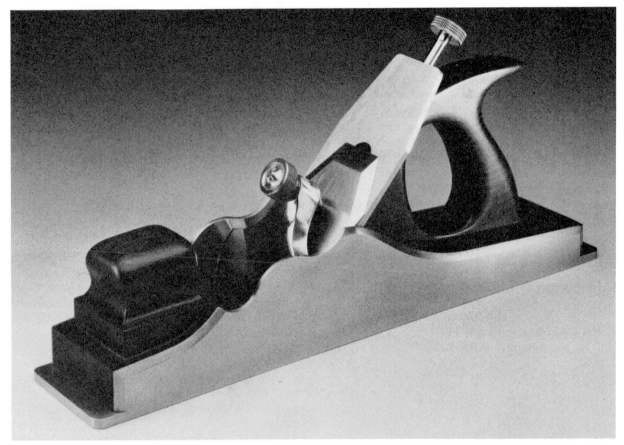

Fig. 277. Panel plane by R.H. Wood.

The Planes of Geoff Mather

Since the days of Leonard Bailey and his contemporaries, many planes have been designed to assist in the continuing romance of man with wood. Though many of these planes have been fit for a particular purpose, some are strangely ugly and ill-fitting in the hand of the user. A number of planes have been ill-conceived, their terms of reference either incorrect or incorrectly interpreted.

None of these failings can be placed at the door of Geoff Mather who lives in North Ashton in Lancashire, England. A visit to his workshop reveals a fair genius of a man, skilled at many crafts using a diverse range of materials. His love of music and his interest in all instruments, particularly those of the past, undoubtedly serve to encourage him to design and make his own planes and other tools for the skill of instrument making. The master stringed-instrument makers of the past invariably fashioned their own planes; some of these early designs have been mass-produced and can still be obtained. The Mather planes are, however, individually made to produce perfection in cutting or scraping. At the same time, however, they are economically designed; indeed, they are an extension to the hand.

His skill in tool-making has produced a wide range of planes, scrapers, purfling tools and others. If there is a wood cutting problem, Geoff is equal to the task. At the same time, a beautiful piece of sculpture is created. His carving planes combine a speedy removal of wood with the traditional gentle carving techniques of the old masters. The old-type finger planes tended to cramp the hand; these are perfect. He uses solid drawn brass for the working faces of plane and tool bodies, and chrome vanadium steel for cutting irons and a variety of exotic lumbers. There is nearly a plane for every situation; if there isn't he'll meet his customer more than halfway.

His breastplate arching planes are beautiful working sculptures, mainly carved in exotic woods with brass sole plates. Many variations of spherical radii to the sole are available in planes from 2½ to 4 inches in length and ¾ to 1½ inches in width of cutting iron. This is perfection in preliminary planing of instrument plates.

Scraper planes come in variety. The S4 is a beautifully sculpted tool; it has a 7-inch-long hardwood body with a 4-inch solid drawn brass sole.

Thumb planes and scrapers are seen in solid brass with curved or flat soles with optional fine adjustment screws to the cutting iron.

The chisel planes, or chisel-ending planes as Geoff calls them, are a new concept inasmuch as this type of plane is usually seen as part of the bullnose rebate plane (i.e., with the nose removed). They are totally in brass.

The mouse mitre plane has fine adjustment to the cutting iron which is held in place by a thumb-screw that passes through the single handle to form an unusual lever locking. As with all mitre planes, the bevel of the cutter is placed on top. The plane sole is 2¾ inches long and its cutting iron ¾ inch wide.

Fig. 278. Shoulder planes.

Fig. 279. Carving plane.

Fig. 280. Arching planes.

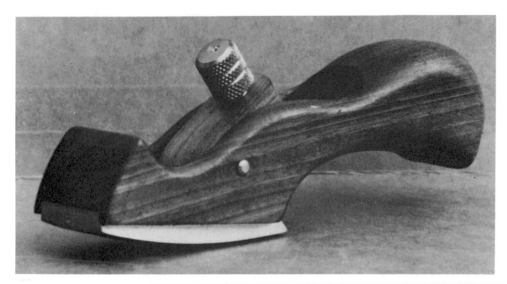

Fig. 281. Side view of arching plane.

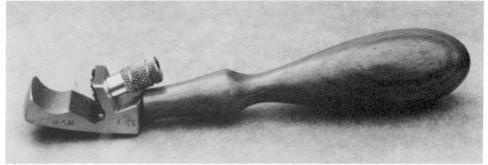

Fig. 282. Forward scraper plane.

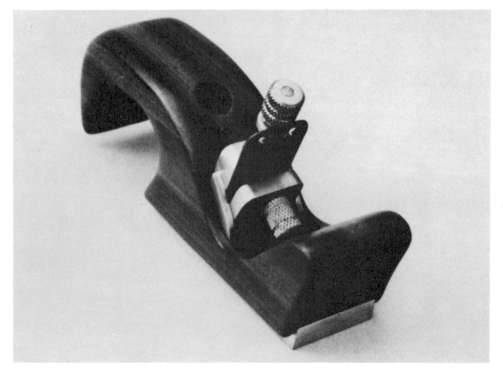

Fig. 283. Scraper plane.

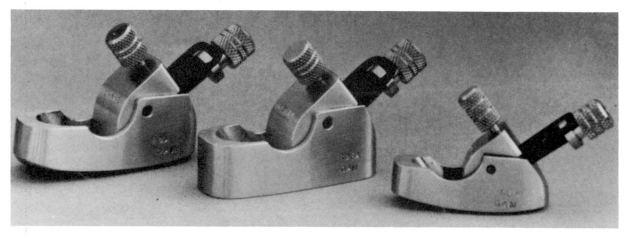

Fig. 284. Heavier quality thumb planes.

Fig. 285. Chisel-ending planes.

Fig. 286. Mouse mitre plane.

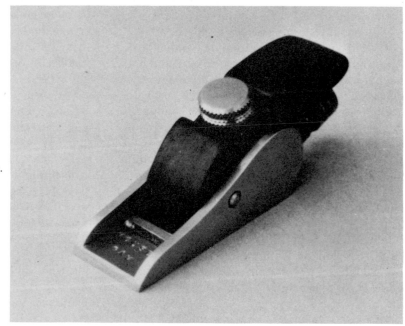

17
Power Planes

The electric hand planes had to come, and research by various companies throughout the world has produced a number of first-rate designs. Long experience in the production of electric hand drills, combined with historical reference to planing machines, helped to bring perfection. Modern production methods have served to reduce costs, and the use of various plastics has reduced the weight. As a result, the hand planer can be seen, not only in use in industry, but also in the home.

One company, Black & Decker, has a DN710 planer with a 3¼-inch cutting width. The cut can be varied in depth from 0 to 0.5 mm (⅟₅₀ inch). Rebates can be cut from ⅜ inch (0 to 8 mm) in depth. A well-fitting side and mitre guide is provided, together with a side guide for rebating.

The plane has reversible high-speed steel blades and a safety park position on depth adjustment so that the blades can be fully retracted into the tool when not in use. A shavings bag and vacuum cleaner adaptor are also available, and the machine can be fitted to a stand for stationary use. Rotation at 19,000 rpm makes for perfection in surfacing, while the two guide grooves assist in effortless chamfering. A front handle is an additional option and makes for easy handling.

The DN750 is a heavier machine with a more powerful motor. Cuts are possible up to .007 inch deep at a single pass. With a cutting width of 3 inches, the machine will rebate up to .8 inch in depth. Two handles with an extra long pole ensure a high degree of control. Cutters are easily removed for sharpening with the aid of an allen key.

A German company, Elu, has the MFF80, a heavier plane of 7.9 pounds (3.6 kilograms), available in 220 or 110 volts. The body is in highly durable polymid, which is a heat resistant and shatterproof plastic. The die-cast aluminum sole plates are skimmed together, ensuring a completely level surface. The front shoe is vee-grooved to give an instant guide for chamfering edges. The plane has a power output of 560 watts, and planing up to a 1-inch depth of cut is possible. A side fence and bevel fence are provided.

The cutter block has taper slots, greatly simplifying the changing of the tungsten carbide knives and increasing the choice of blades. Reversing the blades eliminates the need to adjust and reset. Conventional blades and rustic finish blades are also available.

An inversion stand converts the machine to a bench model, while a shavings bag collects the shavings. Alternatively, an extractor hose can be used. The plane handles beautifully, and can be safely used by the professional or the amateur.

Very heavy-duty planes are designed by Makita of Japan. One has a cutting width of 6⅛ inches and a planing depth of ⅟₁₆ inch, with a cutter speed of 15,000 rpm. There are five planes in this range, all having excellent performances and the usual fitments.

Ryobi of Japan shows one of the biggest ranges, 11 planes in all, varying from a 3¼ inch to a 6⅛ inch width of cut. They have designed a unique blade replacement mechanism, with a quick and easy change. A very clever sharpening kit is available that will serve as a boon to the industrial and home worker alike. Each machine has a blade adjustment gauge available as an accessory.

The most popular of these machines is the

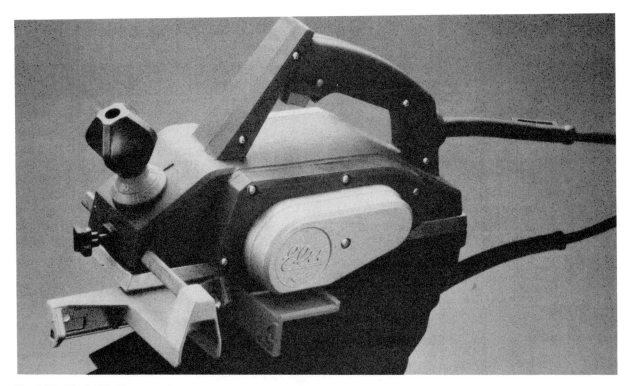

Fig. 287. Elu MFF 80 power plane.

Fig. 288. Elu MFF 80 power
plane in use.

L1323A double-insulated hand planer. This planer has a planing width of 3¼ inches, and cuts to a depth of ⅛ inch. It will cut rebates to a depth of ¹⁵⁄₁₆ inch. The cutter rotates at 14,000 rpm; the input is 710 watts. The depth is set by a knob at the front of the plane, with exact readings taken from the depth of cut plate.

For straight cutting, an attachment is provided so that when it is attached to the side of the planer it rests along the edge of the work being planed. This attachment will permit the planing of an area 2 inches to 3¼ inches wide. The sole has a front shoe, in the middle of which is a precision cut groove. This groove will accurately and safely locate the corner on a length of lumber for perfect chamfering. Another attachment that is fitted along with the cutting guide controls the cutting of rebates.

To convert the plane to a small bench planer, invert it on a bench stand. If the machine is to be used to plane boards wider than the cutter width of 3¼ inches, round both corners off the cutting blade. With this modification, first plane an area equal to one cutter width, then plane a second area adjacent to the first, making sure to overlap the first area. Continue this procedure until the full area is planed.

The cutters can be easily changed, but first unplug the machine from the electricity supply. Remove the hexagonal-headed bolt, blade bender

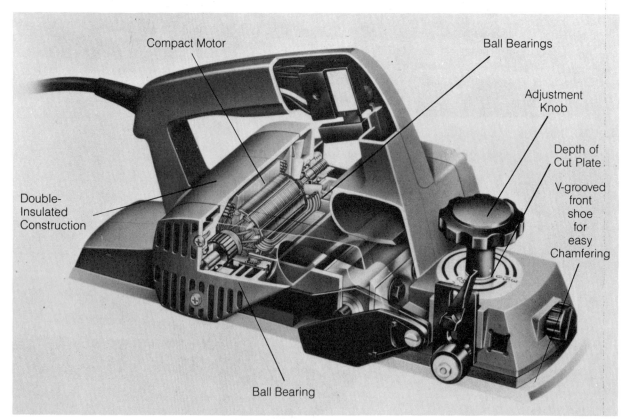

Fig. 289. Ryobi power plane 1323A and its construction details.

Fig. 290. Power plane L1323A.

Fig. 291. Power plane at work, with the left-hand removed to show detail.

Fig. 292. Ryobi 1323 power plane in use.

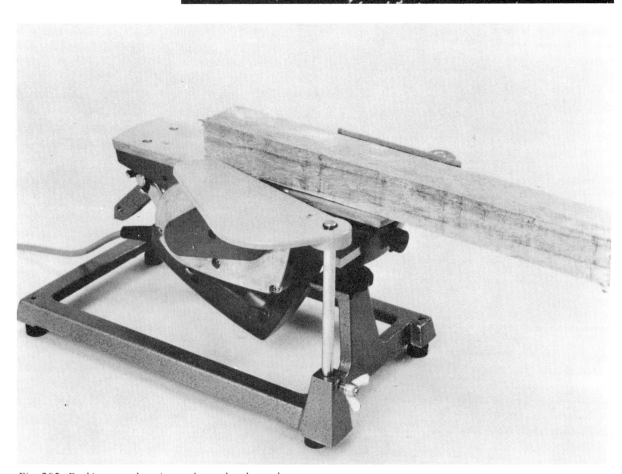

Fig. 293. Ryobi power plane inverted on a bench stand.

Fig. 294. Ryobi power plane cutting a rebate.

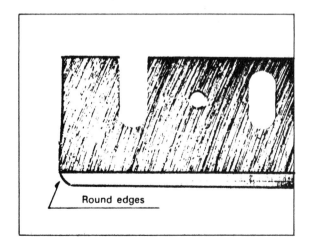

Fig. 295. Rounding the corners of the cutter for planing boards with widths of more than 3¼ inches.

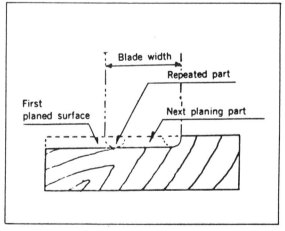

Fig. 296. Planing a wide board: Progressive cutting.

and finally the blades. Replace the new or resharpened cutters on the cutter head, together with the bender and bolt. Set depth of cut to 0 by adjusting on the front knob. Rotate the cutter head until the tip of the cutter is in line vertically with the shaft center. Slacken the hexagonal-headed bolt with the "T"-type wrench, and adjust the cutters using the blade adjusting gauge. The cutter should be level throughout its length with the rear shoe. Tighten down on the bolt.

A special cutter-sharpening device is supplied with the machine. To sharpen the cutters, fasten them carefully to the blade holder, making sure that the edges face in the same direction. Place the cutter edges so that they rest flat on the sharpening stone. Grip the cutter holder firmly and move it along the stone, passing it across the stone at the same time to ensure equal sharpening along the length of the cutters. Use the widest stone possible. Finally remove the cutters from the holder and carefully remove the wire edge.

Some care is needed when using power planers.

Be sure that the work is firmly held either in a vise or clamp, checking that the cutters will be clear of obstruction. With one hand holding the depth-adjusting knob and the other gripping the handle, place the front shoe on the edge of the piece to be planed. Be sure that the cutter is *not* in contact with the workpiece, then start the machine, making sure that the sole of the planer is flat and level on the piece to be worked. Use a slow steady movement with the motor running at full torque. Press at the front of the planer at the commencement of the cut, and on the back at the completion to maintain flat and level cutting. Stand comfortably so that there will be little or no movement of the feet, except only with very long work.

Always clean the machine after use. Occasionally inspect the vee belt by removing the vee belt cover; replace if necessary. Check also the carbon brushes for wear. Replace them should they be worn to the standard line, shown in Fig. 298, or after about 200 hours of operation.

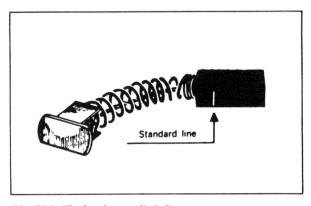

Fig. 298. The brush-wear limit line.

Fig. 297. Sharpening the cutters.

Appendices

Tail vise. Note dog at left hand side of front jaw.

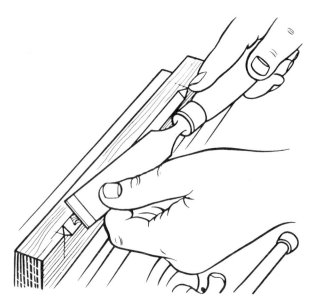

Stopped chamfer.

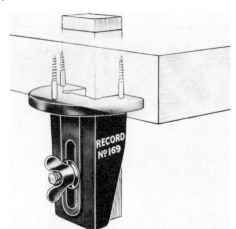

Bench stop.

Bench hook.

GLOSSARY

Adze

A tool like an axe, but with a blade set at right angles to the handle and curving towards it. It was used to smooth wood before the plane was used, and for coarser work for a long time after the plane was in general use. The pleasing texture of much mediaeval work is due to the use of the adze. Though not used much nowadays, the tool is still used skillfully by shipwrights and some of the old-time carpenters. Set the board on the floor and rest your elbow on your knee when using the tool. A skilled man with an adze can leave a smooth surface that compares well with that left by a jack plane.

Aloxite

An abrasive made from the artificial aluminum oxide that is obtained by treating the mineral bauxite in an electric furnace. (See also *Hone*.)

Apron or Apron Piece

A board—shaped or otherwise decorated—stretching between two legs, the sides of a cabinet, etc., the function of which is to give a pleasing line. This type of board is frequently used in construction that helps to keep corners square.

Architrave

A term borrowed from architecture, where it refers to the chief beam that carries the superstructure and rests immediately on the columns. Ordinarily it is the lowest of the three divisions, the other two being the frieze and the cornice. In carpentry, the term architrave is used collectively for the mouldings, jambs and lintels that surround a door or a window.

Astragal

A term also borrowed from architecture which refers to a small moulding of semicircular section. An astragal is used widely for the bars of glazed cabinet doors when it is made with a groove on the reverse side which carries a fillet, thus forming a rebate for the glass on the inner side of the door. The glass is held in this rebate by a bead. Narrow strips of canvas are usually glued in the crossings to strengthen the joints. Architecturally, the astragal appears around the top and bottom of a column.

Baluster

The upright that supports the handrail of a staircase. One of the units of a balustrade. A banister back chair has a back resembling a banister.

Banding

Strips of wood, parallel in length and thickness and often built up in patterns or glued into grooves as inlaid decoration in furniture. When not built up they are usually known as stringing. Bandings can be made by gluing strips of various colored wood, such as boxwood, ebony, walnut, etc., and then cutting "slices" from the end, in the manner of a checkered cake (about a sixteenth of an inch thick). A wide variety are available commercially.

Strings of boxwood, ebony and other woods for corners are usually square in section and are called squares. These can be cut from suitable colored wood very quickly by taking two cuts with the small plow cutter, one from the face side and one from the face edge. The plow is set so that the second cut releases the square. Apart from its decorative effect, a string of hardwood such as ebony tends to save a corner from wear. In the very best work, the string and the rebate each have a saw cut, into which a veneer slip is placed as a key, this strengthening the glued joint.

Bargeboard or Vergeboard

A board, frequently of ornate fashion, suspended from the verge of a gable. The ornament is usually bow saw and spokeshave work, sometimes combined with boring and piercing.

Batten

Properly a piece of squared lumber not more than $7 \times 2\frac{1}{2}$ inches (17.8×6.4 cm); a scantling. However, the word batten also refers to the strip which is nailed across parallel boards to hold them together and to prevent warping, as in a battened door, as well as to a ledge or clamp.

Bead

A narrow semi-circular moulding. This may be carved so as to leave globular members of equal or unequal length. When a short one and a long one alternate, the Jacobean "ball and sausage" moulding is formed.

Bench Hook

A battened board, hooked over the front of the bench to assist in sawing. The best ones have battens fixed with dowels rather than by nailing or screwing.

Bench Stop

A device, widely varying in pattern, which is set in the bench top and against which the wood is held when planing.

Bevel

An obtuse angle, a tool used in setting off this angle and the operation of making it.

Blister

During the process of veneering, a blister can form when the veneer is not properly glued. (It is suggested that animal glue be used for veneering.) To remove the blister, cut through with a very sharp chisel, insert glue with a shaving and apply a hot iron. The object of cutting the blister is the removal of the air.

Block Plane

A small plane, used chiefly in planing end grain (originally the end grain of butchers' blocks), having a single low-set blade which is used bevel-side upwards.

Bolection

A moulding that projects before the face of the work decorated, i.e., a raised panel moulding that projects above the frame.

Brinell Test

A method used to determine the hardness of steel and other metals. The Brinell test measures the resistance to penetration which the material offers when a hardened steel ball of given diameter placed upon it is subjected to a definite load. The depth of the impression made is not measured directly, but the diameter of the cavity is accurately gauged by means of a microscope fitted with a millimetre scale, vernier and cross hair.

From this, the spheroidal area of the impression is calculated and the maximum load in kilograms divided by the area gives a hardness number. This number denotes the degree of hardness of the steel or metal being tested.

Plane cutting irons are tested for hardness in a similar manner except that instead of a hardened steel ball a conical shaped diamond with four flats on it is used. The impression made by the diamond is very small and therefore does not damage the face of the cutting iron.

Brogue

A Scottish term for a bradawl.

Bullnose Plane

A small plane used for planing close to projecting parts, the blade being set close to the nose of the plane.

Butt Joint

The joint made when the two pieces are joined together without overlapping.

Cabinet

A piece of furniture, often ornamented, fitted with drawers, shelves, etc., for the display and preservation of specimens. Display cabinets became very popular with the wealthy classes during the later years of the seventeenth century, as trade with the East grew when, following the example of Queen Mary, there was a vogue for collecting choice pieces of china.

"C" Scroll

A carved motif much used by Chippendale, so called from its resemblance to the letter "C." It is believed this carved motif was introduced by the French.

Capping

A piece of wood generally moulded, topping some other piece of wood as on the post of a bed, etc. A capping plane was a plane that was used mainly for the upper surface of the balustrade of a staircase.

Carcass or Carcase

The skeleton of a piece of work, as the framework of a chest of drawers; also the framework of a house which supports the floor or the roof.

Carpenter

An artificer in wood or one who does the framework of a house, etc., as opposed to a joiner or cabinetmaker who works at the bench.

Cast

A board twisted in its length is said to be cast.

Cavetto

A quarter-round concave moulding.

Cellaret

A compartment of a sideboard for holding wine bottles, or a case of cabinetwork for that purpose.

Chamfer

The surface produced by bevelling off a square edge or corner equally on both sides. Sometimes made concave when it is a hollow. Chamfers may be "through" or "stopped" and very effective edges can be made by working a second chamfer or a bevel on another one. The Record A151 spokeshave is useful for this work.

Chatter

The jumpiness or vibration of a plane, whereby it does not give a smooth, continuous cut. It can be traced to a variety of causes: lack of rigidity, badly machined parts, wrong setting, slack screws, etc. The "Stay-Set" cap iron was in part an attempt to eliminate chatter in smoothing planes.

Check

A Scottish term for rebate. Also used for decoration in squares, particularly inlay.

Choke

When a plane is being used and the shavings stick in the mouth instead of escaping through the plane, the plane is said to choke. A frequent cause of choke is bad setting or slack screwing of the cap-iron screw, causing a shaving to stick between the cap iron and the cutting iron. Insufficient clearance between the blade and the front of the mouth will also cause choke, i.e., when the frog is brought too far forward, with the cap iron as near to the cutting edge as it will go.

Chop Inlay

An early form of inlay, with the pieces fitted into the solid surface. Later veneer was used.

Circular Plane, Compass Plane or Radius Plane

A plane constructed so that it has a convexity or a concavity in its sole, end to end, so that it can work on curved surfaces. The Record circular plane is constructed so that it can be used on convex and concave surfaces. The amount of curvature is adjustable at will.

Clamp, Clam or Cramp

The piece of wood used as a brace to keep one or more pieces together and to prevent warping. It may simply be a piece let into a plow groove or a piece slot-screwed onto the faces, but usually it is grooved and tenoned, as on a pastry board or drawing board. As a fastening it is inferior to panelling, as there is no provision for shrinkage; for this reason it is often discarded in favor of an iron bar, which is let into a plow groove in the edge.

Clapboard

An American term for a lapping weatherboard.

Clap Post

The American term for slamming post—the upright post of a cupboard on which the door claps or closes.

Classical Detail, Moulding, Etc.

As in the architecture of the ancient Romans and Greeks.

Cock Bead

A bead that projects above the ground work.

Column

A cylindrical or slightly tapering body, considerably greater in length than diameter, used vertically as a support. A pillar.

Combination Plane (No. 050, 050C)

A plane capable of plowing, rebating, beading, tonguing and grooving, dado cutting and center beading.

Concave

Hollowed out, opposite of convex.

Contour

The profile or section of a moulding.

Convex

Curving, as the surface of a sphere.

Cord

A pile of wood 4 feet wide, 4 feet high and 8 feet long (1.2 m wide, 1.2 m high and 2.4 m long). Probably originally measured with a cord. Firewood.

Cornice or Cornish

The horizontal moulding that crowns a building or part of a building and the similar moulding running around the wall of a room, etc. To save lumber, these mouldings are often planed from thin boards, the edges of which are planed at 45 degrees, one edge fitting the vertical and the other the horizontal faces.

Corrugated Base

The base of the "C" series of Record smoothing, jack and jointer planes, in which a series of semi-circular grooves is machined longitudinally along the sole. It is sometimes found when planing thin and comparatively wide board. As the surface of these boards becomes true, a suction is created between the face of the board and the sole of the plane, due to a combination of an accurately machined and practically nonwearing sole and accurate work on the part of the user.

The corrugations allow just enough air between the surfaces to break the vacuum and prevent the suction, which can be enough to lift the board with the plane under favorable circumstances. Hence, those who have much face-side planing to do will find that a corrugated base plane will ease the work. The corrugations further assist by holding a little of the lubricant (oil, paraffin wax, etc.), which is applied to the sole of the plane when working.

Cove

A large hollow cornice; a concave moulding.

Cross Grain

A section of wood taken at right angles, or nearly so to the direction of the longitudinal fibres.

Crotch

A term sometimes used for the veneer which is cut from the limb crotch, or for twin trees which have joined together in growth and have a characteristic grain.

Crown Moulding

A moulding having a double curve face. The upper member of a closed cornice placed immediately below the roof proper.

Curl

The characteristic grain of feather formation seen at its best in certain mahoganies.

Dado

A groove cut across the grain. Also called a housing.

Deal

British term for a slice sawn from a log of timber 9 inches (22.9 cm) wide, not more than 3 inches (7.6 cm) thick and at least 6 feet (1.8 m) long. If shorter it is a deal end; if not more than 7 inches (17.8 cm) wide, it is a batten.

The term deal is loosely used for fir and pine wood. White deal is the wood of the Norway spruce, red deal that of the Scotch pine, yellow deal that of the yellow pine; however, much depends on local custom, red and yellow deal often being the same wood, *Pinus sylvestris*.

Deal Frame

A deal frame is a gang saw used for cutting deals.

Dentil

Each of the small rectangular blocks resembling a row of teeth, under the bed moulding of the cornice of the Ionic, Corinthian, Composite, and sometimes the Doric, orders. Hence, loosely a toothed moulding.

Diaper Work

Decoration in squares or lozenges in which there is a repeat pattern.

Dowel

A headless pin, peg, bolt of wood or metal that fastens two pieces of wood together. A round peg.

Drop

A pendant ornament.

Dust Board

A thin partition board between drawers, fitted in plow grooves in the runners. It is slipped in from the back after the carcass is glued up, and is itself not glued in. It is usually made nowadays of thin plywood.

End Grain

The grain of wood which shows when the fibres are cut transversely.

Escritoire

A writing desk; a bureau.

Face Edge, Face Side

The working faces of a piece of wood, guaranteed true and at right angles to each other, and from which squaring, measuring and gauging are done.

Fasces

An ornament resembling a bundle of sticks with a projecting axe (though this is not always present). It may be carved on a bead in a running pattern. It had its origin in the Roman symbol of authority.

Feather Edge

The fine edge of a board that thins off to one side, so as to resemble a wedge in section.

Felloe or Felly

The exterior rim, or part of it, of a wooden wheel, supported by the spokes. The central block, the hub, is called the nave.

Fence

A guide or gauge designed to regulate the movement of a tool, as on a plow plane, where the fence keeps the cutter at an even distance from the face of the work.

Fiddleback

1. A chair in which the back is so shaped as to resemble a fiddle.
2. A characteristic figuring of wood having a ripple pattern, caused by the overlapping of the fibres. It is used on the backs of violins.

Figure

The pattern formed by the grain of wood.

Fillet

A narrow strip of wood fastened upon any surface to serve as a support, etc., or to strengthen an angle formed by two surfaces.

Fillister or Filletster

A rebating plane used in making sash windows.

Flute

A concave channel, resembling the half of a musical flute cut lengthwise, used in the decoration of columns, balusters, friezes, etc. Many cutters for planing flutes are available as extras for the No. 405 multi-plane.

Fore Plane

A plane intermediate in size between a jack plane and a jointer or try plane.

Frame

The woodwork of doors, windows, etc., minus the panels. The skeleton structure of furniture.

Gain

An American term for a mortise or notch.

"G" Clamp

Named because of its resemblance to the letter G.

Geellim or Geelim

Scottish term for a shoulder plane.

Glazed Doors

Doors fitted with glass panels, usually having a pattern formed by the bars between the glass panels. The glass may occupy all or only some of the panels. The beautiful patterns formed by the bars of cabinet doors, etc., are probably the natural outcome of the small size of a glass that was at the time available: As only small panes were possible, the craftsman took advantage of that to introduce pleasing design. Had larger pieces of glass been available, it is possible that we would never have developed the technique of barred cabinet doors and multipaned windows.

Grain

The longitudinal arrangement of the fibres or particles of wood.

Green Wood

Unseasoned wood in which the sap has not been dried out.

Grind

To sharpen by contact with a rotating abrasive wheel. (See Chapter 3.)

Grounding

Removing the background of design in carved work. Routers Nos. 722 or 071 are admirably suited for this work.

Handrail

A rail, as on a stairway, placed for convenient grasping by the hand.

Hardwood

The wood of deciduous trees, as opposed to that of firs and pines. Oak and ash are typical hardwoods, though the softer basswood or lime wood is classed as a hardwood.

Hauflin, Haughlin or Haflin

Scottish term for a try plane.

Haunch

A sudden decrease in width, as in the outer portion of a tenon in a panelled construction.

Heartwood

The more durable wood from the heat of the tree and around it, as opposed to the sapwood which lies immediately under the bark. The heartwood is mature; the sapwood is living wood and of little use as lumber.

Heat Treatment

The heat treatment of steel is the whole of the thermal treatment and conditions to which the material is subjected from the time it is cast until it becomes the finished product ready for use; this includes annealing, hardening and tempering. The great influence heating to varying temperatures has upon the crystaline structure and physical properties of the metal is extremely important.

Annealing removes as far as possible the internal stresses in the metal induced by rolling or forging and brings the metal into the best state to resist fracture. It also produces the maximum degree of ductility and softness.

Hardening is the process of heating the metal to a particular temperature and suddenly cooling it by quenching in water or another medium which will produce the maximum degree of hardness.

The degree of hardness produced in steel by the hardening process is often too hard for many purposes and has to be modified by tempering in order to suit a particular use. This is done by reheating to a temperature that will give the required degree of hardness. *Tempering* reduces the hardness and brittleness and increases the ductility and toughness of the metal; therefore, by varying the conditions of heat treatment any degree of hardness within the capacity of the metal may be produced.

The correct *temper* of a tool is the degree of hardness at which the tool will perform at its best. To measure degree of hardness see *Brinell test*.

Hogging

Taking very heavy cuts. For this purpose the plane cutter is rounded. Lighter hogging may be done with a jack plan by giving the plane a coarse set and adjusting the frog as far back as it will go. The improvements in machine saws in modern times have removed the necessity for hogging nowadays.

Hone and Honing

A hone is a fine siliceous stone for sharpening instruments. Honing is using the stone for this purpose. Other terms for the same things are honestone, whetstone, oilstone and sharpening stone. The best form for sharpening plane irons, chisels, etc., is a rectangular block about 8 × 2 × 1 inch (20.3 × 5.1 × 2.5 cm).

Hones for sharpening curved cutters come in various shapes and sections. Straight-edged cutters are often sharpened by rubbing the stone on the cutter. The cutting action of the stone is due to the presence of quartz or silica; some stones are almost pure quartz. In others, the siliceous matter is intimately mixed with aluminous or calcareous matter, which gives an extremely fine edge on the tool. Minute particles of garnet or magnetite are sometimes present, these assisting the cutting action.

German razor hones were made from slabs of a yellow vein from the slate mountains near Ratisbon. The slabs were cemented to slate for support.

Turkey stones come from Asia Minor via Smyrna. They are found only in small pieces, frequently flawed. Their analysis gives 70 to 75 percent fine silica intimately blended with 20 to 25 percent calcite. A hone of the finest character, Arkansas stone, is found in Garland and Saline counties, Arkansas, United States. This stone is 98 percent silica, with small proportions of alumina, potash, soda and minute traces of iron, lime, magnesia and fluorine. White in colour, they are hard and keen in grit, not easily worn down. A deluxe stone for the woodworker is available in soft, hard or black grade, the latter being the finest.

Washita stone is a second grade of Arkansas that comes from the Washita River, United States. It is more common than Arkansas and probably the most popular of woodworkers' hones.

Charnley Forest stone or Whittle Hill stone was a good substitute for turkey stone, but is now difficult to obtain. Water of Ayr, Scotch stone, and snake stone are too soft for woodworkers' use and are used in polishing marble, copper and in cleaning up silver work. Greenstone from Snowdon, Wales, is used in giving the last edge to lancets.

A stone recently introduced to the American market is the man-made Ultimate Diemond stone. The manufacturers suggest that this stone will never wear out. It cuts slowly, using either oil or water as a lubricant.

Another man-made addition to the sharpening range are rubberized abrasive sticks and wheels. In these, the silicon carbide grit is bonded in neoprene rubber. They produce highly polished bevels together with fine edges.

Horn

The forward handle of mediaeval planes and on continental planes in modern practice, serving the same function as the knob of Record planes.

Housing

A space excavated in one piece of wood for the reception of another, i.e., a shallow groove for a shelf end. Also called a dado.

Inlay

Decoration by setting pieces of wood, brass, ivory, mother-of-pearl, plastics and other materials, forming a pattern into a ground of some other wood, the whole being left flush. Inserts, as a rule, are of veneer thickness.

Intarsia

A form of inlay, known from the 11th century, probably at its best in Italian work of the 15th century. Commencing with geometrical patterns, it gradually developed into representations of classical architecture, views, figures and drapery, and finally emerged as foliaceous scrolls, as in modern marquetry. Many colored woods were used and further color was obtained by scorching some of the woods to get shadow and other effects.

Iron

A term generally used by the craftsman to denote the cutter or cutting blade of a plane. The term to give "too much iron" means to set the plane cutter too low. To give "less iron" is to draw the blade up.

Jack Plane

The term jack is used in many other trades than that of the woodworker, i.e., a motor jack, a jack knife, jack-of-all-trades. In connection with a plane, the word was in use before the close of the 18th century and was doubtless adopted on account of the universality of the tool: It is the tool that is first used to bring the wood to its approximate size.

Joiner

A woodworker who makes joints; a shop worker (as opposed to a carpenter).

Jointer or Jointer Plane

A long plane used in the truing of edges, ready for jointing. A trying plane, as No. 07 or 08.

Keying

Strengthening, as in a joint, by the insertion of a slip of wood, which may be of various forms.

Kit

An outfit of tools.

Knot

A hard mass in wood, rounded and cross-grained, formed at the juncture of a branch. A "live" knot cannot be knocked out; a "dead" knot is loose and can be separated.

Lath

A thin, narrow, flat piece of wood as used in plaster work, tiling, lattice and trellis work, etc. Also a spline or a slat.

Lengthening Bar

A bar which can be fitted to a sash clamp to extend its length. Also called an "eke."

Locking Stile

That part of a door to which the lock is attached. It is opposite from the hanging stile, to which the hinges are attached.

Louvre

A slatted ventilating window, the slats being sloped to keep out the rain.

Malleable Iron

A form of iron which when cast to the desired shape is subjected to heat treatment causing partial decarburization, rendering its structure fibrous and ductile.

Matching or Matched Boards

Boards cut with a tongue on one edge and a groove on the opposite edge; their jointing is called a match joint. The tongues and grooves are made parallel with the grain. On account of the inevitable shrinkage which occurs after assembly, the joint is frequently "broken" by a bead on the tongued edge, or by both edges being slightly chamfered; this improves the appearance. The effectiveness is often further enhanced by a center bead stuck in the middle of each board. The combination plane and the multi-plane are both ideal for the planing of matched boards.

Member

Any part of an edifice, or any moulding in a collection of mouldings, as those in a cornice, capital or base.

Mitre

The joining together of two pieces of wood at an evenly divided angle (not necessarily 45 degrees), as in a picture frame or bars in a glazed door.

Mouldings, Stuck or Planted

A stuck moulding is worked on the frame itself, while a planted moulding is worked separately and later affixed to the work by means of glue, nails or screws. When planted, mouldings are put around a frame enclosing a panel; the nails should only go through moulding and frame, and should not hold the panel. If the panel is nailed, when shrinkage occurs, either the panel will split, or it will draw the moulding away from the frame, in either case leaving an unsightly gap. If the nails miss the panel, the panel is free to shrink without leaving any gap.

Multi-plane

A plane capable of plowing, dadoing, beading, center beading, rebating and fillistering, match planing, sash planing and slitting, with the standard cutters supplied and many other moulding operations with additional cutters.

Muntin

A central vertical member of a frame, between two panels.

Neat's-foot Oil

An oil obtained from the feet of neat (i.e., ox) cattle. It is generally used as a lubricant for the woodworker's oilstone, being slow in drying and remaining longer than most oils on top of the stone. Old-time craftsmen kept a bottle of it hanging near the bench and applied it by means of a stick that remained in the bottle when not in use.

Newel

A post at the top or bottom of a flight of stairs supporting the handrail.

Nosing

The part of a stair tread that projects above the riser.

Nolling

A quadrant section moulding, carved or turned, seen at its best perhaps in Jacobean work.

Ogee

A term borrowed from architecture, indicating a moulding of wave-like character, formed by a convex curve followed by a concave curve. The derivation is uncertain, but is usually considered an English corruption of French *ogive*, a diagonal groin rib, which is a moulding commonly employed. The Latin equivalent is *cyma reversa*.

Oilstone

See *Hone*.

Oilstone Slip

A small, shaped oilstone for sharpening gouges and the moulding cutters of 050, 050C and 405 planes.

Onlay

A term sometimes used for an ornament that is laid on the surface of the wood, as opposed to inlay, which is let into the surface.

Ormolu

Gilded metal used decoratively on furniture.

Ornament

Any addition or part so treated that it adds to the elegance or beauty of the object. Modern design in woodwork largely discards an applied ornament, allowing the construction to become its own ornament, as in the careful planning of dovetails in rhythmical sequences, the chamfering of through tenons, etc., and relying on proportions and the natural grain of selected woods for major effects.

Ovolo

A term borrowed from architecture, indicating a moulding with the curved part composed of a quarter of a circle, or of an arc of an ellipse with the curve greatest at the top. The word comes from the Latin word *ovum*, an egg, and may be compared with oval, which means egg-shaped. In carpentry a sash ovolo has a flatter curve than a common ovolo. The ovolo is frequently further decorated with carving in the form of an egg and dart, or an egg and tongue.

Panel

The board of a wainscot, door or shutter, which is set in a frame, and is sunk below, raised above or flush with the general level.

Panel Board

One which contains the heart of the tree. Such a board will not warp, though it may shrink in thickness at the two edges.

Parting Bead

The bead used between two sliding doors or sashes to keep them apart.

Pediment

The triangular part, like a low gable, crowning the front of a building in the Grecian style. Hence, it is a similar part in later styles of furniture, though its shape may have varied, i.e., on a wardrobe. The word is probably a workman's corruption of the word pyramid.

Peg

A wooden pin or dowel. A mortise-and-tenon joint may be pegged by boring through the completed joint and inserting a round wooden pin (a trenail).

Pilaster

Another word adapted from architecture. A right-angled columnar projection, frequently decorated with fluting.

Plinth

Again, a term adapted from architecture. The projecting part of a cupboard, immediately above the floor. In modern design, the plinth is often seen as receding; it is not subjected to accidental damage from footwear and provides an interesting shadow line. Further emphasis is often attained by veneering such a plinth with the grain vertically placed, contrasting with the horizontal grain of the covering frame.

Plow or Plough

A plane for making grooves, usually parallel with the grain.

Plow Strip

A strip of wood into which a plow groove has been stuck. Its principal use is in drawer making.

Quirk

A term borrowed from architecture, indicating an acute angle or recess, usually in connection with the narrow grooves forming part of a moulding. The derivation is uncertain, but it is probably connected with an obsolete English word quirt, meaning to turn.

Rebate or Rabbet

The two terms are used to indicate a groove cut on the edge of a board in such a manner that the original corner is taken away. (A rebate has one wall and a bottom; a plow groove has two walls and a bottom.)

Rail

The horizontal member of a door frame or carcass. A door may have a top rail, lock rail or bottom rail. The vertical members are called stiles, and those in the middle are muntins.

Riser

The board set on edge which connects the treads of a stair.

Rod

A narrow board on which length, breadth and height of the object to be made are set out separately and full size, together with the details of panelling, doors and other work. It is especially useful when such things as cupboards have to be repeated and where drawings would be too large to have around.

Router

The hand tool known as a router is a two-handled tool used for cutting and smoothing depressed surfaces. An older form consisted of a chisel-like blade inserted in a block of wood, usually beech, secured by a wood wedge and called by craftsmen "the old woman's tooth." The modern router is motorized and can be fitted with router bits in many sizes and shapes.

Sapwood

The young and living wood that is found immediately under the bark and outside the heart-wood. It is of little value in construction.

Sash

A window frame.

Sash Bars

The strips of a sash window that separate the panes.

Scant

Bare measure.

Scantling

Small sectioned lumber such as 2 × 2 inches (5.1 × 5.1 cm) or 3 × 2 inches (7.6 × 5.1 cm). In the 17th century a carpenter's measuring rod was called by this name.

Scratch Block or Scratch Stock

A tool used by cabinetmakers for inlaying strings and bands, and less frequently for making small mouldings. It consists of a stock made of hardwood that is slotted lengthwise to carry a steel blade, the latter being secured by screws which tighten-up the slot. The blade is filed to the desired section, the cutting edge being 90 degrees.

The stock is so shaped that it forms a bearing on the edge of the wood being worked, and the tool is moved backwards and forward to allow the blade to scratch or scrape the desired groove or moulding, clearing the scrapings frequently. Another form of the tool has an iron body somewhat similar to a spokeshave, with an adjustable fence screwed to the sole. The blade works as in the wooden tool.

Set

The adjustment of a plane blade and its cap iron to a desired setting.

Shake

A split in lumber due to seasoning, causing a separation of the wood between the annual rings. When the shake is annular, it is called a cup shake.

Single-Iron Plane

One with no cap iron.

Skew

Oblique. A skew plane has its cutter at an oblique angle to the side of the plane body.

Skirting Board

The narrow board placed around the wall of a room covering the plastered wall where it meets the floor.

Slamming Style

The vertical strip against which a door abuts when closed, and onto which the lock shoots.

Slitting Cutter

The cutter of a No. 405 multi-plane which is used to cut off narrow strips, instead of sawing them off.

Spalt

Wood that is brittle, short-grained and breaks easily through dryness or decay.

Spokeshave

A type of double-handed plane with a narrow face used for curved woodwork. It may have a flat sole for convex curves or a rounded sole for concave curves. Originally used for shaping or shaving spokes.

Spurs

Used on grooving and rebating planes when cutting wood across the grain. In the operative position, the spur or spurs project below the bottom of the plane and act as a knife to cut the top fibres of the wood ahead of the plane cutter; this ensures clean, sharply cut work.

Square

At right angles.

Staff Bead

The bead which holds a sash window in place.

String

One of the inclined members of a staircase, into which the treads and risers are fitted.

Stringing

Strips of square or rectangular wood of small section which are used for inlaying. (See also *Banding*.)

Stub Tenon

A short tenon; one whose mortise does not go right through.

Tail Vise

A vise placed at the end of the bench used in conjunction with dogs, which can be inserted at intervals along the bench top.

Temper

See *Heat Treatment*.

Tenon

A projection at the end of a piece of wood inserted into the sockets or mortise of another to hold the two together, forming the familiar mortise-and-tenon joint. Its origin is lost in obscurity; the Egyptians used it, as shown by its appearance in their wooden beds. Our words are from the French (*tenon, tenir*, to hold; and *mortaise*), but their ancestry is probably much more ancient than this.

Toat

A plane handle. It may be an open toat or a closed toat. The derivation is obscure.

Toothing

Scoring the surface of the wood (ground) on which a veneer is to be laid. The toothing removes plane marks, and provides a better bite for the glue. It is done diagonally across the ground, both ways, and the operation is speedily worked with the toothing cutter of a No. 080 scraper.

Torus

A convex moulding of approximately semi-circular section, generally used as a base moulding.

Trench

A housing, a dado. (See *Housing*.)

Tungsten

A metal found in certain minerals, chiefly wolframite. In colloidal form, it is used in electric lamp filaments. As tungsten carbide, it is a constituent part of the steel used for making Record plane cutters.

Veneer

A thin layer of wood glued on to other wood for decorative effect. Rare woods are thus made to go further, and grain effects that would weaken constructions are made available without affecting strength. Veneers may be saw cut of knife cut, the latter being much thinner. Saw-cut veneer is more tedious to lay, but it can be repaired and restored if need be; many of the modern knife-cut veneers are so thin that repair is impossible. Some are so thin they are very susceptible to damage. It is not good practice to lay veneer on to very inferior wood.

Vise Clamps or Clams

Fibre grips fitted with steel lugs to fit the jaws of metal working vises so that delicate or highly polished articles may be gripped without damage.

Wainscot

A lining of interior walls, usually panelled.

Warp

The natural distortion of wood due to drying out.

Weather Boards

Overlapping boards used as an outside covering to buildings, with a tapered end section. The thicker edge may be rebated to receive the thinner edge of the next board.

Wind

A twist in a board or surface. To test for wind, use winding strips. Many craftsmen take great pride in making their winding strips, planing them up from choice hardwood and often inlaying strips or blocks of contrasting wood or ivory so that coincidence is more clearly apparent.

METRIC EQUIVALENCY CHART

MM—MILLIMETRES   CM—CENTIMETRES

INCHES TO MILLIMETRES AND CENTIMETRES

INCHES	MM	CM	INCHES	CM	INCHES	CM
⅛	3	0.3	9	22.9	30	76.2
¼	6	0.6	10	25.4	31	78.7
⅜	10	1.0	11	27.9	32	81.3
½	13	1.3	12	30.5	33	83.8
⅝	16	1.6	13	33.0	34	86.4
¾	19	1.9	14	35.6	35	88.9
⅞	22	2.2	15	38.1	36	91.4
1	25	2.5	16	40.6	37	94.0
1¼	32	3.2	17	43.2	38	96.5
1½	38	3.8	18	45.7	39	99.1
1¾	44	4.4	19	48.3	40	101.6
2	51	5.1	20	50.8	41	104.1
2½	64	6.4	21	53.3	42	106.7
3	76	7.6	22	55.9	43	109.2
3½	89	8.9	23	58.4	44	111.8
4	102	10.2	24	61.0	45	114.3
4½	114	11.4	25	63.5	46	116.8
5	127	12.7	26	66.0	47	119.4
6	152	15.2	27	68.6	48	121.9
7	178	17.8	28	71.1	49	124.5
8	203	20.3	29	73.7	50	127.0

Index

A

Abrasive belt, 34, 35
Abrasive stick, rubberized, 36
Adze, 11, 167
Aloxite, 167
Annealing, 175
Apron, 167
Arching planes, 155, 156
Architrave
   cutting a, 109
   definition of, 167
Arkansas Fileset, 36
Arkansas sharpening stones, 35, 175, 176
Astragal moulding
   definition of, 167
   making a, 52, 93

B

"Badger" planes, 75, 153
Bailey, Leonard, 20, 21, 69, 103, 132
"Ball and Sausage" moulding, 168
Baluster, definition of, 167
Banding, definition of, 168
Bargeboard, definition of, 168
Batten, definition of, 168
Bead cutter
   making multiple reeds with a, 51
   sharpening a, 39
Bead cuts
   with a combination plane, 94
   with a multi-plane, 105
Beads
   cock, 66, 118, 171
   definition of, 168
   making, 51, 52, 66
   parting, 179
   staff, 182
Beardmore, Alan, 151
Belshaw power hone, 34
Bench hook, 168
Bench planes, 24–31, 73–76

cutters for, 33
frog screws, adjusting, 29, 30
parts of, 27
reassembling, 26–28
rebate, 74
wooden, 133–140
Bench stop, 168
Bevel cut, 54
Bevel, definition of, 168
Black & Decker planes, 158
Blister, 168
Block planes, 69–72, 145
Bolection beads, 51, 169
Box construction, with rebates and grooves, 79
Box scraper, 132
Brinell Test, 169
Brogue, definition of, 169
Bullnose planes, 81, 82, 83
   definition of, 169
Butt joints
   definition of, 169
   making, 42, 43–44, 45, 146

C

Cabinet, definition of, 169
Cabinet ends, with rebates and grooves, 72
Cabinetmaker's plane, 17th century, 13
Cabinetwork, shapings in, 127
Cap iron, 11
   Bailey, 21
   for a circular plane, 121
   Record "Stay-Set," 30–31
Capping, 169
Carborundum®, 35
Carcass, definition of, 169
Carcass joint, 78
Carpenter, definition of, 170
Carpenter's dogs, 44
Carpenter's Tool Chest, The, 15
Carving plane, 155
"Cast" boards, 147, 148, 170

Cavetto, definition of, 170
Cellaret, definition of, 170
Center beading, 48, 49, 94, 101
Chamfer, definition of, 170
Chamfering, 54
    with a bench plane, 25
    with a spokeshave, 125, 126
Chariot plane, 150, 153
Charnley Forest stone, 35, 176
Chatter, definition of, 170
Check, definition of, 170
Chests, evolution of, 85
Chisel planes, 136, 137, 155
Choke, definition of, 170
Chop inlay, definition of, 170
Circular plane, 120–123, 170
Clamp, definition of, 170, 171
Clapboard, 171
Clap post, 171
Classical detail, 171
Cock bead, 66, 118, 171
Collins, A.H., 12
Combination plane, definition of, 171
Combination plane No. 050, 92–96, 97
    assembly of, 94, 95–96, 97
    cuts with the, 93, 94
    cutters, sharpening, 38, 39
    functions of, 92–93
    handling, 93
Combination plane No. 050C, 97, 98–102
    assembling the, 98
    cuts with the, 102
    cutters, sharpening, 38, 39
    setting up, 98–102
Combined spokeshave, 126
Compass plane, 120, 170
Concave cutting, 121
Concave, definition of, 171
Contour, definition of, 171
Convex cutting, 121
Convex, definition of, 171
Convex spokeshave, 126
Cooper's jointer plane, 16, 17
Cord, definition of, 171
Corner joints, making, 57–58, 59
    with rebate planes, 79
Corrugated base, definition of, 171
Corrugations, removing, 142
Cornice, definition of, 172
Cove, definition of, 172
Craftsmanship, ancient, 8–10
Cross grain, definition of, 172
Crotch, 172
Crown moulding, 172
"Crucible process," of melting steel, 23
"C" scroll, definition of, 169
Cup shake, definition of, 181
Curl, definition of, 172
Curved groove, making a, 114

Cutters
    maintenance of, 32–40
    toothing, 131, 132
    with anti-backlash adjustment, 134

D

Dado cuts, 53
    with a combination plane, 93, 94, 100, 101
    with a multi-plane, 104, 105
    with a rebate plane, 78
    with a router, 115
Dado; definition of, 172
Deal, 172
Deal frame, 172
Defiance block planes, 69
Dentil, 172
Demi-varlope, 15, 16
Denford horizontal grinder, 33, 34
Diaper work, 172
"Donkey's ear," 146, 147
Doors
    edges of, meeting, 63
    flush, 62, 63
    frames for, easing rebates in, 83
    glazed, 174
    panels for, 60, 61, 62, 118
Double iron plane, 11
Dovetail plane, 137
Dowel, definition of, 172
Dowelled joints, making, 49
Drawer fronts, decorative applications for, 65, 66, 67
Drawer slip, making a, 55, 56
Drawers, 64–68
    fitting, 67, 68
    fronts of, decorative applications for, 65, 66, 67
    lipping, 65
Dressers, panelling backs of, 64
Drop, definition of, 172
Dust board, 173

E

E.C. Emmerich planes, 134, 135–141
Edge beading
    with a combination plane, 101
    with a multi-plane, 105, 106
Edge planing, 43
    with a bench plane, 26
Egyptians' shop, model of, 9, 10
"Eke." See Lengthening Bar
Elu dry grinder, 35
Elu planes, 158, 159
End grain
    definition of, 173
    moulding on, 108
    planing, 24, 144, 145
English planes, 17th century, 15
Escritoire, definition of, 173
Evans, George Franklin, 122

F

Face edge, of wood, 42, 173
Face side, of wood, 42, 173
Facing, 64
Fasces, definition of, 173
Feather edge, definition of, 173
Felloe, definition of, 173
Fence, definition of, 173
Fiddleback, definition of, 173
Figures, definition of, 173
Fillet
   definition of, 173
   planing a, 53
Fillister plane, 136, 137
Fillisters
   cutting, 76, 94
   definition of, 173
Finishing, 130
Flute, definition of, 173
"Fore" planes, 24–25, 174
Forward horn, emergence of, 12
Frame, definition of, 174
French iron plane, 17, 18

G

"Gains," 116, 117, 174
Galère, 15, 16
Gaynor, Jay, 149
"G" clamp, definition of, 174
Geellim, definition of, 174
German plane, 16th century, 13
Gimson, Ernest, 69, 70
"Glazing," 37
Glues, 45
Goncalvo alves, 141
Grain, definition of, 174
Greenstone, 176
Green wood, 174
Grind, definition of, 174
Grinding machines, 33, 34, 35
Grooves, cutting, 46, 50
   with a combination plane, 93, 94, 99, 100
   with a multi-plane, 104, 105, 106, 107
   with a plow plane, 86–88
   with a rebate plane, 78
   with a router, 114, 115–117, 118
Grounding, definition of, 174

H

Half-round spokeshave, 126
Handrail, definition of, 174
Hardening, of steel, definition of, 175
Hardwood, definition of, 174
Haulflin, definition of, 174
Haunch, definition of, 174
Haunched tenons, starting, 50, 51
Heartwood, definition of, 175
Heat treatment, of steel, definition of, 175

Henley planes, 21, 151–152, 153
History of the plane, 8–23
Hogging, definition of, 175
"Holed" moulding plane, 16
Hone, definition of, 175
Horn, definition of, 176
Housing, cutting. Also see Dado
   stopped, 53
   with a combination plane, 100, 101
   with a multi-plane, 195
   with a router, 113, 115, 116
Housing, definition of, 176
Hutchins, Joseph, 149

I

India® stone, 35
Infil planes, 21
Inlay, definition of, 176
Intarsia, definition of, 176
Iron
   malleable, 177
   use of, 22
Iron planes, 10, 16, 17, 18
Iron-sheathed planes, 19th century, 19, 20
"Irons," 22, 23, 28, 32, 36, 37. See also Cutters
   definition of, 176

J

Jack planes
   bench, 24–25
   definition of, 176
   rebate, 74
   17th century, 15
   wood, 20, 134
Jamestown planes, 149–150
Japanese water stone, 34
Joiner, definition of, 176
Jointer, definition of, 177
Jointer plane, 17, 141

K

Keying, definition of, 177
Kit, definition of, 177
Kunz planes
   spokeshaves, 126, 127
   scrapers, 132

L

Lath, definition of, 177
Lengthening bar, definition of, 177
Lipping, 65
Locking stile, definition of, 177
Louvre, definition of, 177

M

Makita planes, 158

Mark Two Sharpening System, 34
Marples plane, 133
Matched boards
    beading, 106
    definition of, 177
    tonguing, 106
Match joint, definition of, 177
Mather, George, 154–157
Mechanick's Workbench, The, 149
Member, definition of, 177
Metallurgy, 22
Metropolitan Museum of Art (New York), 9
Miller, Charles, 103
Mitre, 146, 147, 177
Mitred boxes, making, 59, 60
Mitred corners, strengthening, 59
Mitre planes, 19, 21, 151, 152, 155, 157
Model making, planes for, 72
Mortise-and-tenon joint
    15th century, 69
    haunched, 61
Mortises, starting, for haunched tenons, 50, 51
Moulding planes, 17th century, 14, 15, 16
    irons for, 11
Mouldings, definition of, 177, 178
Mouldings, making, 52, 55
    with a combination plane, 96
    with a multi-plane, 108, 109
Mouse mitre plane, 157
Multi-plane, 103–111
    cuts with a, 104, 105–106, 107, 111
    cutters for a, 38, 107, 108, 110
    definition of a, 178
    parts of a, 103
Multiple reeds, making, 51
Muntin, definition of, 178

N

Napier, Jas., 22
National Museum of Antiquities, 11, 14
Nave, definition of, 173
Neat's-foot oil, 36, 178
Newel, definition of, 178
19th century plane, homemade, 17, 20
Nolling, definition of, 178
Norris planes, 21, 152
Norwich plane, 17
Nosing, definition of, 178
Nosing tool, 110
Nouveau Manuel Complet du Charpentier, 15
Novaculite, 35
Novaya Zemlya smoothing plane, 14, 15

O

Off-set boards, 45
Ogee, definition of, 178
Oilstones, 35, 36
    resurfacing, 40
    storage of, 39

Oilstone slip, definition of, 179
"Old woman's tooth." See Router planes
Onlay, definition of, 179
Open box dovetail, 70
Ormolu, definition of, 179
Ornament, definition of, 179
Ott, George, 140
Oval rod, planing a, 49
Ovolo, cutting a, 93, 96, 97, 107
Ovolo, definition of, 179

P

Panel board, definition of, 179
Panel, definition of, 179
Panelled constructions, 85
Panel plane, 20, 154
Parting bead, definition of, 179
Pediment, definition of, 179
Peg, definition of, 179
Petrie, Flinders, 10, 11
Philips, Russel, 85
Pilaster, definition of, 179
Planted mouldings, 178
Plinth, definition of, 179
Plowing cuts
    with a combination plane, 93, 98, 99
    with a multi-plane, 104, 105, 107
Plow planes
    assembling, 90
    cuts with, 89
    cutters, sharpening, 38, 39
    definition of, 179
    parts of, 89
    setting up, 90, 91
    uses of, 85–88
    wooden, 139, 140
Plow strip, definition of, 180
Pompeii planes, 10
"Pot life," 45
Power planes, 158–164
Preston, Edward, 151
Primus planes, 134, 135–141

Q

"Quirk," 105, 108

R

Radius plane, 170
"Raggle," 115
Rail, definition of, 180
Raised panel, making a, 50
Razor hones, 175
Rebate cuts, 50, 65, 74
    with a combination plane, 94, 99, 100
    with a multi-plane, 105
    with a power plane, 163
Rebate, definition of, 180
Rebate planes, 73–84, 141

Record planes, 20–23, 144–146
   block, 70–72
   bullnose, 81
   circular, 120–123
   combination, 92–102
   jack, 146
   multi-planes, 103, 104
   plow, 85, 86–91
   rebate, 73–84
   router, 112–114
   scrapers, 130–132
   spokeshaves, 124–126
Reeds, multiple, making, 51
Resin glues, 45
Return beads, making, 51, 52
R.H. Wood planes, 153, 154
Richards, Henry, 21
Rijksmuseum, 14
Riser, definition of, 180
Rods
   definition of, 180
   making, 53
   planing, 49
Roman civilization, 10, 11
Round rods, planing, 49, 53
   with a spokeshave, 127
Router planes, 112–119, 138
   definition of, 180
Ryobi planes, 158, 160–162, 163

S

Sapwood, definition of, 180
Sash bars, definition of, 180
Sash cutters, 110
   sharpening, 39
Sash, definition of, 180
Scant, definition of, 180
Scantling, definition of, 180
Scotch stone, 176
Scrapers, 40, 130–132, 155, 156
Scratch block, definition of, 181
Scratch tools, 85
Scroll, 13
Secret lap dovetail, 70
   trimming the mitre on a, 80
Serpentine fronts, construction of, 122
Set, definition of, 181
Shake, definition of, 181
Sharpedge grinder, 34
Sharpening stones, 35, 36
Shooting boards, 67, 68, 144, 145, 146, 147
Shoulder planes, 79, 80, 81, 149, 151, 152
Side fillet plane, 138
Side rebate planes, 75, 83, 84, 152
Silchester iron plane, 10, 11
"Skate," 104
Skew, definition of, 181
Skirting board, definition of, 181
Slamming style, definition of, 181

Slitting cutter, definition of, 181
Slitting, with a multi-plane, 107
Smoothing planes, 12, 14, 15, 21, 24, 26, 134, 135, 152, 153
Snake stone, 176
"Snicking," 142
South Kensington Museum, 14, 19
Spiers planes, 21
Spokeshaves, 124–129
   cutter holder for, 35
   definition of, 181
Spon's Mechanic's Own Book, 20
Spurs, definition of, 181
"Squares," 168, 182
Staff bead, definition of, 182
Stanley planes
   router, 118, 119
   scraper, 132
Stanley Rule and Level Company, 20, 21, 103
Steel, 22, 23
Stiles, definition of, 180
Stopped chamfer, 54, 126
Stopped groove, making a, 114, 116, 117
Stopped housing, making a, 53, 54, 116
Stop rabbet plane, 136, 137
String, definition of, 182
Stringing, 168, 182
Stub tenon, 70, 182
Stuck mouldings, 177, 178

T

Tabletops, mouldings for, 55
Tail vise, 182
Tempering, definition of, 175
Tenons
   definition of, 182
   haunched, 50
   stub, 182
Through dovetail, 70
Thumb plane, 150, 152, 153, 157
Toat, definition of, 182
Tongued-and-grooved boards, 48, 49
Tongued-and-grooved joints, making, 47, 48
Tongued board, beading a,
   with a combination plane, 101
   with a multi-plane, 106
Tongued joints, making, 45–47
Toothing cutters, 131, 132
Toothing, definition of, 182
Toothing plane, 139
Torus bead
   definition of, 182
   making a, 52
Traut, J.A., 21, 103
Trenails, 69
Trench. See Housing or Dado
Try plane, 18, 24–25, 136
Tungsten carbide, 23
Tungsten, definition of, 182

Tungsten steel, 23
Turkey stone, 35, 175
Two-tongued mitre, 59

U

Ulmia planes, 140
Ultimate Diemond stone, 35, 176

V

Veneer, 139
  definition of, 183
Vergeboard, definition of, 168
Vertical inlays, for drawer fronts, 66
Victor block planes, 69
Vise clamps, definition of, 183
Vise, definition of, 182

W

Wainscot, definition of, 183
"Warped boards," 147, 148
Warren, G.A., 20

Washita stone, 35, 176
Water of Ayr stone, 35, 176
Weatherboard, definition of, 183
Wheelwright's plane, 17th century, 123
Whittle Hill stone, 176
Wind, definition of, 183
Winding strips, 41
Wood
  green, 174
  knot in, 177
  spalted, 181
  squaring, 41, 42
  warped, 183
Woodcraft Supply Corporation, 34
Wooden bench planes, 133–140
Wooden planes, with iron sheathing, 17, 22
Wood, R.H., 153
Worral, Thomas, 103

X

Xenix hone, 34

Acknowledgments

The thanks of the author and publisher must be expressed to Mark Alexander and R.H. McKears, the then directors of Record Ridgway Tools Ltd., for permission to write this book using much of the information contained in *Planecraft*, first written by C.W. Hampton and E. Clifford in 1934.

Thanks also to:

The present Directors of Bahco Record Tools for the use of halftones and line drawings.

E.C. Emmerich of Remschild-Hasten, Germany, and Georg Ott of Ulm, Germany, for halftones and line drawings used in Chapter 14.

Elu Machinery Ltd., Luton, England, for power plane halftones.

Hagermeyer (London) Ltd. for Ryobi planes.

Stanley Tools, Sheffield, England, for assistance with special planes not in the Record range.

Ann and Don Wing, The Mechanick's Workbench, Marion, Massachusetts, for the Jamestown Planes.

Geoff Mather, maker of carving planes, Ashton-in-Makerfield, England.

Alan Beardmore, Henley Planes, Reading, England, for help and halftones.

Gustav Kunz of Hannover Wülfel, Germany.

Black and Decker, Maidenhead, Berkshire, England.

R.H. Wood, Historical Woodworking Tools, Wakefield, England.

Woodcraft Supply Corporation, Woburn, Massachusetts, for the Mark II sharpening system.

Ron Proctor, former colleague and great plane man of Record, who devoted a great deal of time and effort looking over the growth of material relating to metal planes. Thanks to him also for reading the proofs.

My son, Richard J.A. Sainsbury, M.A., Dip. Arch., R.I.B.A., for his help.

Adrian Small, sometime captain of the *Nonsuch*, now safely in its museum in Winnipeg, Canada, for his infinite care in making the drawings.

"My lady of the keys," Beth Flowerday, for infinite care in deciphering my longhand, correcting the syntax and typing the manuscript.

And last but not least, my wife, for living with it.

Other Books by John Sainsbury

Woodworking Projects with Power Tools

Craft of Woodturning

Sainsbury's Woodturning Projects for Dining